ANTISEMITISM IN THE END TIMES

OLIVIER J. MELNICK

HARVEST PROPHECY
An Imprint of Harvest House Publishers

Cover design by Bryce Williamson

Cover images © Anna Bergbauer, ideeone / Getty Images

Interior design by KUHN Design Group

For bulk, special sales, or ministry purchases, please call 1-800-547-8979.
Email: CustomerService@hhpbooks.com

Antisemitism in the End Times

Published by Harvest House Publishers
Eugene, Oregon 97408
www.harvesthousepublishers.com

ISBN 978-0-7369-9185-8 (pbk)
ISBN 978-0-7369-9186-5 (eBook)

Library of Congress Control Number: 2024951615

Printed in the United States of America

25 26 27 28 29 30 31 32 33 / BP / 10 9 8 7 6 5 4 3 2 1

"Olivier Melnick helps readers understand what has been called the longest hatred and how to respond to it with the longest love found in Yeshua the Messiah. Going back to Genesis 3:15, he unpacks the satanic origins of antisemitism, traces its history, and explains its current versions on campuses and in churches today. This helpful book offers a timely word with answers on how to take a bold biblical stand to fight against this vile hatred."

—**Tim M. Sigler,** PhD, CEO of Ariel Ministries

"In this thoroughly documented work, Olivier Melnick does a masterful job of exposing humanity's historical hatred of the Jewish people. Sadly, this disdain for Jews has also been an undercurrent in the Christian church for centuries. With discerning insight, Olivier reveals specific ways our enemy is targeting Israel and individual Jews in these last days, and most importantly, what you can do about it."

—**Jeff Kinley,** *Jeff Kinley Live* and *The King is Coming*
TV host, podcaster, speaker, author of 40+ books

"In his timely book *Antisemitism in the End Times*, author and friend Olivier Melnick shares unique, critical insight regarding the history, roots, and harsh realities of antisemitism through the church age. Then he masterfully unpacks the biblical reasons for the current rise of antisemitism around the world and how it connects to the prophecies and conditions of the end times. Finally, he offers clear, practical guidance for how Christians can take a stand against antisemitism and provide tangible support and encouragement for Jewish people everywhere. Every Christian needs to read this book!"

—**Todd Hampson,** author of The Non-Prophet's Guide™ series, founder of Timbuktoons, cohost of the *Prophecy Pros Podcast*, speaker

"In *Antisemitism in the End Times*, Olivier Melnick exposes how the world's oldest hatred, antisemitism, is reemerging on a global scale, paving the way for the tribulation and a future Holocaust under the Antichrist. With theological clarity and historical insight, Melnick explains how a new form of global antisemitism has overtaken classical antisemitism. He masterfully lays out the prophetic roadmap found in Scripture, showing how Satan is using this ancient, yet now global, hatred in a calculated effort to destroy the Jewish people and eliminate Israel from the world. This book is not merely a historical or theological analysis but a wake-up call. Confronting antisemitism is one of the defining challenges of our time, and the issue of Israel remains the true north for understanding God's prophetic program. Melnick also offers practical guidance on what you and I can do in response to the growing tide of global antisemitism. *Antisemitism in the End Times* is a must-read for every Christian seeking to stand with Israel during this critical moment in prophetic history."

—**Brandon Holthaus,** Tip of the Spear Ministry and Rock Harbor Church

"Sadly, antisemitism has historically found fertile ground within Christendom. Thus, fresh investigations into the horrific subject of antisemitism are much needed and appreciated. Olivier Melnick has furnished such an analysis in this book. If you want to become aware of the common thread of antisemitism throughout human history (past, present, and future), then this book is for you. It receives my highest recommendation."

—**Andy Woods, PhD**, pastor-teacher, Sugar Land Bible Church; president, Chafer Theological Seminary

This book is dedicated to
my mother Evelyn Melnick (née Weinzveig),
who survived World War II and the Holocaust.
She is part of the "NEVER AGAIN" generation,
and yet she lived long enough to witness
a world turning against the Jews
AGAIN!

ACKNOWLEDGMENTS

This book wouldn't be possible without the encouragement and friendship of Jeff Kinley and Todd Hampson, who first introduced me to Harvest House Publishers.

I am so grateful to Steve Miller, who from our first meeting forward was very positive about such an important book for such a time as this. Steve truly understands the Bible, Israel, and the issues covered in this book, making the writing and editing process so much easier. Simply put, he gets it!

I am thankful for my wife, who has always helped me to look at both sides of every story, and has never complained in spite of the long hours I spent on this project.

Most of all, my thanks go to my Messiah Yeshua, who saved me, keeps me strong, and gives me hope for the future.

CONTENTS

LOOKING FOR ANSWERS: WHY IS HATRED GROWING?

Hatred against Jewish people, and now against Israel as well, has continued to burn, like smoldering embers. What society has tolerated as acceptable against Jewish people has now spread like a virus against the false notion that antisemitism had died with the Holocaust.

"The longest hatred," as antisemitism is often called, goes back to ancient and biblical Jewish history, and has never ceased. It might have slowed down or partially disappeared at times, but in recent decades, it was simply swept under the rug of political correctness and multiculturalism. This hatred keeps morphing into more of a beast, as we will see in the rest of this book.

Multiculturalism, the coexistence of disparate cultures without the assimilation of underlying values, is turning out to be more than a disappointment. The values of mutual respect, the rule of law (rather than of men), and constitutional freedoms are basic to Western civilization. Turning back the clock to the Middle Ages and barbarism is not acceptable, and on that point, most civilized free-world citizens can agree.

A good example of the failure of multiculturalism is the attempt at integrating North African (Tunisian, Algerian, and Moroccan) Muslims into the French community since the 1950s. The first generation of migrants who came to France were given many jobs that French citizens didn't care to have, such as street sweepers and trash collectors. They settled in France the best they could and started building their families. The subsequent generations weren't as flexible as their parents and started to push back. The youth, especially in the greater Paris area, started to grow and join or form gangs. Eventually, they started their own families, and between the high numbers in unemployment and their insistence on retaining Muslim values at odds with European values, the societal chasm grew wider. The more the French governments allowed the Muslim communities to do of their own accord, the more they asked for and the less they cooperated or assimilated. Today, France has the largest Muslim population in all of Europe, and this population is out of control and very anti-Jewish.

The question remains: What is the alternative to unbridled multiculturalism? Tracing the hatred toward Jewish people is one way to look through history and see the disturbing patterns of unchecked hatred. The Jewish people have served as the "canary in the mine."

Back in the old coal mining days, when miners went into a mine, they would take with them a canary in a cage. Someone would be assigned to keep an eye on the canary, which would die very quickly if a gas leak were to occur in their work area. The ever-present danger of an underground gas leak leading to a lethal explosion could then be avoided. The unfortunate crisis of the canary dying was their sign that they had to evacuate the mine immediately, or they could be next.

The irrational persecution of the Jewish people over the millennia is well documented, and the growing boldness and acceptance of those who have come against the Jews in hatred is hard to deny, although some persist in doing so. Like the gas levels rising to the point the canary dies, the forces of dark hatred have gathered and concentrated. Many others are in danger of being affected by this hatred. We know God is not on the side of antisemitism or hatred of any kind, much less hatred against His people. Because we have the freedom to do so, we must come to grips with the many aspects that threaten our biblical values of dignity, decency, and morality—all of which are under satanic attack. Education is our friend! Turning from hatred to intelligent understanding is essential.

WHAT DOES THE BIBLE SAY ABOUT ANTISEMITISM?

My understanding of the basis of antisemitism started with an in-depth study of Asaph's Psalm 83 on the enemies of Israel conspiring against the Jewish people and, by proxy, against the God of Abraham, Isaac, and Jacob, also known as the God of Israel. To be sure, the Bible is replete with affirmations about God's special relationship with Israel, as in Genesis 12:3; 17:7-8; Leviticus 26:40-45; Deuteronomy 11:12; Psalm 89:30-37; Jeremiah 31:35-37; Ezekiel 36–39; and many other passages.

The first five verses of Psalm 83 set the stage for understanding the dynamic of hatred of God's people that we can also find elsewhere in the Bible. It is, in reality, a hatred of God.

> O God, do not remain quiet;
> do not be silent and, O God, do not be still.
> For behold, Your enemies make an uproar,
> and those who hate You have exalted themselves.
> They make shrewd plans against Your people,
> and conspire together against Your treasured ones.
> They have said, "Come, and let us wipe them out as a nation,
> that the name of Israel be remembered no more."

> For they have conspired together with one mind;
> against You they make a covenant.

It is quite a powerful statement to assert that hating the Jews equates to hating God, yet this is exactly what this passage of the Tenach (Old Testament) is saying.

Psalm 83 lists ten people groups as the confederate states against Israel. This list is considered by some to be a literary device used by the psalmist to paint a picture of the grave and imminent danger surrounding Israel.[1] While the list of countries can still be a stylistic way of saying that Israel was at risk, some also see a prophetic meaning in this passage. They claim that the list of ten countries could very well be a literal, geopolitical alliance, specifically coming against Israel, even before the war of Gog and Magog mentioned in Ezekiel 38–39. I tend to believe that Psalm 83 uses the enemies of Isreal as a literary device used by Asaph to declare his concerns to the Lord about the general hatred against his people. Either way, Psalm 83 is a warning to those who loathe Israel and the Jewish people.

The warning is clear and simple: Don't mess with Israel and the Jewish people. This goes back to the promise made by God to Abraham in Genesis 12:3, when He declared,

> I will bless those who bless you,
> and the one who curses you I will curse.
> And in you all the families of the earth will be blessed.

This pivotal scripture has been described as God's foreign policy as it pertains to Israel. We can see God punishing those who curse Israel, like Haman in the book of Esther or the Pharaoh who didn't know Joseph. God promises to go after those who go after Israel, and He is not ambiguous about it.

In Zechariah 12:3, God tells us that eventually, all the nations will turn on Israel: "It will come about in that day that I will make Jerusalem a heavy stone for all the peoples; all who lift it will be severely injured. And all the nations of the earth will be gathered against it." God also tells us in Zechariah 12:9 that "in that day I will set about to destroy all the nations that come against Jerusalem."

God will not leave any stone unturned when it comes to punishing the enemies of Israel and the Jewish people, and Asaph knew that when he wrote Psalm 83, as he emphasized in verses 13-15:

> O my God, make them like the whirling dust,
> like chaff before the wind.
> Like fire that burns the forest
> and like a flame that sets the mountains on fire,
> so pursue them with Your tempest
> and terrify them with Your storm.

WHAT DOES HISTORY TEACH US ABOUT ANTISEMITISM?

In my 2007 book *They Have Conspired Against You,* I exposed what I called the new antisemitism as I compared it to classical antisemitism. Both had similarities, but what I called the new antisemitism had both new boundaries and new methodologies. The oldest hatred had gone global and was no longer racially motivated—as erroneous as it had been anyway. Hatred has a way of multiplying when it is not opposed and overcome, and that has been the pattern through the ages.

Classical antisemitism came to its ominous apex during the Holocaust era (1933–1945) as racially based. Hitler believed in the pseudoscience of eugenics[2] and was convinced that the Jewish race was so inferior that it had to be eradicated. Classical antisemitism took 2,000 years to grow and morph, but by the time Hitler got involved, it became a racial problem. To him, the Jews had become subhuman, and as such, had to be eliminated to do the world a great service.

The new antisemitism has plagued the Jewish people for several decades now. It started to develop under the leadership of Palestinian Liberation Organization (PLO) leader Yasser Arafat in the mid-1960s, after two decades of respite when the whole world was processing the horrors of the Holocaust. While the false Palestinian narrative of turning the perpetrators into the victims and vice versa received some pushback at first, eventually it was accepted, and is now received as truth by many.

Three important criteria help to define this new iteration of the longest hatred. It has new boundaries, new methodology, and new perpetrators.

While the cancer of classical antisemitism was mostly localized to Europe, the new antisemitism is a cancer that has metastasized over the entire planet. Classical antisemitism went as far as the railroad system would allow in the 1940s, but the advent of satellite communications and the internet and social networks has allowed the new antisemitism to go global in no time at all. The boundaries have greatly expanded.

The methodology is also different. The victims and the perpetrators have been completely switched. Up to the time of the Holocaust (1938–1945), the victims were the Jewish people wherever they were (mostly in Europe), and the perpetrators wherever either the Nazis or those who collaborated with the Nazis were, as was the case for the French Vichy government under maréchal Philippe Pétain. Within two decades after the end of World War II in 1945, a role reversal began. The Palestinians became the new perpetrators. To be sure, not every single Palestinian desires to kill Jews, but the leaderships of both Fatah and Hamas (Palestinian political and military organizations) are corrupt to the point of using their own people as human shields. It has been part of the new methodology to paint the Palestinians as "victims" and the Israelis as "the new Nazis" of the Middle East. A myriad of cartoons have been published to push that narrative, and the story is always the same no matter what: It depicts Israelis killing poor Palestinians, and Jews controlling the world.[3]

The source of antisemitism remains the same. It was, is, and will continue to be Satan, who hates what God loves and loves what God hates. Over the centuries, he has creatively used people from all walks of life and is constantly subcontracting his agenda of hatred to new groups. So currently, we have new perpetrators of antisemitism covering the entire political spectrum from hard left to extreme right.

Those who promote this new kind of Jew hatred comprise a seemingly mismatched and mixed group of radical leftists, Christians, extreme-right activists, and Muslims. When we think of it, these are groups that would be unlikely allies in any other situation; but in the case of loathing Israel and the Jewish people, they seem to agree. The ancient adage "The enemy of my enemy is my friend" seems appropriate in that context as, for instance, we have seen liberals and Islamists work together against the Jewish people, like in the case of Queers for Palestine.[4]

My fears about the new antisemitism have now been confirmed. It is not going away, and in fact, it has picked up quite a bit of momentum during the last few years. To most people, this resurgence of global antisemitism might only appear to be increasing in numbers and frequency. I believe this is true, but I am also convinced that we are currently going through an exponential increase in the intensity and gravity of those acts, especially since the horrific terrorist attack of October 7, 2023.

PART I

A SURVEY OF DEFINITIONS, FACTS, AND MYTHS

CHAPTER 1

TOWARD A CLEAR UNDERSTANDING OF ANTISEMITISM

Antisemitism has been a problem for many centuries. And in recent decades, it has become manifest in new ways. For this reason, a new term had to be coined—the new antisemitism. When we consider that all of this is happening in the context of a world that is rapidly approaching the end times, we can rightly call this phenomenon end-times antisemitism, a theme that will be developed throughout this book.

This newest breed of antisemitism is highly irrational. To be sure, I am not saying that any sort of Jew hatred has ever been rational in any way. A powerful illustration of how ludicrous antisemitism is and always will be is conveyed in the following story:

In a park in Europe during WWII, a Jewish man was sitting reading a book when a Nazi officer approached him and engaged in conversation.

> "I tell you; those Jews are subhuman; they are the scum of the earth and we should get rid of all of them," said the German officer. The Jewish man did not respond and continued to read. "They control everything, and we must cleanse the world of this venomous race; we must kill them all," added the Nazi officer. "Yes," nodded the old Jewish man, "we must get rid of all the Jews and the bicycle riders." "Why the bicycle riders?" asked the officer with a puzzled look on his face. "Why the Jews?" added the Jewish man.[1]

Antisemitism is indeed irrational, yet surprisingly, it has recently reached new levels of irrationality. When trying to connect all the dots, one can only come to this conclusion: The various acts of Jew hatred that we have witnessed lately seem to be part of some final act in a program to eliminate Israel and the Jewish people.

That very goal is part of the agenda of Israel's archenemy, Satan. He is writing the final chapter in antisemitism in front of our very eyes, and if he could have his way, he would eradicate all Jews on a global scale, once and for all.

Satan is a very real individual. He is not a mythical figure or a spirit or some kind of force. He is a fallen angel who, because of his rebellion against God, lost his privileged position in heaven. He has become "the ruler of this world" (John 12:31; 16:11; see also 1 John 2:13-14). He is nothing like the monstrous being portrayed by Hollywood. On the contrary, to be believable, he disguises himself as "an angel of light" (2 Corinthians 11:14) to deceive as many people as he can (Revelation 12:9). Satan is to be taken very seriously, but believers are not to fear him.

Is it possible that the reason we are seeing a resurgence in antisemitism—with a great emphasis on the irrational aspect of it all—is that Satan knows that his days of glory are coming to an end very shortly? The "ruler of the world" is about to be deposed by the King of kings, the Prince of Peace. But Satan's approach to his last moment of fame is that if indeed he goes down—and he is going to go down—he will redouble his efforts to take Israel and the Jews with him in a final effort to spit in God's face, if possible.

The God of the Bible unconditionally loves Israel and the Jewish people to the point of promising great blessings to those who bless Israel and curses to those who curse Israel, as seen in Genesis 12:3:

> I will bless those who bless you [Abraham and his descendants], and the one who curses you [Abraham and his descendants] I will curse.

For people to recognize the rise of a new kind of antisemitism is only the tip of the iceberg. Many are not seeing this tip and realizing that, according to the Bible, the world is heading for another Holocaust of gigantic proportions.

Israel was, is, and always will be at the center of God's master plan for humanity. God certainly does not need mankind to recognize Israel and the Jews for Him to preserve them, but it would help us if we did. The first book of the Bible, Genesis, sets the stage for God's program for mankind. Out of 50 chapters, 11 deal with mankind in general, and 39 deal with Abraham, Isaac, Jacob, and his sons in great detail. God has always had His eyes on Israel and the Jewish people.

God has promised a bright future for Israel and the global Jewish community. But until that glorious day comes, more Jewish blood will be shed. How much will be shed could actually be up to us.

End-times antisemitism is Satan's desired epilogue in his saga against the Jews, and it will be written. But if Bible-believing disciples of Yeshua[2] the Messiah have anything to say or do, this chapter can be shorter and much less damaging to my people.

In a sense, I am counting on you to read on and learn more about this newest mutation of antisemitism, to identify the new players and join the battle against the enemies of the people whom God calls "the apple of His eye" in Zechariah 2:8. Too many people, including Christians, have chosen the safer road of apathy, but for committed believers, that road shouldn't be an option. Would you join me on this difficult journey?

I wrote my first book, titled *They Have Conspired Against You,* because of my grandfather and those who came to take him. I have written this one because of my fears that they might come back.

KEY DEFINITIONS FOR UNDERSTANDING ANTISEMITISM

In an age when words are being redefined and history is being revised, it is critical to establish a few working definitions for the terminology that will be used in this book, starting, of course, with the word *antisemitism*. Once we understand that the word *Semite* has a different meaning depending on whether it is used by itself or within the word *antisemitism*, we are able to get clearer insight into how the Jewish people are specifically targeted for hatred.

Who Are the Semites?

At first glance, it would appear that antisemitism targets anyone who is of Semitic descent. To be of Semitic origin simply means to be a descendant of Shem (one of Noah's three sons).

> Genesis 5:32—"Noah was five hundred years old, and Noah became the father of Shem, Ham, and Japheth."

> Genesis 6:10—"Noah became the father of three sons: Shem, Ham, and Japheth."

The family of Shem went on to include people groups such as the Akkadians, Ugarites, Chaldeans, Arameans, and the Hebrews, among many others. For a more complete listing, we can go to Genesis 12:21-32, where all of the descendants of Shem are listed by name.

To simplify the lineage from Shem, we can accurately say that Semites include both Jews and Arabs. Yet the term *antisemite* has *never* been used to describe a hatred of the Arab people—only a hatred of the Jewish people. So, in spite of the prefix *anti* (against), the words *Semitic* and *antisemitic* are not necessarily direct opposites.

When Did the Word Antisemitism *First Appear?*

While actions that would qualify as antisemitic go back thousands of years and are documented in the Jewish Bible as early as the book of Exodus, the word itself is much younger. Many theologians, philosophers, pseudo-scholars, and historians have published numerous works vilifying the Jewish people throughout history, but it was not until the late nineteenth century that the word *antisemitism* was coined.

The first usage of the word can be traced to 1860,[3] but it was truly first popularized by German journalist Wilhelm Marr,[4] who in 1873 published a pamphlet titled *The Victory of the Jewish Spirit over the Germanic Spirit. Observed from a non-religious perspective.*

Marr was convinced that Jewish people were on a mission to take over the world, including Germany. In the pamphlet, he didn't hesitate to use an old Middle Ages diatribe about Jewish greed: "There is no way to deny that the abstract, money-oriented, haggling mind of the Jews has contributed much to the flourishing of commerce and industry in Germany."[5] While this sounds like a compliment at first, it is actually a strong, stereotypical statement meant to put Jews in a negative light.

Marr was so convinced that Jewish people controlled the politics, the press, and much of the government of Germany at the time of his writings that he stated, "The same goal, disintegration of the Germanic State for the benefit of Jewish interests, is consistently pursued everywhere."[6]

In his pamphlet, Marr used the words *Semitismus and Judentum* interchangeably to describe Jewry or Jewishness. The usage of the word *Semitismus* led to the coining of the word *Anti-Semitismus,* which he used in another pamphlet, entitled *The Way to Victory of the Germanic Spirit over the Jewish Spirit.* In this pamphlet, Marr clearly stated his feelings about the Jewish people. In 1879, Marr removed all doubts when he founded the first German organization dedicated to fighting the "Jewish threat" to Germany, thus *The League of Anti-Semites* was born.[7] The usage of the word continued to spread and was widely accepted by 1885.[8]

What Is the Definition of Antisemitism?

Below are four definitions for antisemitism:

1. Edward H. Flannery, Catholic priest and historian

   "Antisemitism is attitudes, words or actions that embody a hatred or contempt of the Jewish people as such."[9]

2. Merriam-Webster Dictionary

   "Hostility toward or discrimination against Jews as a religious, ethnic or racial group."

3. Dan Cohn-Sherbok, rabbi and author

   "Anti-Semitism is hostility toward both Judaism and the Jewish people."[10]

4. My definition

   Antisemitism is an irrational and satanic hatred of the Jewish people and Israel, characterized by destructive thoughts, words, and actions against them.

We must understand that antisemitism goes further, as it is the only kind of hatred that includes contempt for the people, the land, and the law. No aspect of Jewish life, customs, or culture and no aspect of the Jewish homeland is exempt from the vitriol of antisemitism. This will become clear when we review the history of the Jewish people through the eyes of antisemitism. It is a history that goes back to Genesis 3:15, describing the original animosity between the seed of the serpent (Satan) and the seed of the woman (Yeshua). It continued to develop further with Haman in the book of Esther, and with the enemies of the Hebrews known as the Amalekites. Eventually, after the closing of the biblical canon, many of the early church fathers contributed to the birth and development of Christian antisemitism.

Because the hatred of the Jewish people and Israel has satanic roots, Christians should not agree with or condone anti-Jewish or anti-Israel sentiments in any way, shape, or form.

How Do You Identify a Jewish Person?

Adolf Hitler tried profiling Jewish people based on the now-debunked pseudoscience known as eugenics. The use of despicable caricatures as a way to promote hatred is not new and continues on today, with demeaning and demonic caricatures being taught today to school-aged children and young adults to indoctrinate them in the hatred of Jewish people.[11] This quote from Hitler demonizes all Jewish males:

> The black-haired Jewish youth lies in wait for hours on end, satanically glaring at and spying on the unsuspicious girl whom he plans to seduce, adulterating her blood and removing her from the bosom of her own people. The Jew uses every possible means to undermine the racial foundations of a subjugated people.[12]

It is amazing that this practice is overlooked whenever political correctness sets in, almost as though to acknowledge the vileness of antisemitism would eliminate a basis for peace. In reality, hatred counteracts peace and itself eliminates the basis for peace.

Much confusion occurs when one is asked to describe exactly what it means to be a Jew. The answer can be religious, ethnic, political, cultural, or any combination of these four aspects. The safest place to find a good definition is from God's Word.

Genesis is a good place to start. I agree with Dr. Arnold Fruchtenbaum, who defines who is a Jew in the first chapter of his book *The Remnant of Israel.*[13] He bases his definition on the Abrahamic covenant first stipulated in Genesis 12:1-3 and further established in Genesis 13:15-16 and 15:4-5. Fruchtenbaum sees the biblical definition of who is a Jew based on the Abrahamic covenant, through Isaac and Jacob.

> From the Abrahamic Covenant a simple definition of Jewishness can be deduced. It lies in the repeated statement that a nation will come through the line of Abraham, Isaac and Jacob and thus defines Jewishness in terms of nationality... Biblically speaking, the Jewish people are a nation. Today we are a scattered nation; but we are, nevertheless, a nation. We are a nation because we are descendants of Abraham, Isaac and Jacob. The implication of this definition is that no matter what a Jew does, [a Jew] can never become a non-Jew; no matter what the individual Jew may believe or disbelieve, he/she remains a Jew.[14]

Furthermore, that covenant is ratified through Abraham's son Isaac (Genesis 26:2-5) and Isaac's son Jacob (Genesis 28:13-15). This points to the relationship between God and the Jewish people. Thus, from these passages, we understand that a nation will come from Abraham through Isaac and through Jacob. Jacob had 12 sons who were the fathers of the 12 tribes of Israel.

A Jew is then a physical descendant of Abraham, Isaac, and Jacob through one of the twelve tribes of Israel. This is how Jewishness—an ethnic state—is defined.

What Is Judaism?

Compared to Jewishness, which is an ethnic state, Judaism is a religion with practices and traditions. You do not have to be ethnically Jewish to be an adherent of Judaism. Judaism and Jewishness are not synonymous.

KEY POINTS FOR UNDERSTANDING ISRAEL

Biblically speaking, Israel can mean the Jewish people or the land of Israel.

When referring to the geographical land given by God to Abraham and his descendants, that land is called by many names, including Israel, Land of Promise, Canaan, the United Kingdom, and the Divided Kingdom. Specifically, when referring to the Northern Kingdom, the term *Israel* is used (see 2 Samuel 2:9; Hosea 5:3).

The same Abrahamic covenant from which we draw the definition of a Jew also tells us that God has promised a land to the Jewish people with some specific boundaries. In Genesis 12:7, God is brief and to the point: "The LORD appeared to Abram and said, 'To your descendants I will give this land.'"

God repeats that promise in Genesis 13:15, and gives more details in Genesis 15:18-21:

> On that day the Lord made a covenant with Abram, saying, "To your descendants I have given this land, from the river of Egypt as far as the great river, the river Euphrates: the Kenite and the Kenizzite and the Kadmonite and the Hittite and the Perizzite and the Rephaim and the Amorite and the Canaanite and the Girgashite and the Jebusite."

Because the Abrahamic covenant is unconditional *and* eternal,[15] that promise is still intact today. According to the biblical boundaries stated in Genesis 15, Israel's much larger biblical makeup has yet to be fulfilled. The current borders based on agreements made in 1948, 1967, or at any other time come nowhere near God's promised real estate boundaries. Based on these biblical facts, I disagree with the term *Occupied Territories* and prefer to call them the *Disputed Territories.*

In this book, I will speak of Israel either from a biblical or secular standpoint as it relates to its unalienable right to the land given by God. Biblically speaking, Israel is also the name given to Jacob after he wrestled with the Angel of the Lord at Bethel (Genesis 32:24-32); and, incidentally, the following passage is another place where God confirms His promise of a Jewish people and their own land:

> God appeared to Jacob again when he came from Paddan-aram, and He blessed him. God said to him, "Your name is Jacob; you shall no longer be called Jacob, but Israel shall be your name." Thus He called him Israel. God also said to him, "I am God Almighty; be fruitful and multiply; a nation and a company of nations shall come from you, and kings shall come forth from you. The land which I gave to Abraham and Isaac, I will give it to you, and I will give the land to your descendants after you" (Genesis 35:9-12).

The same promise is also stated in Genesis 32:28; 1 Kings 18:31; and 2 Kings 17:34.

Since its modern rebirth as a state, Israel as a piece of land has become a bone of contention for the whole world.[16] The modern-day Palestinian people claim historical ownership of that land reaching back to before the Jewish people lived there. The current dispute promotes the misconception that the Palestinian people are an ethnic group, which is not the case.

In the next chapter, we'll take a closer look at what this dispute is all about, and the reasons this land is Israel's homeland.

CHAPTER 2

MYTHS AND FACTS ABOUT THE PALESTINIANS, ZIONISM, AND THE ISRAELI HOMELAND

To better understand the true meaning of *Palestine,* we must go back in history much earlier than the mid-1960s, when the Arabs who lived in the land began to use the term to identify themselves.

While the exact origin of the term *Palestine* is still debated, there are aspects of the word's meaning that we can know for sure. It possibly once described a people group known as the Philistines, but that people group was in no way connected to the Palestinians as we know them today—not ethnically, not linguistically, and not culturally. The very first time that the word *Palestine* is mentioned in any literature is in in the fifth-century BC Greek work *The History of Herodotus* by Herodotus, where it is mentioned five times to describe a coastal area inhabited by the ancient Philistines.

It was about 600 years later that the real damage started. In AD 132, a Jewish revolt took place against the Romans. This was known as the Bar Kochba revolt (Shimon Bar Kochba was a false messiah in Israel at the time[1]). Things didn't end well for the Jewish people. After a bloodbath of gigantic proportions, Israel was renamed *Palaestina* by Emperor Hadrian of Rome. The rebranding of the land with the name of Israel's ancient enemies, the Philistines, was an effort to undermine Jewish history and humiliate the Jewish people. In addition, Hadrian renamed Jerusalem, calling it *Aelia Capitolina.* The name *Palestine* stuck and continued to be used after that time. The term is not found in the Bible itself, and appears only in the map section of Bibles, meaning the term is not part of God's inspired Word.

When the British were in control of this region from 1922 to 1948, the area was governed under what was known as the British Palestine Mandate. In the original text of the Mandate itself, written in 1922, we read this:

> Whereas recognition has thereby been given to the historical connection of the Jewish people with Palestine and to the grounds for reconstituting their national home in that country.[2]

I must clarify that I do not have an issue calling Israel *Palestine* as long as the term is used in a geographical sense to describe the land mass of Israel up until the mid-1960s. Up to that time in history, the term *Palestine* simply described a piece of land in the Middle East. Even after Israel became a state in 1948 and the name *Israel* was applied to the land and nation, the word *Palestine* was not an issue. Not until under the leadership of Yasser Arafat—the chairman of the Palestinian Liberation Organization—did the definition for Palestine go from geographical to political, and describe an allegedly displaced people group that became known as the Palestinians. Arafat worked hard at redefining the word. When he spoke of displaced Palestinians, he expected people to understand that he was describing

Arabs whose land had been stolen by Jews, Arabs who supposedly had been deprived of their ancestral land. However, before the 1960s, historical documents were replete with descriptions of Israel as Palestine, including the British Mandate quoted earlier. These documents confirm the term was geographical in nature.

If we look at article 4 of the British Mandate, we find two words in the same passage that any modern-day Palestinian would be hard pressed to associate in a positive light: *Palestinian* and *Zionist*. In the context of the mandate, it was to the current leaders of the Zionist movement that the administration and government of Palestine were entrusted. Here is what the mandate says:

> An appropriate Jewish agency shall be recognized as a public body for the purpose of advising and cooperating with the Administration of Palestine in such economic, social and other matters as may affect the establishment of the Jewish national home and the interests of the Jewish population in Palestine, and, subject always to the control of the Administration to assist and take part in the development of the country.
>
> The Zionist organization, so long as its organization and constitution are in the opinion of the Mandatory appropriate, shall be recognised as such agency. It shall take steps in consultation with His Britannic Majesty's Government to secure the cooperation of all Jews who are willing to assist in the establishment of the Jewish national home.[3]

So, until the early 1960s, Palestine was always synonymous with Israel, the Jewish State. Arabs in neighboring countries never called themselves Palestinians, but rather, Syrians, Lebanese, Jordanians, Egyptians, etc. Most Arabs in the early 1900s would have argued that Palestinian Arabs were simply Syrians, as Mitchell Bard documents in his well-researched book *Myths and Facts: A Guide to the Arab-Israeli Conflict.* He writes:

> Prior to partition, Palestinian Arabs did not view themselves as having a separate identity. When the First Congress of Muslim-Christian Associations met in Jerusalem in February 1919 to choose Palestinian representatives for the Paris Peace Conference, the following resolution was adopted: We consider Palestine as part of Arab Syria, as it has never been separated from it at any time. We are connected with it by national, religious, linguistic, natural, economic and geographical bonds.[4]

While God uses different names for the land of Israel, such as "the land of Canaan" (Genesis 17:8) and "the land" (Exodus 6:8), and while this land is commonly known as the Promised Land or the land of promise (see Genesis 50:24), nowhere in the Bible is Israel ever called Palestine except three inconsistent times solely in the King James Version (Exodus 15:14; Isaiah 14:29; and Joel 3:4), when it translates the Hebrew *Peleseth* into "Palestina" or "Palestine" instead of "Philistia."

Even the Qur'an (Sura Maida 5:21-22) mentions the "holy land" in the context of Moses and the spies preparing to enter the land of Canaan; but never does it call the region Palestine. Jerusalem isn't even mentioned by name in the Qur'an.[5]

Until the mid-1960s, the name Palestine was always synonymous with Israel. It described the same piece of real estate that became the Jewish State in 1948. As we just saw, the idea of Palestine as a legitimate country for a displaced people known as the Palestinians was introduced and heavily promoted by the late Yasser Arafat, who started and headed the Palestinian Liberation Organization.

Somehow, a revived anti-Jewish agenda was growing fast globally. This was partially in response to what was seen by Arabs as a Zionist existential threat to the Arabs, where Jewish settlers and pioneers were perceived as land grabbers willing to stop at nothing—including the killing of Arabs—to colonize Palestine. This perception is false—for decades, Jewish settlers have bought malaria-infested swamps at very high prices from Arab landowners. Jews have been accused of stealing land from local Arabs,[6] but only 45,000 acres were acquired without a sale—through governmental agreement—out of 463,000 acres acquired. The vast majority of acres were purchased, and much of it at very high prices.

A CLOSER LOOK AT ZIONISM

The terms *Zionism* and *Zionist*[7] were coined in 1890 by Jewish activist Nathan Birnbaum (1864–1937), who also played an important part in the first Zionist Congress held in 1897 alongside its first president, Theodor Herzl. The word *Zion* comes from the Hebrew *tzion*, a reference to Jerusalem and often, by extension, to the land of Israel itself. *Zion* is first mentioned in 2 Samuel 5:7: "David captured the stronghold of Zion, that is the city of David." According to scholar Mitchell Bard, Zionism is "the national movement for the return of the Jewish people to their homeland and the resumption of Jewish sovereignty in the Land of Israel."[8]

Political agendas combined with religious convictions provide us with many possible questions about Zionism, such as the following:

- When and where was Zionism born?
- Who were the major key players in the birth and furtherance of Zionism?
- Is Zionism racism?
- What is Christian Zionism?

In the upcoming pages, we will answer these questions.

Zionism, Born out of Necessity

Since the early church fathers, European Jews have suffered significantly at the hands of many popes, kings, and the masses. Antisemitism, in many shapes, from theological to social to ethnic, has punctuated Jewish life throughout the centuries, limiting if not eliminating any semblance of normalcy within the Jewish communities of Europe. The Crusades, the crushing hatred unleashed by false claims of blood libel against the Jewish people,[9] the 1492 Spanish Inquisition, and the creation of the first Jewish ghetto in Italy, to name a few, were ominous milestones of terror against the Jewish people on the timeline of Jewish history. Things went on to become much worse with the Russian pogroms (massacres during fomented riots against the Jews in the ghettos) and the Holocaust (1938–1945), a systematic extermination in which six million Jews were murdered by the Nazis.

After all this persecution and devastation, something had to change. Jewish people felt they had to "leave the ghetto" not just physically, but spiritually and emotionally as well, and they saw a glimmer of hope with the advent of the *Haskalah* (Jewish Enlightenment).

This movement among European Jews of the seventeenth and eighteenth centuries advocated a more secularized way of life, hopefully leading to their emancipation and thus better integration into non-Jewish societies. Moses Mendelssohn (1729–1786) was a German-Jewish philosopher and the father of the *Haskalah*, which introduced a new emphasis on Jewish culture and history, much of it apart from religion. This emphasis was applied in various Jewish communities across Western and Eastern Europe. For a short while, there seemed to be a period of respite for the Jewish people. Emancipation was working…or was it?

THEODOR HERZL, EARLY PROPONENT OF ZIONISM

Along with Leon Pinsker (1821–1891) before him, Theodor Herzl (1860–1904), an Austro-Hungarian Jewish reporter, had a vision for a homeland for the Jewish people. An incident in France, beginning in 1894 and continuing through 1906, brought Herzl on the scene as a correspondent for an Austrian newspaper. This incident became known as the Dreyfus Affair and proved that the Jewish attempt at gaining acceptance through secular assimilation was not working.

The Dreyfus Affair, the Catalyst for Zionism

In 1894, French Alsatian Jew Alfred Dreyfus, a French army officer, was wrongly accused of treason against the French government and sentenced to life in prison. In 1896, new evidence surfaced that could exonerate Dreyfus, but antisemitic officials suppressed the evidence.

In 1899, Dreyfus was brought up for retrial. In a vitriolic explosion of hatred, antisemitic mobs took to the streets of Paris, screaming, "Death to the Jews!" Even though Dreyfus was later cleared and even fully reinstated as an officer in 1906, in France, the climate had changed. What is known today as the Dreyfus Affair was the catalyst for conceiving of and pursuing Zionism.

The Vienna newspaper *Neue Freie Presse* sent Theodor Herzl to cover the Dreyfus Affair. To be sure, Herzl's obsession with Jewish existence in a land of their own predated the Dreyfus Affair. But it is the very mistreatment of Dreyfus and, by association, the Jews of France, that prompted Herzl to compile his work of several years into the historic pamphlet *Der Judenstaat*, or *The Jewish State*, published in Vienna in 1896. In it, he stated:

> Palestine is our unforgettable historic homeland...Let me repeat once more my opening words: The Jews who will it shall achieve their State. We shall live at last as free men on our own soil, and in our own homes peacefully die.

> The world will be liberated by our freedom, enriched by our wealth, magnified by our greatness. And whatever we attempt there for our own benefit will redound mightily and beneficially to the good of all mankind.[10]

Herzl was convinced that the only viable solution was a mass exodus of the Jews of Europe back to Israel, the land of their ancestors. He further stated: "Political principle will provide the basis, technology the means and the driving force will be the Jewish tragedy."[11]

Herzl, if not the originator of the concept of Zionism, was definitely the visionary, catalyst, and leader of political Zionism. Ernst Pawel, in *The Labyrinth of Exile: A Life of Theodor Herzl*, explained what Herzl contributed to the Zionist movement:

> He brought to it leadership, organization and a unique blend of fantasy and practical realism, but his most important contribution by far was the messianic image of himself, his stature in the eyes of the Jews and in the eyes of the world.[12]

The First Zionist Congress

In 1897, the First Zionist Congress convened in Basel, Switzerland. It wasn't without struggles that Herzl was able to organize this historic event. Most of the Jewish leaders of the time demonstrated some resistance, while the masses expressed interest and even excitement. The message of "We are a people" found in *Der Judenstaadt* resonated with the Jews of Eastern Europe, who were looking for any hopeful escape from the pogroms and the difficult Eastern European *shtetl* (hamlet) life.

At this first congress, Herzl and the delegates adopted the Basel Program and declared:

> Zionism aims at establishing for the Jewish people a publicly and legally assured home in Palestine. For the attainment of this purpose, the Congress considers the following means serviceable:
>
> 1. The promotion of the settlement of Jewish agriculturists, artisans and tradesmen in Palestine.
> 2. The federation of all Jews into local or general groups, according to the laws of the various countries.
> 3. The strengthening of the Jewish feeling and consciousness.
> 4. Preparatory steps for the attainment of those governmental grants that are necessary to the achievement of the Zionist purpose.[13]

Herzl, who was elected president of the First Jewish Congress in 1897, convened six more yearly events until 1903. The Congress's location was moved to Geneva in 1936.

Lobbying for a Return to the Homeland

Herzl started lobbying for the Jewish people's return to a safe land of their own. He first met with German Kaiser Wilhelm II in Istanbul in 1898 to convince him to help secure land in Israel. But Herzl wasn't taken very seriously; and the Kaiser, influenced by his own antisemitic tendencies, flatly rejected Herzl's appeals for a Jewish homeland.

Disappointed and frustrated but not discouraged, Herzl met with British Colonial Secretary Joseph Chamberlain, who, as a compromise, offered the Jews the country of Uganda in East Africa. Eventually, in 1903, during the Sixth Zionist Congress, and by now rather discouraged, Herzl proposed the move of the Jewish people to Uganda as a temporary solution until Palestine could be secured. The Jewish people who followed his leadership reacted immediately and, at the sight of a possible split within the Zionist movement, Herzl decided against the compromise.[14]

Herzl died a year later in Vienna at age 44, having spent most of his adult life fighting for a Jewish homeland. In Vienna in 1897, he had written in his diary, almost prophetically: "At Basel, I founded the Jewish State...In five years, perhaps, and certainly, in fifty years, everyone will perceive it."

ZIONISM AFTER THEODOR HERZL

One could argue that during Herzl's life, Zionism was mainly a political movement relying on diplomacy for any sustainable existence. But even Herzl saw that political Zionism and practical Zionism, while having the same goal, had different methods. The chasm would divide further as the Jewish homeland became more of a reality and Jews continued to return to their ancestral land following the First Aliyah (1881–1903).[15]

Herzl had worked hard at gathering funds, yet they hadn't been disbursed significantly, and a move from the theoretical to the practical was necessary. In addition, there was a serious push for a Hebrew renaissance. The idea of a cultural Zionism, mostly introduced by Russian Jews, appealed to a wider spectrum within the Jewish community, while political Zionism left many of the more religious leaders unsatisfied and unable to relate to the cause.

A key player who had not always seen eye to eye with Herzl was Russian Jewish essayist Asher Ginsberg (1856–1927), who went by the pen name of Ahad Ha'am, Hebrew for "one of the people." Ha'am is known as the father of cultural Zionism, and his vision was for "a Jewish State, and not merely a State of Jews."[16] He felt that the Jewish people should return gradually to Palestine, with Diaspora Jews being given a vision of the new homeland, making them jealous and thus drawing them to move.[17]

Another important figure in the fight for a cultural rebirth was Hebrew lexicographer and journalist Eliezer Ben-Yehuda, who immigrated to Israel during the First Aliyah[18] in 1881. He dedicated the rest of his life, not without tremendous hardship, to the rebirth of Hebrew as a modern tongue.[19]

Robert St. John, Ben-Yehuda's biographer, wrote of him in *Tongue of the Prophets*:

> In twenty years, he had fathered ten children. Five had died but five still lived. Two of them spoke fluently the language he had spent so much of these twenty years trying to bring back to life. More important, the streets of Jerusalem, the marketplaces, the villages scattered over the desert were thronged with other Jews who spoke this same revived language.[20]

In the decade following Herzl's death, Zionist influx continued in the Holy Land, and about 100,000 pioneers lived there. Times were hard, workdays were long, and poverty was rampant; but the spirit of hope kept Zionism alive. On the eve of World War I, Zionism had become a reality—a fragile one, but a reality nonetheless.

THE FIRST WORLD WAR AND ZIONISM

June 28, 1914, saw the assassination of Archduke Franz Ferdinand of Austria in Sarajevo. This precipitated events that led to the beginning of World War I, and the face of Europe changed forever. At the beginning of the war, 80 percent of the ten million Jews of Europe lived in the Russian and Austro-Hungarian Empires.[21] The Jewish communities of Europe had grown accustomed to hardship and had endured many forms of antisemitism. Unfortunately, the advent of World War I worsened their condition as their lives once again became punctuated by lootings, pogroms, and expulsions.

As the war progressed, the Allied nations ratified various treaties and worked on agreements to share the spoils they obtained. One such agreement was that the Ottoman Empire would have to be divided, which included the region of Palestine. By the end of the war, the British had conquered this area. Amid all negotiations, Britain officially endorsed the Zionist program, and almost overnight, Zionism started to take root in the Holy Land. This was a major step in the right direction for the Jewish people, yet the surprise of a British endorsement would eventually be overtaken by the shock of a British about-face.

The Balfour Declaration

As World War I came to an end, the British government acted favorably toward the idea of a Jewish homeland. One important figure of that time who would also become Israel's first president was Chaim Weizmann (1874–1952). Diplomacy continued to play a part in the furtherance of the Zionist agenda, and Weizmann was good at it.

In 1906, Weizmann had just helped the British by sharing his formula to better produce acetone, which is related to the production of explosive propellants. His invention helped greatly with the war effort. Consequently, he became close to Lord David Lloyd George, who would later become prime minister of England. But it was not until Weizmann had a meeting with Lord Arthur James Balfour that things began to crystallize toward the establishment of a Jewish homeland.

Balfour, who had tried to convince Weizmann that the Uganda proposal for a new Jewish homeland was a good deal, somehow ended up convinced by Weizmann that only the land of Palestine would be acceptable. From that point on, Balfour became a Zionist. Weizmann met Balfour again when Lloyd George was prime minister, and

Balfour told him, "You know, I was thinking of that conversation of ours in 1906 and I believe that when the guns stop firing, you may get your Jerusalem."[22]

In 1917, after having become a British citizen in 1910, Weizmann became the first president of the British Zionist Federation and worked feverishly with Lord Balfour to develop what would be known as the Balfour Declaration. This milestone for Zionism vindicated the works of Theodor Herzl, Chaim Weizmann, Nahum Sokolow, and other key Zionist leaders. Things appeared to be looking up for the Jewish people for the establishment of a Jewish homeland in Palestine. In less than 70 words, the Declaration stated:

> His Majesty's government view[s] with favour the establishment in Palestine of a national home for the Jewish people, and will use their best endeavours to facilitate the achievement of this object, it being clearly understood that nothing shall be done which may prejudice the civil and religious rights of existing non-Jewish communities in Palestine, or the rights and political status enjoyed by Jews in any other country.[23]

In 1919, Balfour reiterated Britain's favor of the establishment of a Jewish homeland in Palestine, and included a commitment from France, Italy, and the United States:

> The Four Great Powers [Britain, France, Italy, and the United States] are committed to Zionism. And Zionism, be it right or wrong, good or bad, is rooted in age-long traditions, in present needs, and future hopes, of far profounder import than the desires and prejudices of the 700,000 Arabs who now inhabit that ancient land. In my opinion that is right.[24]

As former deputy prime minister of Israel Abba Eban said, "The Balfour Declaration is the decisive victory of the Jewish people in modern history."[25]

In 1922, following the historic concept found in the Balfour Declaration, the League of Nations (an organization charged with using diplomacy to maintain peace, and a precursor of the United Nations) had a say. It approved the British Mandate for Palestine, giving Britain jurisdiction over the Holy Land and thereby authority to help with the securing of a Jewish Homeland.

The Origins of a Two-State Solution

By the time World War I was over in 1918, similar promises had been made to both the Arabs and the Jews in the Middle East because of the complicated negotiations of the 1916 Sykes-Picot Agreement and the controversial 1917 Balfour declaration. As a result, the establishment of a Jewish homeland was delayed, which contributed to the annihilation of millions of Jewish people during the Holocaust in World War II.

While Zionist pioneers continued to settle in Palestine, the world was about to enter into a new global conflict. And once again, the Jewish people would become the scapegoats of humanity—this time, in proportions that had never been reached before.

The large influx of Jewish people fleeing a pre-World War II Europe for Palestine led to the Arab revolt of 1936–1939. This nationalistic uprising for independence from the British wasn't successful for the Arabs, but it led the British forces to pay attention to some of the Jewish groups present in the area, including the paramilitary organization known as Haganah, which later was integrated into the Israel Defense Forces (IDF).

After witnessing the failed Arab revolt, Britain became concerned and responded by appointing a royal commission, known as the Peel Commission, which recommended that Palestine be partitioned into

Arab and Jewish lands. The Peel Commission led to the publishing of the "White Paper of 1939" by Britain. This would change the promises made by Lord Balfour and seriously limit Jewish immigration into Palestine at a time when Jewish people were being led in droves to the Nazi gas chambers. This closed the door to a safe place for Jews to settle and was poor timing, to say the least!

The Aftermath of World War II and the Jewish State

"The war against the Jews," as author Lucy Dawidowicz[26] called World War II, eventually ended in 1945 with the capitulation of Germany. Three years later, in 1948, another milestone of prophetic proportions was about to take place. Israel would be reborn as a modern nation. Was this as a result of the Holocaust, or the persistent toiling of the early Zionist fathers? Or both? It is impossible to say with certainty, but this rebirth had to happen so that future, unfulfilled Bible prophecies could eventually come to pass. The fact remains that much of the groundwork laid out by visionaries such as Herzl, Weizmann, Ha'am, and Ben-Yehuda was about to pay off, yet not without a further sacrifice that is still being felt today in the twenty-first century.

ZIONISM IS HERE TO STAY

Many followers of Yeshua[27] look at the Bible and clearly see that God is *not* done with Israel. They see a glorious future for the people and the land (Jeremiah 31:35-37; Zechariah 8:20-23). They understand that the promises of Genesis 12:3 still stand, and they want to be in the center of God's will by blessing the people that He calls "the apple of His eye" (Zechariah 2:8).

Believers in Jesus who recognize Israel's right to the land and the Jewish people's right to return to it are often called Christian Zionists. In the Bible, God Himself declared His plan for the Jews to have this land as an everlasting possession (Genesis 17:8; 48:3-4; Psalm

105:10-11). Thus, Christian Zionism is a noble cause and should be promoted by every Bible-believing Christian.

There is a lot of scriptural evidence that factually validates the claims of Zionism. What's more, in Leviticus 25:23, God Himself said that He alone owned the land: "The land, moreover, shall not be sold permanently, for the land is Mine; for you are but aliens and sojourners with Me."

The foundation for Zionism was established by the very first Zionist—God Himself—in the book of Genesis. And it continues to run like an uninterrupted thread through the tapestry of Jewish history. If Zionism has existed for a long time, we also cannot deny that God has used people like Herzl, Ha'am, Ben-Yehuda, Weizmann, Ben-Gurion, Golda Meir, and many others to further promote the right of the Jewish people to the land of Israel. What God has established, no man can destroy (Jeremiah 31:35-37). In the words of Abba Eban, Israeli ambassador to the United States, a diplomat and politician:

> Zionism is nothing more—but also nothing less—than the Jewish people's sense of origin and destination in the land linked eternally with its name.[28]

PART 2

A TIMELINE OF HATRED

CHAPTER 3

ANTISEMITISM FROM THE CHURCH FATHERS TO THE EARLY MIDDLE AGES

Eschatology is the study of theology that pertains to the last days of humanity as described in the Bible. The term is comprised of two Greek words: *eschatos*, which mean "last," and *logy*, meaning "the study of."

In the context of this book, eschatological antisemitism refers to a new kind of antisemitism related to the final chapter of human history and the mounting antagonism against Israel and the Jewish people.[1] We should not be surprised to see this unfold in a new unleashing of global distrust, hatred, and failure to honor God's Word.

As a result of the original sin, hatred has come about despite God being good, His Word being true, and His love being clearly expressed for the world. Tracing the rise of antisemitism gives us a way to track the rise of hatred and gives us the opportunity to consider what type of future we wish for ourselves and others. Awareness about the past, honesty about the present, and hearts shaped by the love of Yeshua will lead us reliably toward the right direction for the future.

Like all other kinds of hatred, antisemitism didn't come about in a vacuum. We are where we are today because of an ongoing progression of historical events against the Jewish people that have mushroomed into a worldwide jihad against them—the State of Israel in particular, and the West in general. In the Jewish writings (Tanach), the roots of this hatred can be traced as far back as Israel's interaction with the Amalekites (Exodus 17:8-16; Deuteronomy 25:17-19). Exodus and even the events in the book of Esther also document this (Exodus 1:15-22; Esther 3:8-9; 5:13-14; 9:25).

Hatred started as brother against brother with Cain and Abel, and Cain's murder of his brother illustrates the effects of anger and hatred in the real world. The potential to hate and murder is part of the sinful nature of mankind. The Amalekites are an example of hatred that arises from an enemy, an outside source not of our clan. This type of hatred has been recognized since ancient times in the wars and conflicts recorded throughout history. The Bible tells us that such conflicts will continue until the Prince of Peace returns to Jerusalem, as we see in Micah 4. This type of hatred is typical of racial hatred, of one tribe against another tribe. The Bible also foretold how, in the end times, nation will rise up against nation (Matthew 24:7). Today, we are seeing this type of hatred all around us.

THE EARLY CHURCH FATHERS

We will start our historical overview of hatred with the first century AD, a time that overlaps with the ministry of the apostle Paul, also known as Rabbi Saul. Keep in mind that a vast array of scholarly work has already been produced on the history of the early church, and it is not within the scope of this book to cover all the major developments. Instead, we will study the sequence of historical events that relate to the progression of anti-Jewish sentiment up to where it is today.

The first five centuries of faith in Jesus Christ (Yeshua the Messiah) saw the rise of many church leaders, theologians, and teachers. Their leadership dominated church life and doctrine for centuries to follow. Much of early Christianity was structured, systematized, and even protected by these men. Even if many of them were greatly responsible for the mistreating of the Jewish people, much is owed to these men, who helped to advance a faith still somewhat in its infancy.

As the early church fathers studied the Tanach (the Old Testament), they came to realize they could benefit from studying with rabbis who spoke and read Hebrew. In doing so, they received invaluable knowledge of the Hebrew Scriptures from their contemporary Jewish sages. Along with that knowledge came some unavoidable exegetical[2] influence from some of their Jewish counterparts.

The destruction of the temple in AD 70 by the Romans presented a dilemma to surviving Jews, who found themselves dispersed from the land of Israel. So many of their practices had rested on the sacrificial system that in order to survive as a religion, a resolution had to be found. The result was a council in AD 90 in which rabbis created a new basis for practicing Judaism, now called rabbinic Judaism. Rabbinic Judaism is a departure from the traditional biblical faith that depended on the existence of the temple to apply it. It focused on three elements: Torah-learning, prayer/fasting, and good deeds. Torah-learning consisted of studying the Hebrew Scriptures (the Christian Old Testament), the traditional oral law of Moses, and the many, many commentaries later codified in the Talmud.

Because of the emphasis on study of the Scriptures, with no Jewish male being exempt, the study as well as interpretation of the Scriptures multiplied. This great body of information, naturally, was seen as a blessing and benefit to the early church fathers as they began to build a theology for the newly founded church that would increasingly become influenced by Gentiles. It emerged in the fourth century with its own council to decide how faith should be applied. Ironically, rabbinic (as opposed to biblical) Judaism and Christianity grew up side by side, influencing one another.

What happened to the Jewish believers in Yeshua? As from the beginning of faith in Yeshua, they were persecuted by both Jews and Gentiles! Yeshua prophesied that His followers, who at the time were part of the Jewish community, would be kicked out of the synagogues (John 16:2). That prophecy began to be fulfilled after Stephen gained attention for performing miracles. When he was summoned to give his testimony before the Sanhedrin, he preached to the Jewish leaders, chastising them for following in the footsteps of their ancient fathers, who had killed the prophets and stood proudly against God, hard-hearted and unyielding to the Holy Spirit (Acts 7:2-53). Their response was to explode with anger and stone Stephen (verses 54-58).

Some Christian teachers have made the mistake of using Stephen's speech to the Sanhedrin to justify hatred of the Jews. Ironically, Saul (his Hebrew name), who was also known as the apostle Paul (his Roman name), was the young man who minded the robes of those who stoned Stephen (verse 58). In Saul's early career of persecuting fellow Jews who came to faith in Yeshua the Messiah, he likely was following the lead of his elders within the Sanhedrin. When the Messiah appeared to Saul on the road to Damascus, notice that He did not ask him why he was persecuting the Jewish believers. Rather, He asked, "Saul, Saul, why are you persecuting Me?" (Acts 9:4). When people persecute God's beloved, He takes it very personally (see also Psalm 83:5).

There are four different approaches to rabbinic exegesis of the Hebrew Scriptures, going from literal to mystical. Rabbis would almost always favor one approach over another, but often use more than one. Nevertheless, rabbinic schools of thought started to develop over the centuries, and as a result, different interpretations of the Hebrew Scriptures became available.

Not only did this mean that the church fathers were receiving many different interpretations from literal to mystical from their rabbi mentors, but inevitably, they also started to adopt some of the exegetical methods of Western rhetoric that originated from the Greco-Roman culture that surrounded the early church.

Greek rhetoric began and has continued in the West as the basis for education, theology, law and government. It is a two-edged sword, literally. This type of rhetoric was developed to assist leaders in taking action by appealing to common values. Rhetoric can rouse nations to protect their homelands or to build education systems that produce tomorrow's leaders. However, it can also be used to castigate and ostracize enemies while praising heroes. These techniques can be twisted and misused to gain consensus to eliminate or sideline perceived enemies. Hitler took his lessons in doing so from Plato's *The Republic* and applied them to 12 million helpless "undesirables," including 6 million Jews.

The next unfortunate but logical step was for many of the church fathers to apply their newfound methods of interpretation to entities like the church, Israel, Christians, and Jews.

What had started as a rather literal approach to God's Word by the followers of Messiah and the apostolic fathers slowly morphed into a more allegorical and even mystical approach, thus opening the door for the first wave of anti-Judaism.

This early wave of anti-Jewish sentiment was mostly theological, and we could label it theological antisemitism or theological anti-Judaism.

How Flawed Theology Paved the Way for Hatred

Some of the early church fathers had a distorted understanding of biblical Judaism. From their perspective, Israel had been a continual disappointment to God, who had done so much for them.

They needed to separate the "sinful" from the "holy," so these church fathers started to ostracize the Jewish people.

Christianity would soon claim all the virtuous actions in the Old Testament for a kind of preexistent church. If not by name, certainly conceptually, replacement theology[3] emerged as a new doctrine. And the views espoused by this theology influenced legal actions taken against the Jews early on.

Many of the church fathers have left a negative legacy of their understanding of the Jewish people. By promoting flawed doctrine that we will soon examine, the early church fathers introduced a major source of hatred into the church. Jewish history has been punctuated by harmful actions based on this early departure from the truth. While the origins of this way of thinking were theologically driven, antisemitic hatred, and the basis for tolerating hatred toward others, was borne out of the least likely of all places: the church itself.

Let's look now at a short chronological list of some of the church fathers' writings as they relate to the Jewish people. These represent quite a departure from a balanced, literal, and contextual interpretation of the Bible. While most of the church fathers would not have condoned the systematic killing of Jewish people, their words carried a lot of weight, and the negative effects of their words have lasted much longer than they could have imagined. Their views became the foundation of a much more aggressive form of Jew hatred that kept growing and morphing over the centuries and persists today. They helped to develop the false notion that the Jewish people were "Christ killers," a term that almost every Jewish person has heard at one time or another.

Five Early Theologians Who Opened the Door to Hatred

Ignatius, Bishop of Antioch (circa AD 35–50 to circa AD 98–117)

Ignatius of Antioch was an apostolic father, the third Bishop of Antioch, and was also a contemporary and student of the apostle John. He wrote:

> For if we are still practicing Judaism, we admit that we have not received God's favor...It is wrong to talk about Jesus Christ and live like Jews. For Christianity did not believe in Judaism, but Judaism in Christianity.[4]

Here, the reader is simply told that it is wrong to practice Judaism because it has apparently been replaced by Christianity. The suggestion is planted that Christianity preceded Judaism, although, of course, history shows that Christianity was a Jewish movement that Gentiles joined.

Tertullian (AD 160–220)

Tertullian was a Christian author who produced a large body of literature in Latin. He was also an apologist who taught against heresy. Tertullian has been called "the father of Latin Christianity" and "the founder of Western theology." He was one of the first church fathers to formulate trinitarian terminology.

In his work *Adversus Judaeos,* or *Against the Jews,* Tertullian's theological anti-Judaism is purely ideological. He uses the Hebrew Scriptures to methodically disprove the relevancy of the Mosaic law and then goes on to prove that all blessings to ethnic Israel have been passed on to the "other nation" of God: the Christians.

Writer David Efroymson, in his work on Tertullian's influence and legacy, stated that many followed after Tertullian with their anti-Jewish diatribes. Efroymson made the following profound statement, alluding to the distant but destructive impact that Tertullian's teachings had: "The road from here to Auschwitz is long and may not be direct, but one can get there from here."[5]

Origen of Alexandria (AD 185–254)

Origen was a church father who contributed to the early formation of Christian doctrines. He further developed the allegorical method of interpretation, always looking for deeper mysterious meanings in Scriptures that were not literal. He often painted the Jewish people as "Christ killers." In his work *Contra Celsum* (*Against Celsus*), Origen wrote,

> One fact, then, which proves that Jesus was something divine and sacred, is this, that Jews should have suffered on His account now for a lengthened time calamities of such severity. And we say with confidence that they will never be restored to their former condition. For they committed a crime of the most unhallowed kind, in conspiring against the Saviour of the human race in that city where they offered up to God a worship containing the symbols of mighty mysteries. It accordingly behooved that city where Jesus underwent these sufferings to perish utterly, and the Jewish nation to be overthrown, and the invitation to happiness offered them by God to pass to others—the Christians...[6]

Origen's use of the allegorical approach opened a can of worms that allowed subjective interpretations to creep into theology. The result is a disconnect from God's Word and His salvation story from Genesis to Revelation regarding Jews and Gentiles. Origen had to ignore much of the Jewish context of the Bible to arrive at his conclusions.

John Chrysostom (AD 344–407)

Chrysostom is still considered one of the greatest of all church fathers and is known as "the golden-mouth orator." Much of what was written against the Jews by previous church fathers was dwarfed by Chrysostom's contribution. His descriptions of the Jewish people were extremely abrasive. He even went as far as calling Jewish practices a disease.

> The synagogue is worse than a brothel...It is the den of scoundrels and the repair of wild beasts...The temple of demons devoted to idolatrous cults...the refuge of brigands and debauchees, and the cavern of devils. It is a criminal assembly of Jews...a place of meeting for the assassins of Christ...a house worse than a drinking shop...a den of thieves, a house of ill fame, a dwelling of iniquity, the refuge of devils, a gulf and abyss of perdition...I would say the same things about their souls...As for me, I hate the synagogue...I hate the Jews for the same reason...Men who are lustful, rapacious, greedy, perfidious bandits...inveterate murderers, destroyers, men possessed by the devil...they have surpassed the ferocity of wild beasts, for they murder their offspring and immolate them to the devil.[7]

Augustine (AD 354–430)

A contemporary of John Chrysostom, Augustine was a Christian theologian and philosopher who influenced Western Christianity in ways still felt today. He was unique in the fact that his treatment of the Jewish people reflected some ambivalence. He highly respected the writings of the apostle Paul and often quoted Romans 9–11, yet he could not understand, let alone accept, the Jewish people's blindness and animosity toward Christianity. With regard to the Jewish people's treatment of Yeshua, he wrote:

> The Jews hold Him, the Jews insult, the Jews bind Him, crown Him with thorns, dishonor Him with spitting, scourge Him, overwhelm Him with revilings, hang Him upon the tree, pierce Him with a spear.[8]

Starting with Constantine and under Augustine's rule, laws began to be passed against the Jews. The church fathers, then, were the starting point of a long line of judicial actions aimed at controlling, ostracizing, and ultimately, annihilating the Jews.

In addition, the council of Nicaea decided to alter the celebration of the Jewish Passover by adding the celebration of Easter, and changing the timing of the celebration to a solar calendar event instead of keeping its place on the lunar Jewish calendar, as done in Scripture.

Until that time, the Christian celebration of the death and resurrection of Messiah was closely related to the Jewish Passover celebration. After all, the Last Supper was Yeshua's last Passover seder of the three that He observed during His public ministry.

THE ROMAN EMPIRE

The unfortunate but logical progression of hatred is that once it is incorporated into government as an institution, it works to isolate, reject, and persecute a marginal group. This is what happened when the long history of theological anti-Judaism within the church got incorporated into the Roman Empire under Constantine. The unholy marriage of a powerful, centralized government with a church preaching anti-Judaism eventually resulted in the passing of legislative measures against the Jews. As we will see, this set the stage for even greater persecution and destruction of the "scapegoats of humanity."

Following Augustine's mixed response to Judaism and the Jewish people, Emperor Constantine made some major changes to the Roman Empire and to the church. He was able to reunite the Roman Empire under one emperor. In AD 313, Constantine issued the Edict of Milan after publicly claiming to be a Christian. Until then, Christianity was the enemy of the state; but as it became one and the same with the state, the state persecution of Christians nearly came to a stop (outside of a few isolated cases). Incidentally, it was during Constantine's reign that the cross became the official Christian symbol. While the persecution of Christians largely came to a stop under Constantine, that wasn't true for the Jewish people.

Initially, Constantine was satisfied with placing Christianity and heathendom on equal footings. After he came to power and granted Christianity legal status, he didn't repress heathen practices. His leanings toward a more pagan Christianity were clearly shown in the results of the first ecumenical council at Nicæa in AD 325. Constantine's measures against the Jews were milder than those of some of his Christian predecessors, yet they announced the end of the toleration that Jews had enjoyed in the Roman Empire. Until that time, Jews were sort of second-class citizens, somewhat protected by law but merely tolerated. These somewhat "good old days" for the Jewish people were about to come to an end.

Paul's advice about how believing Gentiles were to treat the Jewish people was ignored. In Romans 11:11, he directed Gentile believers to provoke the Jews to jealousy by their grace-filled relationship with God through Yeshua: "I say then, they did not stumble so as to fall, did they? May it never be! But by their transgression salvation has come to the Gentiles, to make them jealous." Instead, the Jewish people were provoked to anger, at best, by a constant stream of persecution coming from blinded and ignorant Christians.

Most of the imperial laws affecting the Jews since the days of Constantine can be found in the Codex Theodosianus[9] (a compilation of laws in the Roman Empire developed by Roman emperors since AD 312) and in the Code of Justinian (AD 529). Both huge works are crucial to understanding the history of the progressive deterioration of Jewish rights in public life.

While the Codex Theodosianus didn't always spell bad news for the Jews, it put in place many laws that would later be revised and enforced. While Judaism was still considered a tolerated religion in the Roman Empire, Jews were treated as second-class citizens and the treatment of them grew progressively worse.

Other rulers and church leaders picked up where Augustine and Constantine left off and added their antisemitic contributions to the chronicles of church history. Here are a few more milestones along that road:

- AD 337: Emperor Constantius II created a law that made the marriage of a Jew to a Christian punishable by death.[10]
- AD 367–376: St. Hilary of Poitiers referred to Jews as "a perverse people whom God has cursed forever."[11]
- AD 418: Jerome (the only early church father with Origen who could read Hebrew) created the Vulgate translation of the Bible in Latin. In one of his works, he wrote that "the Jews mocked God crucified, the Gentiles honoured Him."[12]

The decline of Judeo-Christian relations over the centuries shouldn't be missed. First came the theological discourse from some of the early church fathers based on shaky allegorical interpretations of the Bible. Lacking a solid Jewish foundation to discern God's message, laws were enacted to protect Christians and ostracize Jews. Later, physical abuse against whole Jewish communities broke out, complete with harm to their properties and persons—based on reactions to the new laws. Theological anti-Judaism that started with harsh words became legal antisemitism in deeds and formed the foundation of medieval antisemitism and at times violence, which was rampant during the murderous Crusades.

THE EARLY MIDDLE AGES

The Middle Ages is the historical period that followed the Age of Antiquity, also called the Classical Age. The Middle Ages spanned from the fifth century to the fifteenth century. The most commonly accepted start date for the Middle Ages is AD 476, when Romulus Augustus, the last Roman emperor in the West, abdicated.

The Early Middle Ages can also be referred to as the Dark Ages, and indeed they were—especially for the Jewish people. As a general rule, the Middle Ages meant one thing for Christians and a completely different thing for Jews. As Europe was striving for unification and as the church was gaining ground, Jews continued to be ostracized and opposed.

From pope to bishop and from emperor to mob, all across Europe, Jewish people became targets. Laws continued to be passed beyond the Theodosian Code and the Code of Justinian, and animosity ended up leading to violence.

The anti-Judaism of the early church fathers, coupled with pagan antisemitism from the Roman Empire, proved to be an explosive mix for the Jewish communities of Europe. *Anti-Judaism in theory became antisemitism in practice during the Middle Ages.*

In his book *The Anguish of the Jews*, Edward Flannery summarizes the situation well:

> By the middle of the fifth century, the transformation of the Jewish status was complete. The struggle with the church was lost, and Hellenistic trends in Judaism defunct...In the eyes of the Church, the Jew was a guilt-laden unbeliever resistant to grace and a destroyer of souls. To the Empire, he was still a citizen protected by law but now merely tolerated as a second-class citizen...A new era in the history of Judaism was opening.[13]

Ideological and intellectual opposition had turned to stereotyping and pure hatred. The Jews were not only accused of being wrong, they were viewed as being evil and cursed by God as Christ-killers to remain a witness-people damned for all eternity.

The concept of a witness-people evolved from the early Christian accusation that all Jews were responsible for Yeshua's crucifixion. By early Christian standards, the Jews should have ceased to exist soon after the AD 70 destruction of the temple, but they continued to grow and flourish in various global communities of the Diaspora. This was puzzling to many Christians, who thought that rejecting Christ and crucifying Him should have been enough to have God condemn and destroy them. So the question arose: Why are the Jewish people still here? The logical answer, in many minds, was that they existed only to be a witness-people. They would supposedly admit they were wrong at the time that they "witness" the second coming of Yeshua.

Being Jewish in a Christian world went from bad to worse, and unfortunately for the Jewish people, the world was entering the Dark Ages, which truly were dark for the Jewish people.

Following is a list of some of the actions carried out against Jews during this time. While there were some periods during which the Jewish people were treated more kindly, the dominant attitude was one of hatred, with devastating results.

Forced Baptisms and Conversions

The practice of forced baptisms introduced a tragic new element in already-weakening Judeo-Christian relations. Christianity was so closely meshed with the state that Jewish unbelief was considered a grave crime against the state.

Heraclius (AD 575–641), emperor of the Byzantine Empire, made an attempt at unifying the empire through Jewish conversions to Christianity, but did not get the results he hoped for. Occasionally, a Christian leader would loosen the empire's grip on the Jewish community and treat Jews somewhat fairly.

The Second Council of Nicaea, in AD 787, declared that all baptized Jews who secretly continued to practice Judaism should no longer be admitted to the church or permitted to participate in the holy sacraments, but they were allowed to practice Judaism freely. The church made some early attempts at letting the Jewish people practice Judaism, but the desire of leaders and the masses to bring about greater religious and cultural unity influenced many to continue forced conversions and baptisms, which came to an apex under King Ferdinand and Queen Isabella of Spain during the fifteenth century.

The Limited Tolerance of Pope Gregory the Great

Jewish people who lived in Western Europe during the Middle Ages benefited from a different group of leaders than those living in Eastern Europe. The Western leaders, for the most part, made Jewish life more tolerable. Jews were considered Roman citizens and thus left alone, at least in principle, if not always in reality.

Pope Gregory the Great (AD 540–604), who was no great friend of the Jews, still made some minor attempts to treat them somewhat fairly. His devotion to the Theodosian Code and its proper practice was counterbalanced by his desire to see Jewish people convert to Christianity—a Christianity that, by then, had been corrupted by a myriad of man-made Catholic traditions throughout Europe.

Of all the Western European countries of that era, Spain is unique in that it never truly experienced the Reformation and has therefore had a continuous association between Catholicism and the monarchy, which continues today as a parliamentary constitutional monarchy. As a result, Jewish people had a different relationship with their respective Spanish communities which we will look at next.

Spain Switches Gears Against the Jews

King Reccared was the Visigoth leader of Hispania (the Spain of the Middle Ages) from AD 586 to 601. Prior to that period, Spain had been a rather welcoming haven for the Jewish community, which had thrived there demographically and had acquired substantial wealth in the process. After Reccared converted to Christianity in AD 587, he became instrumental in establishing some new restrictive policies regarding the Jews.[14]

As one king replaced another, the Jewish people saw their rights progressively being taken from them. Eventually, King Recceswinth (who ruled AD 649–672) denounced Judaism before the Eighth Council of Toledo. He was quoted saying that "Judaism was abominable, detestable and a pollution." He campaigned for Jewish "blasphemers" to be forced to sign an oath making the daily practice of the Jewish faith impossible. Violators were either stoned to death or burned at the stake.

In AD 711, Muslim soldiers landed in Gibraltar and were able to take over Spain. Hardly conceivable in our twenty-first century, the eighth-century invasion of Spain by Islam had received some help from the Jewish community, who perceived their brief and limited partnership with Islam as an opportunity to combat a common enemy. The concept of joining forces against "Christianity" was appealing to both sides.

The next seven centuries became known as the Golden Age of Spain. Jews fared better in Spain than in the rest of Europe, where they rarely could settle down peacefully.

The Calm Before the Storm

Jewish people in France experienced somewhat of a respite under most of the Carolingian dynasty that was started by the descendants of Charles Martel (686–741), a ruler of France from 718 until his death, who got his name from the Latin for "Charles," or *Carolus.* The Carolingians reigned from the late 580s to the early 1120s.

Under the Carolingian rule, the laws of the Theodosian Code were ignored, but Jewish life was still not without problems. During the ninth century, Jews were regularly accused of treason by Christians. A custom was then developed that on Good Friday, each Jew must receive a blow to the face as a price to pay for having crucified the Lord. This would continue as a Christian custom for at least 300 years.

While the latter part of the first millennium AD was not without incident in Jewish history, the ninth and tenth centuries ended up being a period of relative calm between the early centuries of anti-Jewish theological tirades by the church fathers and the upcoming dark eras of the Crusades and Inquisition.

In an era punctuated by unjustified atrocities in the name of Messiah, some of the greatest Jewish minds were born. Their contributions to Jewish history shaped Judaism as we know it, all the way into the twenty-first century. Among the many contributors to the advancement of mankind in general, and Jewish life in particular, were two major Jewish thinkers: Moses Maimonides (Spain)[15] and Rashi[16] (France).

Moses ben Maimon, or Maimonides, also known by the acronym Rambam for **Ra**bbi **M**oshe **B**en **M**aimon, was a famous medieval Jewish philosopher and one of the greatest Torah scholars and physicians of the Middle Ages. He was born in Cordoba, Spain, in 1135, and died in Egypt in 1204. About Moses Maimonides it was said, "From Moses to Moses, none arose as Moses."

Shlomo Yitzhaki (1040–1105), also known by the acronym Rashi for **Ra**bbi **Sh**lomo **I**tzhaki, was a medieval French rabbi famous for the first comprehensive commentary on the Talmud, as well as a very thorough commentary on the Tenach. Within worldwide Judaism, Rashi is considered the foremost commentator, so much so that few religious Jews today would consider studying the Torah or Talmud without his commentaries.[17]

Both Rashi and Rambam were influential within the Jewish community during the earlier Crusades, and they were involved in trying to counteract Jewish conversion to Christianity. For the Jewish people, aside from the Holocaust, it is difficult to find a year more fateful than 1096, which marked the beginning of the First Crusade. Some of the most violent and bloody massacres in Jewish history were about to take place, staining the church forever.

CHAPTER 4

ANTISEMITISM FROM THE CRUSADES TO THE SPANISH INQUISITION

Few events in the history of the Jewish people were more catastrophic than the Crusades. The First Crusade began in 1096, at which time Rashi was 56 and in the prime of his writing years. The sudden outburst of violence against the Jewish communities of Europe at the hands of nobles, knights, monks, and peasants came as a surprise because the official purpose of the Crusades was to push the Muslim infidels out of the Holy Land.

THE CRUSADES

On November 27, 1095, at the council of Clermont,[1] Pope Urban II (circa AD 1042–1099) summoned Christians to retake the Holy Land and Jerusalem from the Muslims. A combination of religious, economic, and social motives resulted in the overwhelming response that became known as the First Crusade.

Christian knights and peasants joined forces in the First Crusade under a Christian banner with the motto "God wills it." They departed from Western Europe and headed to the Holy Land. It was not long before the Crusaders realized that they could start by fighting some other "infidels" in their own backyards. As they marched through Europe on their way to Jerusalem, they went after Jewish people. Some Crusaders in Rouen, Normandy, were quoted as saying: "We desire to combat the enemies of God in the East; but we have under our eyes the Jews, a race more inimical to God than all the others. We are doing this whole thing backwards."[2]

Seven more Crusades would take place for a total of eight through 1270. While not all of them were as lethal to the Jews as the first one, they were always accompanied by a viral desire by European peasants, princes, and Crusaders to eliminate "the enemies of Christ."

Money Lending: The Inevitable Outcome

By this time, Jewish people were finding it increasingly difficult to conduct business. They were progressively forced out of owning property or large parcels of land for agricultural purposes. They were no longer allowed to belong to a guild.[3] Jews were also forbidden to own slaves, which made it almost impossible for them to do agricultural work. Not necessarily by choice, some members of the Jewish community became deeply involved in money lending.

Christians were allowed to borrow money *only* from Jews, who, in turn, would collect the money back with interest. Kings in Europe started taxing the Jewish moneylenders on their profits. Because taxes kept rising, the Jewish moneylenders had to increase their interest rates just to keep pace. This process went on for a while and gave birth to the myth of the "greedy Jew." Some Jewish moneylenders did raise their rates too high in attempts to take advantage of needy Christians, but they were not in the majority, and they ended up with poor reputations in both the Christian and

Jewish communities. These individuals happened to be greedy first and Jewish second.

As money lending became more common, antisemitism amongst the masses became more of a reality. Poor peasants, who were always in need of money and borrowing often from Jewish moneylenders, ended up becoming resentful because they were borrowing from "unbelievers." Their anger almost always led to physical abuse and killings. Princes and nobles would protect the Jewish moneylenders as long as they could benefit from them; but if the borrowers or mobs attacked the Jewish community, the princes and nobles would conveniently abandon "their Jews."

By the end of the thirteenth century, Jews had been expelled from France, England, and most of Germany, mainly because of issues relating to moneylending.

The road to the Holocaust continued as falsehoods mounted up against the Jews.

The Ritual Murder Libel

The twelfth century introduced a new charge against the Jews that would be added to the list of reasons they should be converted, ostracized, abused, or even killed. This charge, known as blood libel or blood accusation, was fabricated from beginning to end for the sole purpose of stigmatizing Jewish people and demonizing them. Accusations are still being leveled against the Jewish people by antisemitic groups and people across the globe.

What was blood libel all about? Supposedly, Jews would kill Christian children during Holy Week for ritual purposes. More than 150 false charges of blood libel were recorded throughout history—mostly during the Middle Ages—resulting in the deaths of many Jewish people.

The first claim of blood libel arose in Norwich, England, in 1144, according to the Catholic Encyclopedia.[4] The dead body of a boy was found on Good Friday. The boy was later referred to as William of

Norwich. The testimony of a monk (Thomas of Monmouth) was the only record of the event. He accused the Jewish community of draining a young Christian boy of his blood to make unleavened bread for Passover. No proof was ever found to substantiate the accusation.

The William of Norwich incident was responsible for a crowd attacking a Jewish delegation coming to the coronation of Richard the Lionhearted in 1189. The following year, most of the Jews in Norwich were slaughtered. More accusations of ritual murder and blood libel followed throughout England. Jews were eventually expelled from England in 1290, and they were not allowed to return until 1656 under Oliver Cromwell.

The ritual murder libel claims picked up momentum and spread across the English Channel to France and Germany.

The charge later reemerged in Poland in the late eighteenth century, as well as the late nineteenth century in France, Germany, and Russia. The same accusation has appeared more recently, in New York in 1928, in Nazi propaganda during World War II, and even in a booklet entitled *Jewish Ritual Murder* published in Birmingham, Alabama, in 1962. In 2007, Italian author Ariel Toaff, in *Pasqua di sangue,* brought the controversial topic back to the forefront.[5] While these claims are absolutely ludicrous and impossible to prove, they continue to be propagated today, mostly in the Middle East by antisemitic Muslim countries.

Already viewed by many as unbelievers and usurers, the Jews graduated to the level of being accused of ritual murders. This lie became responsible for the violent deaths of many Jewish people during the Middle Ages and thereafter.

The Badge of Shame: A Distinctive Dress for the Jews

Even though many popes had shown respect to the Jewish community over the years, much harm was still being done. Pope Innocent III (1160–1216) enforced a papal constitution stripping Jews of their rights. Bringing forth the accusation of deicide, Innocent III convoked the Fourth Lateran Council in 1215 to further ostracize the Jews.

One of the measures introduced would change the status and the safety of Jews for the next 700 years. The Jewish people of Europe were now required to wear a badge on their garments (and later, a pointed hat known in German as the *Judenhut*) to facilitate their identification on the by-ways of Europe.[6] The badge quickly became known as "the badge of shame," and Jewish people made many attempts to hide or not wear it, risking their lives in the process. Over time, twelve councils and nine royal ordinances of the Catholic Church reinforced its use.

The badge was first introduced in France as *la rouelle,* a yellow circle sown on the chest and the back of all garments worn by Jews. Nazi Germany would pick up on the idea and take it to a new level with the infamous yellow star that led to the deaths of six million Jews.

Host Desecration

During the Fourth Lateran Council, Pope Innocent III also formalized the Catholic doctrine of transubstantiation, making it an official part of the Catholic Church. This doctrine taught that in the course of observing the Lord's Supper, the chalice of wine contained the very blood of Messiah, and the wafer, or host, became the very body of Messiah. Yet there isn't a biblical foundation for the doctrine of transubstantiation.

Yeshua spoke symbolically of His body and His blood as He was closing the Passover Seder in the upper room and linking what He was about to do for the world to the cup of redemption (third cup) and the unleavened, broken matzoh (leaven almost always symbolizes sin in the Bible) as seen in Luke 22:14-20. His whole teaching on the bread and cup was meant to symbolize His body and blood.

The year 1243 marked the beginning of the accusations of "host desecrations" in Belitz, near Berlin, where all the Jews of the town were killed. For centuries to follow, more accusations prevailed throughout all of Europe, from France to Poland and from Prague to Berlin. As a result, Jews were burned at the stake.

Persecutors said the Jews would desecrate communion wafers by piercing them, supposedly because the blood of Yeshua would then pour out, allowing the Jews to reenact the crucifixion for which they were said to be guilty. The accusers completely ignored the Bible, which stated that Yeshua gave His own life so that He could take it back (John 10:14-18).

Accusations of host desecration led many Europeans, especially Germans and Austrians, to go from community to community and slaughter Jews. This led to the deaths of about 100,000 Jews in more than 140 different communities. These massacres were the first historical attempt at holding European Jewry corporately responsible for a crime, a pattern that would repeat itself several times until its apex during the Holocaust.

The Myth of Poisoning the Wells of Europe

In 1321, a rumor was spread that the king of Tunisia, some infidels, and some lepers from the Jewish community had conspired together to end Christianity. They were accused of preparing a poison made with urine, herbs, human blood, and a sacred host. Several centuries before the birth of the *Protocols of the Learned Elders of Zion*, this myth of Jewish world conspiracy came to life, and it led to the killing of 5,000 Jews at the time.[7]

By the mid-1300s, the combined efforts of church and state, as noble as they might have been, were powerless against the tidal wave of mob anger toward Jews and their communities. With the advent of the black death or black plague, the legend of the poisoning of the wells of Europe had found a fertile ground.

The black plague was the most devastating pandemic in the history of mankind, responsible for the deaths of an estimated 75 million people worldwide (25 million in Europe alone[8]) from 1347 to 1351. It was four years of horror for the Jewish communities of Europe. As the continent appeared to be on its way to total extinction, people looked for a cause to blame, and it was not long before the Jews once again became the convenient "scapegoats of humanity."

Jewish people also died during the black death, but generally in lesser numbers. Three factors were responsible for the smaller death tolls in Jewish communities: the kosher laws that forced them to maintain a stricter hygiene, the separation of Jewish communities from other communities, and the Jews' liturgical washing of the hands. But that didn't stop the masses from slaughtering Jewish people and destroying more than 200 Jewish communities.

Still another source of persecution for the Jews was the Spanish Inquisition. With it, antisemitism would move up another notch and add the notion that the Jewish "problem" was an ethnic one.

Early in the fifteenth century, one individual who was aggressive about Jewish conversions to Christianity was Vincent Ferrer, who travelled from synagogue to synagogue. He is credited with the baptisms of some 25,000 Jews, and in one instance, reportedly 4,000 conversions in one month. When Jews declined to convert, he was severe toward them, and it is believed that he may have come up with the original concept of the Jewish ghetto.[9]

The issue that Christians had with Jews morphed into an issue with conversos,[10] who were Jewish converts to Christianity. They were now becoming numerous. However, many conversos had not truly converted and had not broken their ties with Judaism. They had professed Christianity to escape persecution, but secretly continued to practice Judaism as crypto-Jews (from the Greek term *krypto*, which means "hidden"). Some Christians hated these *conversos nuevos* (new converts) even more than they hated unconverted Jews.

These Jews became known as Marranos ("swine"). The double

standard imposed on the Marranos created a tidal wave of hatred from the pulpits of Spain, and anti-Marranism was added to antisemitism. They started to feed upon one another with the idea that they both came from *mala sangre*, or "bad blood" because of hereditary Jewishness.

For the first time in Jewish history, *Judaism was no longer a theological problem but was becoming an ethnic one.*

Brutal attacks against the Marranos of Spain became more and more common, and many Franciscans and Dominicans called for the reintroduction of the thirteenth-century Inquisition.

As antisemitism continued to grow from the fertile soil of theological anti-Judaism and social ostracism, its roots also became deeper as the issue of ethnicity was introduced. Another 500 years would go by before the Holocaust came along, but the road toward ethnic hatred continued to be built, and its progress would be greatly aided by the advent of the Spanish Inquisition.

THE SPANISH INQUISITION

By 1479, King Ferdinand and Queen Isabella of Spain had succeeded in uniting the two kingdoms of Castile and Aragon, which gave them hope of a unified Christian Spain as well. Isabella's Dominican confessor, Thomas De Torquemada, immediately pushed for a reestablishment of the Inquisition to rid Spain of the Marranos once and for all. After some resistance, the Inquisition was reintroduced. The first *auto da fé* (meaning "act of faith") was held within a year, resulting in six Jews being burned at the stake. *Auto da fés* were rituals in which condemned heretics and apostates were required to do public penance. For the Marranos, that took place *after* their punishment was decided. This public humiliation was usually followed by imprisonment or an execution conducted by civil authorities.

In 1483, Torquemada was appointed Inquisitor General. For years to come, Marranos and all Spanish Jews lived in a constant state of terror. The procedure was almost always the same:

- Investigation: from town to town, information was gathered.
- Trial: always favoring the prosecution (church).
- Torture: hanging by the wrists with weights on the ankles.
- Punishment: prison, confiscation of property, death.

The Inquisition failed to completely eradicate the Marranos and expanded to persecute all the Jews in Spain. Torquemada noticed the bond between orthodox Jews and Marranos who were Christian converts in name only, and when he realized he couldn't control the Marranos problem, he asked Ferdinand and Isabella for the complete expulsion of all Jews from Spain. Initially, they refused, but he insisted.

In 1492, a decree was issued that required all Jews to leave Spain within six months. There is a legend that scholar, financier, and tax collector Isaac Abravanel is said to have offered a large sum to King Ferdinand to bribe him into allowing the Jews to stay in Spain. The king was known for his love of money. It is reported that when Torquemada found out about the offer, he went to the king and said, "Judas Iscariot sold Messiah for thirty pieces of silver; will your highness sell Him for thirty thousand ducats? Here He is; take Him and sell Him!"

The king held fast to his decree, and an estimated 300,000 Jews had to leave. Most of them went to Italy, Turkey, and Portugal. Those who went to Portugal ended up facing persecution again under the Portuguese Inquisition against Marranos.

By the end of the fifteenth century, the Jew had become, in the view of medieval culture, an undesirable agent of Satan, as noted by the widespread use of demonic terms in association with Jewish people.

The terms *Jewish* and *diabolical* were now synonymous. Understandably, to Jews, the cross became known as the symbol of disaster.

Medieval antisemitism left a mark that still has an effect in the twenty-first century. As the world emerged from the darkness of the Middle Ages and into the modern era with the beginning of the Renaissance, many positive changes stirred in the European world. With this new era came much progress in almost all areas of life, including science, medicine, music, literature, and art. Yet for the Jewish community, the modern era didn't bring much hope of a better life. People still held to the view that if Jews couldn't be converted or changed, they had to be contained and controlled.

CHAPTER 5

ANTISEMITISM FROM THE REFORMATION TO THE FIRST WORLD WAR

Introduced during the birth of the Renaissance, humanism was instrumental in the coming onto the scene of several Christian Hebraists.[1] In addition, the invention of the moveable-type printing press by Johannes Gutenberg in 1440[2] was a big help toward increasing the availability of Bibles and Talmuds.

All of a sudden, as Talmuds became more available, some Christians feared that the Jewish denigration of Christianity would gain more momentum. Thus, several attempts were made to have the Talmud declared illegal.

THE PROTESTANT REFORMATION

The feud over the Talmud and the Bible brought the Catholic Church to a place where its oppressive power and growing corruption were exposed. This led to the major shift known as the Protestant Reformation. Christendom found itself at the bloody crossroads of Roman Catholicism and the Reformation; and once again, the Jews were caught in the crossfire.

During this time, the Catholic Church increased its influence on Christendom. The overwhelming power of the Catholic hierarchy from priest to pope and the sales of indulgences[3] bothered some within the Catholic Church, such as Martin Luther, who decided to do something about what he felt was an abuse of power. In his eyes, a reformation of Christendom was needed.

Martin Luther, a Catholic priest and professor of theology, started the Protestant Reformation after nailing his 95 Theses on a church door in Wittenberg, Germany, in 1517. Luther was excommunicated in 1521 by Pope Leo X because of his refusal to retract his views, which the Catholic Church saw as heresy. Luther's translation of the Bible into German made it more accessible and had a tremendous impact.

Initially, Luther tried to attract the Jews to a new faith. He felt that stripped of popes, bishops, and priests, Christianity had a lot to offer to all, including Jewish people. In 1523, in his pamphlet titled *Jesus Christ Was Born a Jew,* he wrote some positive remarks about the Jewish people:

> If I had been a Jew and had seen such dolts and blockheads govern and teach the Christian faith, I would sooner have become a hog than a Christian. They have dealt with the Jews as if they were dogs rather than human beings; they have done little else than deride them and seize their property. When they baptize them they show them nothing of Christian doctrine or life, but only subject them to popishness and monkery...If the apostles, who also were Jews, had dealt with us Gentiles as we Gentiles deal with the Jews, there would never have been a Christian

> among the Gentiles...When we are inclined to boast of our position [as Christians] we should remember that we are but Gentiles, while the Jews are of the lineage of Christ. We are aliens and in-laws; they are blood relatives, cousins, and brothers of our Lord. Therefore, if one is to boast of flesh and blood, the Jews are actually nearer to Christ than we are...If we really want to help them, we must be guided in our dealings with them not by papal law but by the law of Christian love. We must receive them cordially, and permit them to trade and work with us, that they may have occasion and opportunity to associate with us, hear our Christian teaching, and witness our Christian life. If some of them should prove stiff-necked, what of it? After all, we ourselves are not all good Christians either.[4]

In 1543, when the Jewish community didn't meet Luther's expectations, he published the book *Of the Jews and Their Lies,* where his venomous description of the Jewish people inspired and possibly encouraged Hitler to proceed with his Nazi agenda of death. In the book, Luther used language that, at the very least, equaled the past and future diatribes against the Jewish people:

> What shall we Christians do with this rejected and condemned people, the Jews?...I shall give you my sincere advice:
>
> First, to set fire to their synagogues or schools and to bury and cover with dirt whatever will not burn, so that no man will ever again see a stone or cinder of them. This is to be done in honor of our Lord and of Christendom...
>
> Second, I advise that their houses also be razed and destroyed. For they pursue in them the same aims as in their synagogues...

> Third, I advise that all their prayer books and Talmudic writings, in which such idolatry, lies, cursing, and blasphemy are taught, be taken from them.
>
> Fourth, I advise that their rabbis be forbidden to teach henceforth on pain of loss of life and limb...
>
> Fifth, I advise that safe-conduct on the highways be abolished completely for the Jews...
>
> For, as we have heard, God's anger with them is so intense that gentle mercy will only tend to make them worse and worse, while sharp mercy will reform them but little. Therefore, in any case, away with them![5]

Several months after publishing *On the Jews and Their Lies,* Luther wrote *Vom Schem Hamphoras und vom Geschlecht Christi*, German for *Of the Unknowable Name and the Generations of Christ,*[6] in which he compares the Jews to little devils sucking on a pig.

Luther also preached several sermons in Eisleben, right before his death in 1546, in which he continued to paint the Jews as enemies of Christianity in need of conversion or expulsion. While none of Europe's rulers enacted all of Luther's antisemitic recommendations, his legacy provoked many riots and massacres after his passing.

Lucy Dawidowicz, in *The War Against the Jews: 1933–1945,*[7] observed that "both Luther and Hitler were obsessed by the 'demonologized universe' inhabited by Jews." Other scholars and historians believe that Luther's view of the Jews had a profound effect on Germans for centuries to come and had a serious influence on Hitler's ideology and his implementation of the Final Solution to the Jewish Question. Connecting the dots between Luther and Hitler is not difficult to do.

As the Jewish people kept being expelled from France, England, Spain, and Portugal, they found themselves wandering through Europe and the Middle East looking for refuge. Their migration took many to the Balkans, Poland, Turkey, and Israel. Poland, in particular, became a place of refuge and saw a tremendous influx of Jews.

In France and England, despite the expulsions, antisemitism continued to flourish. In the words of historian David Nirenberg, "If the Jew did not exist, the anti-semite would invent him."[8] In other words, it didn't matter whether Jewish people were actually guilty or if people had even met a Jewish person in their lives; Jewish people were becoming guilty of the ills of the world simply by virtue of being Jewish.

The Ghetto, an Invention of the Modern Era

Jewish people, by virtue of their religious activities that adhered to so many regulations, had always lived in tight-knit communities. Jewish separatism from others went back to the eleventh century. They lived in some sort of "ghetto by choice," for protection rather than incarceration.

However, the sixteenth century introduced the ghetto or Jewish quarter (the word *ghetto* is from the Italian *ghetto*, meaning "casting," or Venetian *geto*, meaning "foundry"). These ghettos were kept under lock and key. Jews were now forced together in tight quarters, as though they were being put in prison. The ghetto had moved from providing protection to being a form of incarceration, and the results were tragic.

It all happened in 1516, when Venice's ruling council of elders decided to let the Jews remain in Venice as long as their presence was confined to one specific area—namely, the small island known as Ghetto Nuovo. That island became the world's first ghetto. Jews from different communities all across Europe moved into this ghetto and even lived in separate communities within the ghetto itself.

Jews could leave during the day only with special permission and with a stigmatizing yellow circle on their clothes. They also had to return at night before curfew and before the ghetto was locked and guarded by gatekeepers. Ghetto residents were restricted to working at pawn shops, as moneylenders (at very low rates while facing high taxes), or in the textile or medical trades.

The Venetian ghetto and all subsequent others were overcrowded, and always at the mercy of diseases, starvation, and fires.

Later, many more ghettos would be introduced in Frankfurt, Rome, and Prague, all of them following the Venetian model. The main period of ghetto life for the Jewish people took place during the 1940s in Eastern Europe in cities like Lodz, Brakow, Vilna, Minsk, and Warsaw, among many others.

These ghettos brought the image and the status of the Jewish people to an even lower level than before. No longer perceived as the threat that they had appeared to be to Christians during the Middle Ages, the Jews became the target of constant ridicule and vilification.

Poland: A Haven Turned Upside Down

Against the backdrop of multiple expulsions and ghettoization elsewhere, Poland appeared as the only substantial ray of hope for the Jews. It offered the Jewish community a haven of peace that allowed them space for social and spiritual growth like nowhere else.

From the Middle Ages onward, large numbers of European Jews who wanted to escape the Crusades, the blood libel accusations, the black death, and the Inquisition migrated eastward to Poland and Lithuania. The refugees were well received and accepted because their immigration created economic booms for the local economies. They were accepted in all areas of government and business. From 1500 to 1648, the Jewish population of Poland grew from 15,000 to 500,000, and they were granted almost complete autonomy from kings such as Sigismund II (who ruled from 1548 to 1572). Jewish education and Talmudic studies reached such a level of excellence during that time that they influenced European Judaism for years to come.

Even during this period of respite, accusations of ritual murder and host desecration continued to spread and found fertile soil in the new Jewish influx from Western Europe. And tragically, Polish Jewry experienced one of the bloodiest decades in Jewish history, outside of the Holocaust, between 1648 and 1658.

In April 1648, the Ukrainian Cossacks (a group of east Slavic people from Ukraine and Southern Russia) rebelled against the Polish-Lithuania Commonwealth and proclaimed their independence. The rebellion was led by Bogdan Chmielnicki,[9] who allied with the Tartars[10] and led the Eastern Orthodox Cossacks against the Polish Catholics and Jews. The result was the deaths of 100,000 to 200,000 Jews and the destruction of more than 700 communities.

While the massacres were against both Poles and Jews, the atrocities perpetrated against the Jews were far more violent. As a result of the Chmielnicki Massacres and heavy losses of life, European Jewry was looking for relief from any king, including King Messiah Himself.

As it turned out, the sixteenth through the eighteenth centuries proved to be a very difficult time for the Jews of Europe. A few periods of respite aside, there was no place where Jewish people could settle and create a community without the dark cloud of antisemitism hovering over their heads. The European emancipation was around the corner, and with it some changes would be introduced, but not enough to be considered any kind of improvement. This was especially true for the Jews of Eastern Europe, who would find themselves confined to a new and larger geographical ghetto within imperial Russia, known as the Pale of Settlement.

The Pale of Settlement and the Pogroms

The Pale of Settlement[11] (1791–1917) was a land mass that included about 20 percent of European Russia and much of present-day Lithuania, Belarus, Poland, Moldova, Ukraine, and parts of western Russia, and added up to a total of about 500,000 square miles. This territory was acquired by the Russian Empire across the course of several military conquests that took place from 1791 to 1835, and the area was held until the fall of the Russian Empire in 1917.

Within the Pale itself, Jews suffered many restrictions, higher taxes, and hardship. Experiencing very little relief under Alexander I of Russia (ruled 1801–1825), their condition worsened under his successor, Nicholas I (ruled 1825–1855). Russia's own answer to their "Jewish problem" was the "Russification" of the Jews. In 1827, Nicholas I introduced a law for military conscription,[12] forcing all children into the military at the age of 12. This also allowed for the deprogramming of Jewish kids, and often happened through the kidnapping of the youngsters by "snatchers." The result was far from satisfactory, so Nicholas introduced educational reform in 1840, trying to pull Jewish people from their traditions and Talmudic studies. This also had little effect.

About 90 percent of Russian Jews lived inside the Pale, where they grew from a population of 1.6 million in 1820 to 5.6 million in 1910. The 1860s brought the Jewish communities of the Pale some privileges, but they were quickly reversed by the May Laws of 1882, restricting Jews to overcrowded urban areas.[13]

In addition, the pogroms (the Russian word for this means "devastation") of the 1870s through the 1910s created hostile environments that exacerbated the miserable conditions in which the Jews lived. The first pogrom might have been as early as 1821 in Odessa, Ukraine. The official reason given for the hundreds of subsequent pogroms was the assassination of Alexander II in 1881, for which some blamed the Jews.

Pogroms became government-sponsored riots against the Jews, and they claimed the lives of many in the little Jewish villages and hamlets known as the *shtetls* of the Pale. The pogroms and other boycotts and hardships led to the mass immigration of two million Jews to the United States from 1881 to 1914. The *Haskalah* enlightenment movement, seeking to modernize Judaism in hope of better integration, also took place at the same time. Eventually, the Pale of Settlement was dismantled in 1917 after the fall of the Russian Empire.

As the end of the nineteenth century was approaching, Jews were about to experience another major shift in antisemitism. Racial antisemitism was about to become more dominant, as antisemitism was soon to benefit from the "science" of eugenics (a pseudoscience that allegedly aimed to improve the genetic quality of a particular population). Eugenics, even though quickly debunked by scientists the world around, would bring forth a new and more hostile form of political philosophy that would make racism even more deadly.

The Protocols of the Learned Elders of Zion

We learned earlier about one of the biggest hoaxes in the history of antisemitism, the pamphlet known as *The Protocols of the Learned Elders of Zion.* This work has been recognized as a hoax since 1920–1921, and I want to talk more about it here because of its impact on antisemitism during this time period in world history.

The writer, Russian mystic Sergei Nilus (1862–1929), claimed this information came from the minutes of the First Zionist Congress, at which Jewish leaders allegedly planned to take over the world. In addition to being a forgery, *The Protocols* is an early example of literature that engages in conspiracy theories. The pamphlet is filled with clichés and platitudes about Jews taking over the world, yet never offers any details or specifics.

While the pamphlet has long been known to be a fraud, it continues to proliferate worldwide. A tragic early example of someone who propagated its claims is American automobile giant Henry Ford.

From 1919 to 1927, Henry Ford published a newspaper called *The Dearborn Independent.* It published *The Protocols* at the same time that *The Times* in London discredited the pamphlet. But this did not stop Ford, who was quoted as saying, "The only statement I care to make about *The Protocols* is that they fit in with what is going on."[14]

Ford also was responsible for the financing and distribution of 500,000 copies of *The Protocols*. Many of the articles published in the *Dearborn Independent* were reprinted in a later volume known as *The International Jew*.[15] Hitler himself relied heavily on *The Protocols* and even quoted them in *Mein Kampf*, praising and validating them:

> To what extent the whole existence of this people is based on a continuous lie is shown incomparably by *The Protocols of the Wise Men of Zion*, so infinitely hated by the Jews. They are based on a forgery, the *Frankfurter Zeitung* moans and screams once every week: the best proof that they are authentic...Anyone who examines the historical development of the last hundred years from the standpoint of this book will at once understand the screaming of the Jewish press. For once this book has become the common property of a people, the Jewish menace may be considered as broken.[16]

The Protocols helped Hitler to rationalize the destruction of European Jewry. In many ways, *The Protocols* were a catalyst for the Holocaust, as they became part of "the solution to the Jewish question."

In the twenty-first century, *The Protocols* continue to be published and distributed by neo-Nazi fringe groups and radical Islamist groups around the world.

The First World War

After the assassination of Archduke Franz Ferdinand in Sarajevo on June 28, 1914, World War I was declared, and the face of Europe would be changed forever. Eighty percent of the ten million Jews of Europe lived in both the Russian and Austro-Hungarian Empires.

The Jewish communities of Europe had been used to hardship and had endured many forms of antisemitism, yet the advent of World War I worsened their circumstances as their lives were once again threatened by lootings, pogroms, and expulsions.

The greatest hardships occurred in Russia. Jewish men who enrolled in the Russian army to fight Germany were often accused of spying for the Germans, and as punishment, many were sent to Siberia. When Russia started to lose ground in the war, the Jews were blamed.

On the other side, 20 percent of the 600,000 Jews in Germany served in the German army. When Germany started to lose ground, antisemitism grew worse, and the Jews were once again the scapegoats of humanity. They were accused of spying for Russia and charged with treason.

As World War I progressed, the Allied nations ratified various treaties and worked on agreements to share the spoils. One treaty of significance to the Jewish people resulted from the fact the British had conquered the region known as Palestine.[17] In the midst of all the negotiations, Britain officially endorsed the Zionist program, and almost overnight, Zionism started to take root in the Holy Land. This was a major step in the right direction for the Jewish people.

The 1919 Versailles peace treaty also brought some hope for the Jewish communities of Europe. Eastern European Jews were pushing for their religious rights and traditions to be preserved, while Western European Jews desired citizenship rights. Both were partially satisfied.

All the Jews of Europe, aware of their unending status as unwanted citizens, eagerly sought the enforcement of the 1917 Balfour Declaration[18] in the hopes of officially establishing a Jewish home in British Palestine.

While Europe found itself needing to rebuild from its own ashes, the Jews continued to be the targets of antisemitism from every direction. *The Protocols* added fuel to the fire, urging people to eliminate or restrain the Jews at a time of critically needed reorganization and rebuilding.

In 1922, following the 1917 Balfour Declaration and the 1920 San Remo Conference,[19] the League of Nations approved the British Mandate for Palestine, giving Britain jurisdiction over the Holy Land, and thereby authority to help with the securing of a Jewish homeland. But as we learned earlier, during World War I, two different promises had been made by the British government. One was given to the Arabs as a reward for their help against the Ottoman Empire, and the other was given to the Jewish people through the Balfour Declaration.

These conflicting promises ended up hindering the advancement of Zionism and contributed to the annihilation of millions of Jewish people during the Holocaust, which we will turn to next.

CHAPTER 6

ANTISEMITISM FROM THE HOLOCAUST ONWARD

Germany's defeat and humiliation at the close of World War I, brought about by the Treaty of Versailles, led to an economic collapse followed by the hyperinflation of 1923. The country was bankrupt. A strong sense of German nationalism, coupled with economic chaos, provided the conditions for Adolf Hitler's rise to power, but this did not occur overnight.

Hitler (1889–1945) was a German politician born in Austria. He fought in World War I, and in 1923, attempted what became known as the Beer Hall *Putsch*, a failed *coup d'état* in Munich that landed him in prison, where he wrote *Mein Kampf* ("My Struggle"). After being released in 1924, he became the leader of the National Socialist German Workers Party, also known as the Nazi Party. In 1933, he became the chancellor of Germany, shortly after which he became dictator over Germany from 1933 to 1945.

It is an unfair assessment to say that Adolf Hitler was insane, because insanity is too often pleaded to release one of legal responsibilities. It would be more accurate to say he was evil or demon-possessed. He was determined to put his homeland back on the map, but also on the forefront of the European continent by creating a new Germany, the Third Reich, which became a totalitarian regime that sought to create the perfect race. To that end, Hitler misapplied the science of eugenics,[1] which was popular during the early twentieth century.

Between 1923 and 1932, while Hitler was gaining power at an exponential speed and preparing for the extermination of the Jews, numerous Jewish cemeteries and synagogues were destroyed. Antisemitism morphed once again, this time into a relentless multiheaded monster that no one seemed able to stop.

Edward Flannery said, in *The Anguish of the Jews*,

> No longer was the Jew a mere scapegoat or member of an inferior race, but the cause of every problem, the destroyer, the poisoner of Aryan blood, the epitome of evil. And he was all this inherently and ineradicably; neither baptism nor renunciation of Judaism could redeem him. The solution to the Jewish problem was also new and simple, and concisely summarized in the Nazi slogan, "Juda Verrecke!" (Jewry perish!).[2]

After Hitler became chancellor of Germany, laws were put in place against non-Aryans, especially Jews. Non-Aryans were given a legal definition: a person with at least one Jewish grandparent. Thousands of Jews, many of whom had no interaction with Judaism or had even turned to Christianity, found themselves the recipients of this new stigma. Jewish books were collected by German soldiers and burned. The badge of shame of the Middle Ages was reintroduced in the form of a yellow Star of David patch, and Jewish shops were marked with *J* or *Jude* (German for "Jew"). Jewish emigration became the only way to escape persecution. Some 50,000 Jews left Germany by the end of 1933, including Nobel Prize winners and notables such as Albert Einstein. Eventually, even emigration became nearly impossible.

In 1935, the Nuremberg Laws were introduced, and Jewish people lost their citizenship. Marriage and sexual relations between Jews and Aryans were prohibited and severely punished. In addition, guidelines were created to determine who in Germany would qualify as a *mischling* ("half-breed") and who wouldn't.

The Nuremberg Laws set the stage for the final delegitimization of the Jewish people before the Final Solution began to be implemented. By 1935, Hitler was solidly established in power. Few, if any, would dare to contradict him. His obsession with the "Jewish problem" soon led him to the next step in his attempt to destroy European Jewry: *Kristallnacht*!

KRISTALLNACHT: POINT OF NO RETURN

During the night of November 9-10, 1938, violent attacks on Jewish businesses, synagogues, and properties occurred simultaneously all over Germany. *Kristallnacht*, or the "Night of Broken Glass," was a new phase in antisemitism, and it pushed things past a point of no return. As the civilized world voiced its objections to the violent pogroms, Hitler ignored the outrage. More than 1,600 synagogues were ransacked and almost 300 set on fire in one night. While "only" about 200 Jewish people were killed, shortly afterward, the Nazi agenda was implemented, setting the stage for far more deaths.

Hermann Göring, Hitler's second-in-command, met with other Nazi leaders two days after *Kristallnacht* to initiate the Final Solution.[3] Most scholars and historians refer to *Kristallnacht* as the beginning of the Holocaust.

THE FINAL SOLUTION TO THE JEWISH QUESTION

As early as September 1939, the *Einzatsgruppen*—an arm of the German SS paramilitary organization—was tasked with annihilating the

Jews and were responsible for the deaths of 1,300,000 people. Yet Hitler realized that, from his perspective, one bullet per victim was a high price to pay, so the Nazis experimented with using carbon monoxide from a van's exhaust system and cycling it back into the sealed vehicle packed with people. The effort wasn't considered successful because it was too slow, and the victims' agonizing screams "bothered" the German soldiers. Eventually, this gave birth to the gassing of victims in large rooms within the Nazi death camps. At one point the expatriation of Jews to the African island of Madagascar was contemplated, but the idea was quickly abandoned.

Time being of the essence, Hitler decided that Jews should all be exterminated because they couldn't be expatriated fast enough. The next critical step was officially adopted at the Wannsee Conference in a Berlin suburb in early 1942. The meeting lasted only 90 minutes. Senior Nazi officials assigned Reinhard Heydrich as the chief executor of the Final Solution to the Jewish Question. The plan, apparently approved by Hitler, was to send all Jewish captives to forced labor camps to help rebuild Germany and let them die during their work or exterminate the survivors after the work was done.

At first, German soldiers moved the Jewish people to concentration camps, which were similar to labor camps, except that the living conditions were such that the death rate from diseases and starvation was very high. Forced labor was imposed to generate supplies for the war, but the true agenda loomed large over all that happened. It was not long before inmates were transferred to extermination camps or simply remained in work camps that became death camps.

The Holocaust was almost successful in eradicating all Jews from Europe. Very few people who were taken to the camps survived. Hitler set up a train system that allowed him to transport large numbers of Jews to the camps. And he went out of his way to gather Jews who had fled Germany and who lived in other European countries.

Thus, the Holocaust is the only genocide in human history where the perpetrators went out of their way to gather the victims and *transport them back* to their deaths at a great cost.

FROM THE ASHES OF THE HOLOCAUST

World War II against Germany ended on May 7, 1945. Almost four months later, Japan surrendered on September 2. At last, World War II was over, as well as the Holocaust.

Three years later, a milestone of prophetic proportions took place: Israel was reborn as a modern nation on May 14, 1948! How much of this was this made more likely because of the Holocaust? Or was this mostly the result of the persistent toil of the early Zionist fathers? It's impossible to know for certain how much each factor contributed to Israel's rebirth. But we do know Israel had to be reborn to fulfill Bible prophecy. Ezekiel chapters 36–37 foretold of a coming day when the Jewish people would return from the Diaspora in unbelief.

In November 1947, the United Nations decided to partition Palestine. Following that historic decision, on May 14, 1948, the leader of the World Zionist Congress, David Ben-Gurion (1886–1973), declared that Israel was now a state independent of the British Mandate for Palestine. Israel was later accepted as a full member of the UN in 1949.

On May 15, 1948, the very next day after Israel's declaration of independence, neighboring Arab nations attacked Israel. Ever since, Israel has been constantly under attack or at war:

1948–1949: War of Independence

1956: Suez Crisis

1967: Six-Day War

1973: Yom Kippur War

1982: Lebanon War

1987–1993: First Intifada

2000–2005: Second Intifada

2006: Lebanon War

2008–2009: Gaza Operation Cast Lead

2012: Gaza Operation Pillar of Defense

2014: Gaza Operation Protective Edge

2023: Israel-Hamas War

The boundaries of the land of Israel have been in media headlines ever since and have frequently been described as either disputed or occupied territories.

Within a decade of Israel's rebirth, a new narrative was being crafted by those who wanted to delegitimize the Jewish State in the eyes of a broader audience. The goal of this narrative was to redefine the players in a way that would draw the world's sympathy to "Palestinian victims" and demonize the "Israeli colonizers and occupiers." Nobody promoted that shift better than Yasser Arafat.

A TOXIC NARRATIVE: PERPETRATORS AND VICTIMS

The new narrative describing victims and perpetrators in the Middle East took root while Yasser Arafat was the leader of the Palestinian Liberation Organization (PLO). His arrival on the scene changed the face of the Middle East forever. Born in Cairo, Egypt, Arafat (1929–2004) spent much of his life fighting Israel, Zionism, and the Jewish people. In 1959, he founded Fatah, the left-wing secular faction of the PLO, with one goal in mind: the complete eradication of Israel. He was the father and a proponent of "Palestinian self-determination," for which he fought his whole life, "magically" transforming Jordanians, Syrians, Lebanese, and Egyptians into "Palestinian refugees" in need of getting back their own land, "Palestine."

Prior to Arafat and the PLO, the Palestinian people didn't exist, at least in the sense that they are described today. To better understand the true meaning of Palestine, we must go back in history. While the exact origin of the name *Palestine* is still debated, there are aspects of the word's meaning that we can surely know. It may have once described an ancient people group known as the Philistines, but that people group was in no way connected to the current era Palestinians—not ethnically, not linguistically, not historically, and not culturally.

In AD 132, a Jewish revolt took place against the Romans. The Bar Kochba revolt, led by Simon bar Kochba, a false messiah in Israel at the time, didn't end well for the Jewish people. After a bloodbath of gigantic proportions, the Roman emperor, Hadrian, renamed Israel and called it Palaestina. He rebranded the land using the name of Israel's enemies, the Philistines, in an effort to undermine Jewish history and humiliate the Jewish people. Hadrian also renamed Jerusalem, christening it Aelia Capitolina. The name Palestine stuck and continued to be used after that time. It does not appear in the Bible, except for on maps created long after the Bible was written. Of course, these maps are not inspired.

It is fair to say that from 132 to 1948, the word *Palestine* described a land mass known today as Eretz Yisrael (the Land of Israel), and that it was inhabited by Palestinian Arabs and Palestinian Jews. Palestinian Arabs simply considered themselves Arabs and did not view themselves as having a separate identity from other Arabs. This is affirmed by a statement made in 1919 when representatives were selected for the Paris Peace Conference:

> We consider Palestine as part of Arab Syria, as it has never been separated from it at any time. We are connected with it by national, religious, linguistic, natural, economic, and geographical bonds.[4]

In other words, in 1919, the people whom the world now calls Palestinians lived near Syria and considered themselves Syrian Arabs. They didn't call themselves Palestinians.

In 1937, a local Arab leader, Auni Bey Abdul-Hadi, told the British Peel Commission:

> There is no such country [as Palestine]! "Palestine" is a term the Zionists invented! There is no Palestine in the Bible. Our country was for centuries part of Syria.[5]

From that point on, the anti-Zionist propaganda started to grow exponentially. Antisemitism was no longer alone in driving the Judeophobic agenda of the Middle East. Anti-Zionism or anti-Israelism became part of the picture. As documented in the rest of this book, while the terminology might have changed, the foundation of all the new anti-Israel sentiment continues to be antisemitism. The old hatred was repackaged and renamed, but not eradicated.

Arafat and his global supporters worked overtime to create the Palestinian narrative that is now believed as fact by many around the world. This narrative paints Israel as the perpetrator and Palestinians as victims. It led to what many now call the new antisemitism. Even though this hatred against the Jews was actually a continuation of classical antisemitism, it reared its ugly head and became more distinctly evident as the new antisemitism at the start of the Second Intifada (Palestinian Uprising) in 2000.

THE NEW ANTISEMITISM

The new antisemitism has a lot in common with what we can call either the old antisemitism or classical antisemitism, as far as the goal is concerned. It was, is, and always will be the complete destruction of the Jewish people just because they are Jewish. This hatred has been delivered to the world in a new package, making it more believable and easier to accept than its racially motivated predecessor. It has new boundaries, a new source, and a new methodology.

The boundaries of the old antisemitism were European for the most part. Even though history could testify that the hatred against Jewish people had already transcended borders and continents, the big push came out of Germany and extended to various Eastern and Western European countries.

The cancer of Jewish hatred was largely localized to Europe. After the Holocaust, world Jewry began to recover, and in 1948, after the miraculous and prophetic rebirth of Israel as a modern nation, many people believed that the beast of antisemitism had finally been destroyed.

However, Israel and the Jewish people are now exposed to a new antisemitism that is not confined to geographical borders. All Jewish people are targets, as if by proxy, regardless of their geographical location. With the advent of the internet and social media networks, every bit of information has the potential of being global and instant, and as a result, can inflict much greater damage. The cancer has metastasized to the entire planet! And as if the lack of boundaries were not enough, the source and methodology changed as well.

Because the new antisemitism isn't strictly racially motivated, the perpetrators come from a broader spectrum, including atheists, liberals, radical Muslims, and even some "Christians."[6]

It could be argued that Yasser Arafat was the father of the new antisemitism, even though the transition from classical and racial antisemitism has been progressive and difficult to pinpoint. The new narrative started in the mid-1960s and has continued into the twenty-first century.

This new antisemitism is not going away anytime soon. What used to be motivated by a disdain for a "subhuman race" needing extinction is now motivated supposedly by a desire for tolerance, multiculturalism, and world peace. However, the Jews remain the victims even as the world has come to believe it's the Palestinian people who have been victimized and displaced.

This hatred has morphed as part of Satan's last attempt to completely annihilate the Jewish people. What I did not realize at first was that we've reached a new level in Satan's visceral hatred of God's chosen people. Yet it would be a grave mistake to think that we have reached the worst in terms of antisemitism. The liberal left, the extreme right, and radical Islam are all working together now against the Jews. As these most unexpected of allies continue to vilify and persecute Israel and the global Jewish community, a new kind of boldness has emerged from their coalition. The hatred of Israel and of all Jews is now becoming more acceptable, and in some circles, is even expected.

The Cancer Spreads Globally

The Synagogue Bombings in Tunisia

In 2002, a natural gas truck rigged with explosives was driven into the El Ghirba synagogue in Tunisia and detonated. Nineteen people died and more than 30 were wounded. A 24-year-old man acted as a homicide bomber, and later, Al-Qaeda took credit for the attack.

In 2003, several attacks were carried out against a Jewish community center and other sites in Casablanca, Morocco. The explosions claimed the lives of 45 people and wounded another 100. Al-Qaeda took responsibility for the carnage.

A few months later, in Istanbul, Turkey, two synagogues were attacked simultaneously on the Sabbath with a car bomb. Twenty-nine congregants died and hundreds were wounded.[7]

In 2006, a Jewish man named Ilan Halimi was killed. He was kidnapped, tortured for three weeks, and dumped in a forest with cigarette and acid burns over 80 percent of his body.[8] French Jews were shocked by the news of Ilan's death and verbalized their fears and concerns about safety in France. Many even declared that France was finished for the Jews.[9]

A great wave of immigration from France to Israel started at that time and continues to this day. However devastating Halimi's story was, it was yet another case that catapulted France into the next level of antisemitism—the multiple killings of Jews. This occurred in March 2012 in Toulouse, France, and is known today as L'affaire Merah.[10]

The Massacres in Toulouse, France

One March morning, France woke up to the news of the killing of a rabbi and three Jewish children at Ozar Hatorah, a Jewish school in Toulouse, France. The gunman—Mohammed Merah—appeared to have been the same perpetrator who had killed several French paratroopers just days before. The whole country was in shock.

The French media outlets excelled at their attempt to whitewash the crime. Their agenda was made clear as they made every effort to divert public opinion of Mohammed Merah from his identity as a radical Muslim terrorist to an extreme-right terrorist, or even worse, an insane individual. Insanity exonerates responsibility—how convenient!

There should be no room in our minds for doubt about Merah's motives. There should be no excuses for his hatred, and there should be no justification for his actions. Yet, on March 23, 2012, a teacher in Rouen, Normandy, asked her twelfth-grade class to observe "a minute of silence for the victim," referring to Merah.[11]

Mohammed Merah was not a Palestinian, and his victims were not Israelis; but in 2012, it was already well established in the psyche of the Jew-haters around the world that—by proxy—any allegedly negative move made by Israel could bring guilt to any Jewish person on the planet, and so it went. Today, Jewish guilt by proxy is running rampant.[12]

The Robbery and Rape in Creteil, France

In December 2014, three armed men entered the apartment of a Jewish couple in the southeast Paris suburb of Creteil. One guarded the man in the apartment, one raped his female partner, and the third acquired their credit cards and pin numbers to go to the nearest ATM and withdraw cash.

This tragic event drew an outcry from the Jewish community yet was grossly under-reported by the French media networks. What is hard to fathom is that the assailants were working under the assumption that they could get money from the couple because they were Jewish and therefore supposedly wealthy[13]—a stereotype about Jewish people that dates back to the Middle Ages and hadn't been a factor in recent antisemitic crimes.[14] As we saw earlier in chapter 2, this stereotype grew out of the fact Jews had few options for making a living, with one being money lending,[15] and these Jews were taxed heavily by Europe's monarchs, forcing them to charge high borrowing rates.

The Ukraine Expulsion Letter

In April 2014, a leaflet was published and distributed to Jews in the East Ukraine town of Donetsk as they left their synagogue. This happened on the first night of Passover, when Jews worldwide gather with their families to celebrate God's provision and their redemption from Egyptian bondage. The leaflets were written in Russian on government letterhead, and ordered Jews to register their real estate, modes of transportation, and family members over the age of 16. Jews were also asked to pay $50 to have that registration processed, and were told that if they failed to comply, expulsion was inevitable.[16]

As it turned out, the leaflets were forgeries. I wish I could say that Jews shouldn't fear for their safety with a repeat of such trickery, but I see it otherwise. The very fact that such a plot against Jewish people would even cross anyone's mind is evidence that humanity is not getting any better. Jewish people continue to be the scapegoats of humanity for a myriad of reasons, which are becoming more ludicrous and irrational than ever. Jewish people today remain at risk, and as antisemitism heats up to the level known in the 1930s and

1940s, it is clear that a new generation of willing executioners is inevitable, standing by in the antechamber of antisemitism and waiting for opportunities to act out their hatred.

The Day Terrorism Became Heroism

In October 2014, while the French government continued to perform its usual hypocritical game of semantics to reassure the Jews of France that they were safe there, an incident took place that proved the opposite. The old adage "Actions speak louder than words" still holds true.

A man who killed Jews was honored in France. He wasn't viewed merely as a victim, militant, or martyr for the Palestinian cause; that, of course, would be an insult to many. Ironically, in our upside-down world, the terrorist was recognized as a hero and a peacemaker.

The man in question is Marwan Barghouti, an arch-terrorist who, since 2004, has been serving five consecutive life sentences plus 40 years in an Israeli prison for the deaths of five Israelis. Barghouti still exercises much control over Fatah, a faction of the PLO, from his prison cell. He is credited for having led the first (1987–1993) and second (2000–2005) Intifadas, or violent uprisings in which Jewish people are killed. Barghouti is a terrorist, a murderer, and an antisemite.

In 2014, the city of Valenton, on the east side of Paris, named a street Allée Marwan Barghouti.[17] As the street was inaugurated, the mayor unveiled a sign that read:

> Alley Marwan Barghouti, Palestinian deputy, activist, arbitrarily imprisoned in Israel, "The Palestinian Mandela" is an honorary citizen of Valenton.

The final proof of how far people have gone into the irrational is the very fact that in 2016, the same life-sentence-serving Marwan Barghouti was nominated for the Nobel Peace Prize by Belgian lawmakers.[18] So how far do Belgian Jews think their own government would go to protect them against antisemitism?

The Jewish Museum Attack in Brussels

In May of 2014, Medhi Nemmouche walked inside the Jewish Museum in Brussels and killed three people and injured one in a mass shooting. Two of the victims were Jewish. Nemmouche was later apprehended in southern France and was also believed to have ties with the Islamic State.[19]

Murder at a Magazine Headquarters and a Kosher Supermarket in Paris

Who can forget the three days of terror that took place in Paris on January 7–9, 2015? The attacks left a wound that will most likely take years to heal.

The massacre at the *Charlie Hebdo* magazine headquarters in Paris took the lives of 12 people. Two masked men barged into the building and shot most of the staff as they were conducting their weekly editorial meeting.[20] The killings were in response to the magazine's repeated insults targeting Mohammed, the prophet of Islam. The magazine building had been firebombed a few years earlier because of a Mohammed cartoon on the cover of an issue titled *Sharia Hebdo,*[21] a sly play on the magazine's name, *Charlie Hebdo.*

France has a long history of publishing satirical literature, and the incident was a blatant attack on freedom of expression.

About mid-day on January 9, a typical Friday in a very Jewish area of Paris, Jewish residents were doing last-minute shopping before the Jewish Sabbath began at sundown. Just then, Amédy Coulibaly walked inside a kosher supermarket on the southeast side of Paris and took the store hostage after killing four Jewish people. Later that same afternoon, the French police brought an end to the crisis at the kosher store.

France was in shock, and within 48 hours, people from around the world rallied around President François Hollande for what is now remembered as the "Paris march against terror."[22] People in France held "I Am Charlie" signs on the streets. But sadly, what seemed to be momentum toward solidarity against antisemitism quickly faded away.

The Synagogue Attack in Pittsburgh

On October 27, 2018, a gunman opened fire on the Tree of Life synagogue in Pittsburgh, Pennsylvania. Eleven people died and six were wounded in what has been labeled the deadliest antisemitic attack in US history. After the killing spree, the shooter told police that "all these Jews need to die."[23, 24]

That shooting shocked Jewish communities across the United States, making them realize that even in America, Jews were not that safe after all. Indeed, not long after the shooting, various Jewish federations realized that they had to start equipping their communities to provide security during services and High Holy Days.[25] The need for security for Jewish congregants has become a reality across the country.

The Attack at Poway Synagogue, California

In 2019, a man entered a Chabad synagogue in the San Diego area of California, killed one person, injured three including the rabbi and attempted to kill at least fifty more. He was sentenced to life plus 30 years. He had published a letter on an antisemitic site claiming that Jews were plotting a thorough genocide of the European race.

A Growing and Disturbing Trend

The list of antisemitic attacks I've provided here is a short summary of many that have taken place in recent decades. Suffice it to say that antisemitism is extensive, global, and growing daily. This trend has been of great concern to those who monitor antisemitism. Then, of course, October 7, 2023, happened—and the world has never been the same since. Later in the book, we will take a closer look at what took place on that fateful day, and how antisemitism has gotten even worse.

PART 3

A NEW AND MORE DANGEROUS AGE OF ANTISEMITISM

CHAPTER 7

ESCHATOLOGICAL ANTISEMITISM: AN EVEN GREATER DANGER

The word *eschatology* comes from two Greek words, *eschatos*, which means "last," and *logy*, meaning "the study of." Over the years, and at the hand of many scholars and theologians, the Bible has been studied systematically and organized theologically by topics going from God to salvation to angels to the last days. These theological topics have been broadly organized into 12 categories.[1]

Eschatology is one of several parts of theology and is the study of the last days of human history. As such, it deals with future events that will take place and affect humankind prior to what is known as the "eternal order," often identified with heaven.

In relation to antisemitism, it is crucial to understand that what takes place against the Jewish people and Israel during the end times is inevitable, but is not related to one's understanding or adherence to any eschatological position. This is very important because people too often discard the description of prophetic future events simply because the Bible presents these events in ways that we do not completely understand. In fact, we may, as believers, disagree over when we expect these events to occur, the order in which they will occur, and what they may look like.

For instance, people believe that the rapture (the future event when Yeshua comes down from heaven and snatches away His followers from the earth) can happen before, during, or after the seven-year tribulation (a period of great turmoil on Earth during the end of times). Some people believe that there will not be a rapture at all. While all very different, these views reside within the spectrum of what we call orthodox Christianity.

The point here is that if an event is described in the Bible as a real event that has yet to come, those who believe in the inerrancy of Scripture will affirm that this event will take place at some time in the future. When it comes to the last events that will take place against Israel and the Jewish people, we can also assert with absolute certainty that they *will* take place without being dogmatic about the order in which they will occur.

Believing that God's Word is true should alleviate all temptations to reject the future of Israel and the Jewish people simply because of one's theological position. We can settle the issue by looking at what the Bible has to say about the last days.

This being established, we will approach our study of the last events of mankind in general and Israel in particular from a premillennial, pretribulation position. While it is important to determine what these events will be, it is beyond the scope of this book to defend a premillennial, pretribulation view. Let us simply identify the events of the last days from the Bible and place them where they seem to best fit in God's plan according to His Word, leaving it to readers to select a different order if they so desire. Regardless, from God's viewpoint and from the perspective of eschatological antisemitism, the events of God's end-times plan are yet to be fulfilled. We will look at eschatology as it pertains to mankind, Israel, and the Jewish people as well as to followers of Yeshua.

My favored sequence of the events of the last days is as follows:

- Yeshua's midair return to snatch up believers in what is known as the rapture (1 Corinthians 15:51-53; 1 Thessalonians 4:16-18)
- The tribulation or "time of Jacob's trouble," which will last for seven years (Jeremiah 30:7; Daniel 9:24-27)
- The millennial kingdom or messianic kingdom on earth, which will last for 1,000 years (Psalm 72:8; Revelation 20:1-3)
- The eternal order, or the rest of eternity in a new heaven (John 5:24; 6:27)

ESCHATOLOGY: WHAT HAS HAPPENED SO FAR?

After His resurrection (Matthew 28:6; John 20:16-18; Luke 24:38-39) and since His ascension into heaven 2,000 years ago (Mark 16:19; Luke 24:51), Yeshua has been awaiting the day when He will return to Earth to wrap up God's program for mankind. Over the centuries, many people have claimed that their generation was in the last days, yet we are still here on Earth.

According to Yeshua, several events must take place to set the stage for the last days, and we can read about them in Matthew 24:1-8, at the beginning of what is known as the Olivet Discourse. The first event has to do with a global conflict: "Nation will rise against nation, and kingdom against kingdom, and in various places there will be famines and earthquakes. But all these things are merely the beginning of birth pangs" (verses 7-8).

If indeed that passage is a Jewish way of saying there will be world conflict, it then becomes obvious that World War I (1914–1918) was the beginning of birth pangs, and then, within 20 years, World War II took place from 1939–1945. Many historians agree that World War II was a continuation of World War I[2] or that they were closely related, and this pretty much from the time of the Treaty of Versailles in 1919, which imposed sanctions on Germany. Within 13 years, Adolf Hitler was on the scene.

Going back to Matthew 24, we read that famines and earthquakes will accompany those wars (verse 7). While earthquake data can be tricky to compile and can vary from one source to the next, the general consensus, according to the United States Geological Survey (USGS), is that earthquakes have increased since 1900.[3]

In addition, famines occurred between World War I and World War II in China in 1927, 1929, 1943, and again also between 1958–1962, and in the Soviet Union in 1921–1922, 1932–1934, and 1946–1947.[4]

Another key event is the existence of the state of Israel. Simply by virtue of the birth of the modern state of Israel on May 14, 1948, the prophecies that require the Diaspora (dispersion) Jews to return to their homeland are now being fulfilled. The world has witnessed a tremendous influx of Jews into Eretz Yisrael (the land of Israel) since 1948.

Many scholars see one future regathering of the Jews in the land in unbelief, while others see two future regatherings[5]—one in unbelief and a second one for God's blessing at the end of the tribulation (Isaiah 11:11-16; Ezekiel 36:22-28; 37:1-10; Jeremiah 16:14-15; 23:7-8). Regardless of the view you adopt, the regathering(s) couldn't happen if there weren't a physical place for the Jewish people to regather to. But there is, and that happened on May 14, 1948. Yet another event needed to occur for the last days program of God to move forward, and that was the Jewish control of the old city of Jerusalem. That momentous event took place in 1967 as a result of the Six-Day War.[6]

Israel has been spread out by the global Diaspora for a long time and more than once. While it could be argued that the Egyptian captivity was the first diaspora of sorts, the Babylonian captivity in 587 BC describes the first major dispersion of Jews outside of the land of Israel as discipline for disobedience (Deuteronomy 28; Jeremiah 29; Isaiah 45:13; 51:14). The people eventually returned, only to be sent out again after the Roman destruction of Jerusalem and the temple in AD 70. Today, Jewish people can be found in many countries around the globe.[7]

Ezekiel 36:24 clearly tells us that God will bring the Jewish people back to the land, and then later He will regenerate them. In other words, first they will return in unbelief, and then they will express belief in the God of Israel, which is confirmed in Ezekiel 37.

Also, according to Daniel 9:26-27, the Antichrist will come onto the scene and sign a peace treaty with the leaders of Israel. That very signing between the Antichrist and Israel is evidence that their return will be in unbelief and somewhat in rebellion against the God of Abraham, Isaac, and Jacob. But God doesn't break His promises, and regardless of Israel's disobedience,[8] He will bring the people back into the land, as stated in Ezekiel 36:22:

> Say to the house of Israel, "Thus says the Lord GOD, 'It is not for your sake, O house of Israel, that I am about to act, but for My holy name, which you have profaned among the nations where you went.'"

Jerusalem fell back under Jewish control in 1967 as a result of the Six-Day War, and yet the Six-Day War was never prophesied in the Bible. But again, the war was a catalyst for Jewish leadership to take over the ruling of Jerusalem.[9]

We know from the Bible that another Jewish temple will be built in the future. It will be the third temple, often known as the tribulation temple. The reason it needs to be rebuilt and functional is because halfway through the tribulation, the temple will be desecrated (Daniel 9:27; Matthew 24:15; 2 Thessalonians 2:3-4; Revelation 11:1-2). Simply stated, it must first exist in order to cease to exist!

ESCHATOLOGY: WHAT STILL NEEDS TO HAPPEN?

Painting with broad strokes, we can assert that the main eschatological events yet to be fulfilled are (in a pretribulation, premillennial order) these: the rapture of the church, the tribulation, the millennial or 1,000-year messianic kingdom, the second coming, and the eternal order.

The Bible also speaks of an attack on Israel as part of the last-days events. It tells us of an invasion of Israel from the north, which is described in Ezekiel chapters 38 and 39. This great attack is known as the invasion of Gog and Magog and will most likely include Russia, Iran, and a few other lesser countries. Initially it will deliver a serious blow to Israel, but the invaders will quickly be stopped and destroyed by God, who, in the process, will display His power and glory to all the nations. It appears this invasion will take place before the abomination of desolation that occurs at the midpoint of the seven-year tribulation, based on Ezekiel 38:8-14. We also need to understand that there is nothing in today's Israel, Russia, and Iran that would prevent it from happening now.

Furthermore, the world needs to be conditioned to go along with such a drastic agenda of hatred against Israel. Soon, we will take a closer look at this agenda and how it is manifesting itself.

There are several places in the Bible that indicate that the Jewish people will be persecuted in the last days, and two key passages about that are found in Zechariah chapters 12 and 14. The prophet Zechariah says this in Zechariah 12:1-9:

> The burden of the word of the LORD concerning Israel.
>
> Thus declares the LORD who stretches out the heavens, lays the foundation of the earth, and forms the spirit of man within him, "Behold, I am going to make Jerusalem a cup that causes reeling to all the peoples around; and when the siege is against Jerusalem, it will also be against

> Judah. It will come about in that day that I will make Jerusalem a heavy stone for all the peoples; all who lift it will be severely injured. And all the nations of the earth will be gathered against it. In that day," declares the LORD, "I will strike every horse with bewilderment and his rider with madness. But I will watch over the house of Judah, while I strike every horse of the peoples with blindness. Then the clans of Judah will say in their hearts, 'A strong support for us are the inhabitants of Jerusalem through the LORD of hosts, their God.'
>
> "In that day I will make the clans of Judah like a firepot among pieces of wood and a flaming torch among sheaves, so they will consume on the right hand and on the left all the surrounding peoples, while the inhabitants of Jerusalem again dwell on their own sites in Jerusalem. The LORD also will save the tents of Judah first, so that the glory of the house of David and the glory of the inhabitants of Jerusalem will not be magnified above Judah. In that day the LORD will defend the inhabitants of Jerusalem, and the one who is feeble among them in that day will be like David, and the house of David will be like God, like the angel of the LORD before them. And in that day I will set about to destroy all the nations that come against Jerusalem."

Zechariah tells us there will come a day when all the nations of the earth will go against Jerusalem (verse 3). The main point of these nine verses shouldn't be missed; God is going to deliver His people Israel from all those who go after them (verse 9). This infers that Israel will be subject to a massive attack of global proportions prior to being rescued by God. It seems a bit over the top to say that "all the nations" will go against Jerusalem, yet this is exactly what God means, and He even repeats this in Zechariah 14:1-4:

> Behold, a day is coming for the LORD when the spoil taken from you will be divided among you. For I will gather all the nations against Jerusalem to battle, and the city will be captured, the houses plundered, the women ravished and half of the city exiled, but the rest of the people will not be cut off from the city. Then the LORD will go forth and fight against those nations, as when He fights on a day of battle. In that day His feet will stand on the Mount of Olives, which is in front of Jerusalem on the east; and the Mount of Olives will be split in its middle from east to west by a very large valley, so that half of the mountain will move toward the north and the other half toward the south.

This is part of the last chapter of God's program, and it will most likely take place at the end of the tribulation, also known as "the time of Jacob's trouble" (Jeremiah 30:7 NKJV). That time at the end of the tribulation is when the campaign of Armageddon will occur.

The only way to instigate all the nations to go against Israel is to give them contempt for the Jews everywhere in the world, and that is exactly what Satan is working on now. Globally, Jews have become guilty by proxy and are thus worthy of contempt and destruction.

It is beyond the scope of this book to take an in-depth look at all the events of the last days, but there are many excellent works available.[10] Eschatologically speaking, we need to spend a lot less time on speculating about how all these events will take place, and more time on what we should do before they start happening.

ESCHATOLOGY: SATAN, THE MAIN PROTAGONIST

Satan's Longstanding Obsession with Antisemitism

It is important to note that the main protagonist in the end-times program is Satan. We need, of course, to keep this balanced with the fact that God is also allowing for certain things to happen as part of His final program to discipline the Jewish people and bring them to Him (Zechariah 12:10; 13:9).

Like a vicious puppet master, Satan continues to work behind the scenes to completely destroy the Jewish people and Israel as well as many people from the nations. As all of Jewish history has shown us, he is obsessed with his goal of preventing God's program from being fulfilled. He wants to prove that God is a liar. Satan wishes to avoid, or at least postpone, his demise and final abode in the lake of fire for all eternity.

Satan's hatred for what God loves goes all the way back to the first messianic prophecy, which is found in Genesis 3:15—a prophecy about the seed (Messiah Yeshua) of the woman. From the time that Satan realized that God loved the Jewish people, he has labored aggressively to destroy them.

In His humanity, the Messiah would be from Israel. Yeshua was indeed from the seed of Abraham (Genesis 22:18) and from the tribe of Judah (Genesis 49:10). Satan doesn't like the way the story ends, and he is determined to nip the messianic line in the bud and has made repeated attempts toward that goal.

Among the earliest occurred right before the flood, when, in Genesis 6, we witness the intermarriage of "the sons of God" with the "daughters of men." Could it be that Satan was attempting to corrupt the humanity from which Messiah would be born? This would appear to be Satan's answer to the seed of the woman spoken of in Genesis 3:15. The "sons of God," or Nephilim, meaning "fallen ones," intermarried with human women and created a superhuman yet corrupted race in God's eyes.[11] The messianic line couldn't be corrupted; thus the flood took place (Genesis 9), and Noah, his wife, and his three sons and daughters-in-law were protected and humanity was given a fresh, uncorrupted start.

Then of course we have the case of the Pharaoh "who did not know

Joseph" (Exodus 1:8) and wanted to kill all the firstborn males of the Hebrews (Exodus 1:8-22; Acts 7:18-19). We must keep in mind that the biblical way to trace lineage was always through the father. By destroying all the Hebrew males and forcing the females to intermarry with Egyptian men, Satan could put a halt to the coming of the Jewish Messiah. Satan was creative, but the God of Abraham, Isaac, and Jacob had much better plans, and Moses was born.

The Pharaoh who didn't know Joseph panicked when he saw the growth of the Jewish population during the Egyptian captivity. He ordered the killing of all Jewish newborn boys to control Jewish demographics, but Moses was born and spared. Pharaoh's curse of killing Jewish baby boys was used on him and all of Egypt when, in the last of the ten plagues, all the Egyptian firstborn (including Pharaoh's son) died in one night. This was a direct application of the principle that God stated in Genesis 12:3, when He said, "I will bless those who bless you, and the one who curses you I will curse."[12]

But Satan doesn't give up easily, as we see in the case of Israel's archenemies, the Amalekites (Deuteronomy 25:17-19), who were determined to destroy Israel. In one of several battles, the Amalekites cowardly attempted to go against Israel from the rear when Israel's men were "faint and weary" (verse 18). The Amalekites (descendants of Esau, Genesis 36:12) appear to always have been the enemies of the Jews,[13] and even their name, Amalekites, became a symbol of Jewish hatred in rabbinic literature. They continued to go after Israel (Numbers 14:45; Judges 6:33; 1 Samuel 14:48; 15:7; 27:8) until, by God's providence, they were almost completely destroyed by King David (1 Samuel 30; 2 Samuel 1:1) and finally wiped out in the days of King Hezekiah (1 Chronicles 4:41-43).

In the book of Esther, we are introduced to a possible descendant of the Amalekites who remains a major figure in the history of antisemitism: Haman the Agagite (Esther 3:1). What made Haman's hatred for the Jewish people different from previous biblical examples of antisemitism was his irrational contempt for the people of God. Haman was so furious at Mordecai for not bowing down to him that he desired to kill all the Jews in the kingdom of Ahasuerus, which was, of course, a gross overreaction to one man's decision.

> When Haman saw that Mordecai neither bowed down nor paid homage to him, Haman was filled with rage. But he disdained to lay hands on Mordecai alone, for they had told him who the people of Mordecai were; therefore Haman sought to destroy all the Jews, the people of Mordecai, who were throughout the whole kingdom of Ahasuerus (Esther 3:5-6).

Haman didn't hate the Jews because they were a threat to him or they mistreated him. Rather, he hated them simply because they were different. So he plotted to destroy them by turning the king against them:

> Haman said to King Ahasuerus, "There is a certain people scattered and dispersed among the peoples in all the provinces of your kingdom; their laws are different from those of all other people and they do not observe the king's laws, so it is not in the king's interest to let them remain" (Esther 3:8).

Haman then went further and offered to pay money to those who helped him with his evil endeavor. This is revealed in Mordecai's conversation with Hathach, the king's eunuch: "Mordecai told him all that had happened to him, and the exact amount of money that Haman had promised to pay to the king's treasuries for the destruction of the Jews" (Esther 4:7).

It is interesting to note that once again, according to God's promise in Genesis 12:3 to bless and curse people based on how they treated the Jewish people, Haman was hanged on the very gallows that he had built for Mordecai:

> Harbonah, one of the eunuchs who were before the king said, "Behold indeed, the gallows standing at Haman's house fifty cubits high, which Haman made for Mordecai who spoke good on behalf of the king!" And the king said, "Hang him on it." So they hanged Haman on the gallows which he had prepared for Mordecai, and the king's anger subsided (Esther 7:9-10).

Satan has influenced various leaders and people groups against the Jews all through history. In AD 70, the Romans destroyed the temple in Jerusalem, forcing the vast majority of the Jews in Israel to scatter in the Diaspora, and many of them are still in other countries today. Satan constantly searches for new ways to attempt to destroy the Jews; his hatred against the chosen people of God has never subsided. He also knows that he cannot do his work alone, so all through the ages, as we've seen in the Bible and in this book, he has subcontracted his agenda to willing individuals and people groups.

What will hopefully become evident as we start looking at the contemporary players in eschatological antisemitism is the fact that it is highly irrational. End-times antisemitism is much more irrational than its predecessor, which is the main reason I believe there has been a major shift in this hatred. There is never a good excuse for hatred of any kind, but it is easier to understand why a certain person or group would harbor negative feelings toward another people group if they had been cheated, lied to, or even abused by that group. But in the case of Israel and the Jewish people, that is hardly the case. Israel has been falsely painted as a perpetrator and treated as a scapegoat, and in the days to come, this will get much worse.

Satan's Career Will Soon Be Over

Satan has been behind antisemitism from its very inception. He is passionate about it; he is very committed to succeeding at any price. That's because Satan is well aware of his ultimate fate, and he knows that the timing of his fate is connected to Israel's acceptance of Yeshua as the Messiah.

Satan "deceives the whole world" (Revelation 12:9) and is the "father of lies" (John 8:44). He is also the "ruler of this world" (John 12:31-32) and the "evil one" (Ephesians 6:16). These are just a few of the descriptions of Satan found in the Bible. He prides himself at loving what God hates and hating what God loves, and as a result, *he hates the Jews*. It's that simple, which explains why this hatred can be so highly irrational.

Israel's enemy has been overly creative in the ways he has chosen to attack and destroy the Jews, and he continues to be. And we cannot ignore the fact that he uses people to further his agenda.

Satan is not omnipotent (all-powerful) or omniscient (all-knowing), but he knows what the Scriptures say about God, about Israel, and certainly about himself. While he very well knows his final destiny, he is determined to do everything he can to postpone it.

In a nutshell, Satan knows he has already been defeated, and he also knows that when Messiah Yeshua returns at the second coming, his career will be over.

In Revelation 19, we read about Messiah's return to Earth in judgment. He will destroy all His enemies, and that includes Satan. After Yeshua reclaims the earth, Revelation 20:1-3 tells us that Satan will be thrown into the abyss. And after the millennial kingdom, Satan will be thrown into the lake of fire for all eternity (Revelation 20:10).

While Satan knows there is nothing he can do to change his final destination, out of desperation, he figures that maybe he can stop or at least postpone the second coming by incapacitating those responsible for enabling it to take place: the Jews!

If Satan could get the whole world to hate the Jews and want them dead, that would help his agenda. That's why he invented antisemitism and continues to instill highly irrational Jew hatred in the minds of people around the globe. Ironically, many antisemites have never met a Jewish person in their life.[14]

Satan has used both atheists and religious people—as well as people from all kinds of different groups and factions—to adjust his master hatred of the Jews over the centuries. What makes eschatological antisemitism so unique is that Satan is mixing all these people together in his most recent recruiting spree. He is taking the adage "The end justifies the means" to new levels of evil.

A TURNING OF THE TIDE

Have you noticed how today, both sides of the political spectrum agree simultaneously that they hate the Jews and are working together at hurting Israel? We see the extreme right, like the French party Front National or the Jobbik Party in Hungary, working with leftists and liberals toward the common goal of stopping Israel—"the occupier"—of the Middle East.

We also see Christians—and we must use the term loosely—partner with or support Muslims and pro-Palestinian terrorists. What all Christians need to understand is that Muslims who adhere to Islam don't worship the same God as we do,[15] and that radical Islamists hate Christians as much as they hate Jewish people and the West. In a move that appears to be taken straight from a *Twilight Zone* episode—if such a topic were ever covered on that TV show—people who do not see homosexuality as a sin are working with people who behead and murder homosexuals. There is even a small group of American liberals who describe themselves as Queers for Palestine.[16] The absurdity of such a group supporting the Palestinian narrative is evident. Regardless of one's view on homosexuality, it is clear that homosexuals *are not* welcomed by Palestinians or by Muslim countries. Instead, homosexuals are persecuted, tortured, and at times killed. This is as ludicrous and oxymoronic as having groups like Blacks for KKK or Jews for Hitler.

The result is an amalgam of people who can be found across the political spectrum and across the religious spectrum as well. What unites all these people who would otherwise not see eye to eye is their disdain for Israel and the Jewish people. These people are the new players of end-times antisemitism. They are different from the previous protagonists in their identity and in their nearly covenantal partnerships with groups of opposing ideologies.

It is necessary to identify these groups if we want to understand them and counter their erroneous approach to the Middle East and the Jewish people. In some cases, much can be done, in others, less. But in all cases, we absolutely cannot remain silent. Before we identify these groups, it is also necessary to understand what causes them to partner together against Israel.

AN EXPONENTIAL INCREASE OF IRRATIONALITY

In our day and age, as antisemitism continues to worsen, it is important to realize that as irrational as the sentiment has always been, it is now reaching new levels never seen since the 1930s and 1940s.

Could it be that one of the reasons irrationality so greatly characterizes antisemitism is because Satan is getting desperate, and he is throwing every weapon he has onto the battlefield? This may explain why we're seeing antisemitism unify those from the extreme left and the extreme right, and atheists and religious people, and other disparate groups. Anything goes!

Before we identify some of these different groups, let's look at a few examples of the recent surge of irrationality in antisemitism since October 7, 2023, when Hamas carried out a surprise attack against southern Israel from the Gaza Strip.

October 7, 2023: The Day the Jewish World Changed Forever

Early in the morning on the Jewish holy day of Simchat Torah, Israel woke up to the sound of sirens. In and of itself, this is not unusual for the tiny Jewish State, but this time, it was different. The sirens didn't stop; they intensified. It wasn't long before the country was on high alert and tens of thousands of military reservists were called to duty.

Not only Israel, but the rest of the world watched in horror as Hamas terrorists and Palestinian civilians broke through the eastern border fence of the Gaza Strip and went on a bloody killing spree. Within hours, 1,200 innocent Israelis had been murdered and more than 240 had been taken hostage. This turned out to be the highest Jewish death toll in one day since the Holocaust.

For a few days, the world was in shock and people showed their support for Israel after they witnessed the raping, maiming, burning, and brutal killing of Israelis at the Nova Music Festival, Kibbutz Be'eri, and other locations. Then the unthinkable happened, and the world started to turn against Israel.[17] Within a week or so, no one seemed to remember the Hamas terror attack, and everyone started to focus on Israel's allegedly disproportionate response to Hamas in the Gaza Strip. They falsely accused IDF soldiers of brutality and violence against Gazans.

The level of antisemitism worldwide suddenly went off the charts. Especially notable were the many young people on American college and university campuses who chanted, "From the river to the sea, Palestine will be free," clearly showing support for Palestinians and disdain for Israel. We even saw people take sides with Hamas, which is clearly a terrorist organization.

Young people around the globe brandished the modern Palestinian flag everywhere they went, and students even raised it on the campus of Harvard University, the same university whose president said that calling for the killing of Jews was acceptable depending on the context.[18] Claudine Gay ended up resigning not long afterward, yet not because of antisemitism, but plagiarism. She remained part of the faculty.[19]

Within a few months, Martin Griffiths, the UN's undersecretary general for humanitarian affairs and emergency relief coordinator, declared, "Hamas is not a terrorist group for us...It's a political movement."[20]

At a time in history when the world should come to the rescue and support of Israel and Jewish people globally, people are quickly and exponentially turning their backs on the Jewish State. As one writer observed, the double standards that people adhered to with regard to Israel and the delegitimization and demonization[21] of Israel are increasing daily, and the result is the emboldening of antisemites around the globe. Jewish lives are now at risk just about everywhere outside of Israel. This does not mean that Israel is 100 percent safe for Jews, especially since October 7, 2023, but the Jewish State remains the only country in the world where the government diligently seeks to protect its own people from harm. Everywhere else in the world, most people's support of Israel fluctuates somewhere between empty lip service and occasional help.

October 2023: Tearing Down of Hostage Flyers at NYU

Within days of the Hamas terror attack, flyers started to appear around the world, featuring the faces of the Israelis taken hostage by Hamas. Almost immediately, some people at New York University tore down the flyers, which led to a lot of public outrage.[22] The antisemitism behind this act shouldn't be missed. The perpetrators—most of whom were never disciplined—wanted to destroy the evidence that people had been taken hostage. They promoted an agenda of hatred, and in some cases, went so far as to claim the hostages were fake.

These actions, along with the campus riots and pro-Palestinian protests, led up to 64 percent of potential Jewish college students to watch out for antisemitism in their search for the ideal college.[23]

November 2023: Jewish Stars Stenciled on Paris and Berlin Buildings

Within one month after the October 2023 attack, antisemitism started to surface in new ways. Paris and its suburbs woke up one morning to blue Stars of David (Jewish symbols) stenciled on various buildings fronts.[24] This also happened in Berlin on buildings where Jews reside.[25] It remains unknown who did these acts, but it is reminiscent of the identification of Jewish buildings and businesses during *Kristallnacht* in 1938. At the very least, this was an act of intimidation against various Jewish communities.

February 2024: Boycott of Jewish Customers at a Ski Rental Shop in Switzerland

Another very telling event took place in Davos, Switzerland, in February 2024. A small ski equipment rental shop posted signs in Hebrew on the sports shop window. The sign said that because of some past incidents, including theft, "we no longer rent sports equipment to our Jewish brothers."[26]

The Swiss Federation of Jewish Communities sued the shop, which later removed the signs. This was another example of *Kristallnacht*-like actions taken by antisemites. The decision to stop renting to all Jews because of the misbehavior of a few served as an excuse used by antisemitic shop owners and was as irrational as Haman's desire to kill all the Jews in the kingdom of Persia simply because of his hatred of one Jew, Mordecai.

March 2024: Lord Balfour Painting Destroyed in Cambridge, England

Another telling incident took place in Cambridge, England, in March 2024. A student associated with Palestine Action slashed and sprayed a priceless painting of Lord Balfour. As mentioned earlier, Lord Arthur James Balfour is the British politician who was behind the Balfour Declaration, written in 1917. That declaration was a key component in the establishing of the modern State of Israel. Lord Balfour became a symbol, to some, of British colonialism, and to others, of Zionism.

It is concerning to see that a painting of a man who wrote a short letter that was instrumental in the rebirth of Israel could become a thorn in the flesh of those who are opposed to Israel and Zionism. The discomfort of disagreement is understandable, but the destruction of art to promote a political agenda goes too far. This is also indicative of how liberal progressives frequently handle disagreements. They destroy things rather than speaking up, making their case, and civilly walking away, if need be.[27]

November 8, 2024: The Amsterdam Pogrom

In the words of Bible prophecy expert John Haller: "On November 7, the world went to bed in 2024, and on November 8, it woke up in 1938."

This was particularly eerie because November 9 marked the eighty-sixth anniversary of *Kristallnacht*, when a massive pogrom fell upon the Jewish community of Berlin and officially started the Holocaust, also known as the Final Solution.

On November 7 in Amsterdam, a soccer game took place between the Ajax Amsterdam and Maccabi Tel Aviv. After the game, "hundreds of fans" of the Israeli team "were ambushed and attacked," according to the Israeli embassy in the United States.[28] It was as if a full-blown pogrom had broken out against the fans of Maccabi Tel Aviv. So much so that Israeli Prime Minister Benjamin Netanyahu had to charter two El Al planes to rescue the Israeli fans. This happened in 2024, and the attacks were obviously planned and coordinated. And this will not be the last time this happens! The vocal and violent responses against Israel and the Jewish people continue to be off the charts all around the globe.

The *Kristallnacht* of yesterday is anchored in history. Yet more *Kristallnachts* are being repeated today in front of our very eyes, with few reactions from what seems to be an apathetic global community. Will the Jews pay a high price again? While God keeps His promise never to forsake Israel (Jeremiah 31:35-37), He never said this would be accomplished without casualties. So, yes, the latest manifestations of antisemitism could cost the Jewish people dearly, especially if people of good will and Christians remain silent.

The new antisemitism that is rising out of the ashes of the Holocaust is morphing into a more lethal iteration of the longest hatred. It is closely connected to the order of events that have yet to take place in the future, as predicted in the Bible. And it is critical that we understand the direction the world is going and learn how to analyze these events and prepare for them.

End-times antisemitism, as the timeline in chapter 2 proves, isn't an isolated phenomenon. It is the result of more than 2,000 years of Jewish hatred. It is the next level of antisemitism and it includes a plethora of perpetrators, all being used as puppets by Satan to fulfill his destructive agenda against God's chosen people.

By virtue of its very name, end-times antisemitism is related to eschatology or end-times prophecies regarding humankind. To better understand it, we need to look at the order of the events of the last days according to God's Word. And we need to take a closer look at the identities of the new players in antisemitism.

CHAPTER 8

THE NEW PLAYERS IN ESCHATOLOGICAL ANTISEMITISM, PART 1

ISLAM AND LIBERALISM

Scholars often divide Jewish history into two eras: pre-Holocaust (before the 1930s) and post-Holocaust (after 1945). Indeed, the Holocaust was the single most-defining event in Jewish history. When Nazi Germany capitulated and World War II came to an end, only 12 million Jews had survived from 18 million, and almost 80 years later, the global Jewish population still hasn't recovered to the level of pre-Holocaust numbers.

Three significant events took place after World War II that made the world believe antisemitism was dead, and that the new Jewish motto "Never again" was a true testimony to a page of history turned forever.

THREE EVENTS THAT MADE ANTISEMITISM APPEAR TO BE DEAD

The Arrest and Trial of Adolf Eichmann in 1960

Adolf Eichmann was one of the architects of the Holocaust. He met with other Nazi officials at the Wannsee Conference on January 20, 1942, to initiate the Final Solution to the Jewish Question. He was a key player in setting up the death factories of the Holocaust. After a brief detention by the Allies at the end of the war in 1945, Eichmann escaped in 1946 and fled to Argentina under a new assumed name on a Vatican passport. Eventually, in 1962, the Israeli secret service (Mossad) caught up with him, extracted him, and brought him to Israel, where he was tried and hanged in 1962.[1]

Eichmann's trial brought hope to Holocaust survivors who thought that after his arrest, more Nazi escapees would be brought to justice. They hoped for some closure, but to date, only a few Nazi players have been brought to justice. Nevertheless, the Eichmann capture and trial made global Jewry believe—even though briefly—in the possible demise of racial antisemitism.

Vatican II and Nostra Aetate

A few years later, in 1965, Pope Paul VI issued a proclamation titled *Nostra Aetate* ("In Our Time"). In it was an important statement that came from the previous pope, John XXIII. The document declared that the Jewish people could no longer be held corporately responsible for the death of Christ.[2]

The accusation of deicide (the killing of God) had run rampant for almost 2,000 years. The shift in the official position of the Catholic Church regarding that accusation was a major step in the right direction and brought hope to many as to the beginning of the demise of Christian antisemitism. But 60 years later, the accusation lives on within the masses, and other lies have been added to exacerbate the issue even further.

The 1967 Six-Day War

The Six-Day War generated worldwide sympathy for the still-young State of Israel. In that war, Israel was seen—possibly for the last time in its recent history—as the humble and youthful David fighting a mighty Goliath with great success and minimal casualties. But the admiration was short-lived as a false narrative began to be pushed by a newcomer from Egypt who became the leader of the so-called Palestinian people.[3]

Yasser Arafat, born in Egypt, started the Fatah movement in 1959 and slowly became the leader of the Palestinian people and promoter of the Palestinian cause for self-determination. It took several decades to take hold, but the fabricated narrative that says Palestinians are displaced natives is now solidly rooted in the global soil made of a mix of multiculturalism, political correctness, and Jew-hatred. Under Arafat, antisemitism has morphed into a new beast pretending not to be connected to the old one. Antisemitism has become anti-Zionism. People can now claim to be anti-Jewish and anti-Israel without being accused of antisemitism. Incidentally, Arafat wore his keffiyeh (head scarf) pinned to the right side of his body, in the shape of pre-1948 Israel.[4]

While there was some hope that antisemitism had died after the Holocaust, we now know that the oldest hatred had simply been swept under the post-war rug of collective guilt and never ceased to exist.

In the words of Jeffrey Goldberg in *The Atlantic*, after the 2015 attack on the kosher supermarket in Paris, "For half a century, memories of the Holocaust limited anti-Semitism on the Continent. That period has ended." Further in the same article, he says that "the inoculation of the Holocaust has worn off."[5]

Goldberg was right, but the shift goes back to before 2015. The players in the new antisemitism started to act up as they followed the footsteps of Yasser Arafat, and they have continued to gain momentum well into the twenty-first century.

THE NEW PLAYERS BEHIND THE SURGE OF ANTISEMITISM

Islam

For lack of a better way to say it, Arafat made Muslim antisemitism popular, and it has continued to grow up through today. To be sure, there has been a long history of hatred between Arabs and Jews. A brief overview of Islam in relation to Israel and the Jews is necessary to understand the scope of the animosity and the depth of the hatred.

As we know from the biblical account, Abraham was not willing to wait on God for a son. Sarah suggested that he procreate with Sarah's maidservant Hagar, and Ishmael was born (Genesis 16; 25:12-18). Isaac would later be born from Abraham's union with Sarah (Genesis 21). The great hatred between the descendants of Isaac—the Jews—and descendants of Ishmael—the Arabs—had started. Fast-forward to the birth of Islam in AD 610, which has grown over the centuries, and you have a very long history of hatred between the Jewish people and the Arabs.

It is important to understand that not all Arabs are Muslims, and not all Muslims are Arabs. It is also critical to understand that Jewishness is not a religion but an ethnic identity, while Islam *is* a religion that goes beyond simply the Arab people. Incidentally, Islam is much more than a religion. Islam is an ideology that comprises a religion, a political system, a banking system, and many other elements.

Most of the Western world has accepted the fact that the vast majority of the Middle East, North Africa, and the Asian Pacific regions are of the Muslim faith. What seems to be a surprise, however, is how Islam has grown rapidly all over Europe and even in North America.

According to the most comprehensive Pew Research Center survey to date, there are about 1.6 billion Muslims in the world today.[6] This makes Islam the second largest religion after Christianity (2.2 billion),[7] and the Muslim numbers are still growing to the point that by 2050, many countries in Europe and other places around the world will have a Muslim majority.

Islamist terrorist events over the past few decades have given Islam a bad reputation. A lot of people have become fearful of Muslims, especially in countries where they are currently growing but were originally a small minority. By overreacting and painting with the proverbial broad strokes, people can end up categorizing all Muslims as terrorists. They have a kneejerk reaction that we could compare to a general fear of Germans in the 1940s, when some people assumed that every German was a Nazi. Such thinking suffers from an oversimplification or overgeneralization of who Muslims are.

Yet the other side of that coin, blind tolerance, is just as dangerous. Too many people have adopted a postmodern worldview characterized by blind tolerance, embracing multiculturalism without assimilation and a lame political correctness. This naive approach leads people to overlook growing threats to peace and the freedoms of speech and religion. This self-destructive path is often driven by ignorance. That ignorance is either a choice from the West or a result of devious ploys within Islam, sometimes even both. But ignorance can always be remedied with education, provided the educator is an unbiased teacher who isn't trying to fulfill an agenda.

Many people who see Islam as a religion of peace argue that only 15 to 20 percent of the global Muslim population is radically motivated—that is, are Islamists or terrorists. Going with the most conservative figure of 15 percent when applied to the demographic of 1.6 billion Muslims, that means 240,000,000 of them may be radical. That leaves us with a sizeable number of radical Muslims ready to kill and die a martyr's death for jihad. This is not a small number by any stretch of the imagination!

While we must understand that not all Muslims are radicals or terrorists, we must also recognize that Islam isn't necessarily the religion of peace that many are proclaiming. Therefore, what is really meant when we describe Islam as a perpetrator?

Islam is widely promoted by the West as a religion of peace. Anybody who thinks or says otherwise is quickly labeled an Islamophobe and a racist. The first thing we need to understand is that Islamophobia is different from racism. Islamophobia is a fear (phobia), dislike, or even hatred of Islam and what it teaches. In other words, Islamophobia is connected to an ideology, not a people. If one disagrees with the ideology of Islam, one can very well be called an Islamophobe, meaning someone who has a fear or loathing of Islam. But mere criticism or opposition to an ideology is not necessarily an irrational response. Also, opposing an ideology doesn't automatically make a person racist. For instance, if someone specifically targets people simply for being Arabs, they could rightly be labeled Arabophobes, and that can be equated to racism because now a specific people group is being targeted and not an ideology shared by one-and-a-half billion people from many different countries around the world.

As for Islam being a religion of peace, we often hear or read about this Qur'anic verse from Surah Maida 5:32:

> If any one slew a person it would be as if he slew the whole world and if any one saved a life, it would be as if he saved the life of the whole people.[8]

This is a beautiful statement that anyone in their right mind would be wise to adhere to, regardless of their religious inclination or lack thereof. After all, the thought shared in Surah Maida 5:32 is almost a verbatim quotation from the Jewish Talmud:

> Whoever destroys a soul, it is considered as if he destroyed an entire world. And whoever saves a life, it is considered as if he saved an entire world (Mishnah Sanhedrin 4:9—Yerushalmi Talmud, Tractate Sanhedrin 37a).

Yet we must note several things about the context of that Qur'anic verse. The beginning of the verse is seldom, if ever, mentioned. It states, "On that account we ordain for the children of Israel..." So here, the Qur'an seems to be teaching that the principle just mentioned applies to the Jewish people in quite a negative way. By reading the verse as a whole, the meaning changes from one of universal value to one of valuing the killing a Jewish person and seeing it as a deed with merit (slaying one is as if slaying all Jews), whereas allowing a Jewish person to live is seen as saving all Jews, which is seen by radical Muslims as a negative. But everyone should agree that the murder of any one person is an affront to all the living, and saving even one is a benefit to all. No one should agree with the sentiment that murdering Jews, or anyone else, for their ethnicity, is acceptable.

Let us look a bit further, just to make sure that we as Westerners have not misinterpreted the intent of the Qur'anic passage with regard to how it is applied by those who perpetrate terrorism. This direct quote from the Talmud found in the Qur'an evidently applies to the Jewish people, according to Islamic interpretation. So what applies to Muslims? That can be found in the next verse, where the punishment for mischief against God and his apostle is stated:

> The punishment of those who wage war against God and his Apostle, and strive with might and main for mischief through the land is: execution, or crucifixion, or the cutting off of hands and feet from opposite sides, or exile from the land: that is their disgrace in this world, and a heavy punishment is theirs in the Hereafter (Surah Maida 5:33).[9]

What an incredible contrast between the two verses! The one quoted from the Talmud, which is a Jewish commentary on how to interpret God's laws in the Hebrew Scriptures, is a message of benevolence. But when it is quoted in the Qur'an, the connotation is one of wrath. Of course, "mischief" needs to be further defined, but by

Islamic standards, it is fair to say that infidels (non-Muslims) are guilty of mischief by virtue of not following the Qur'an.

But beyond this, there are a few teaching principles about Islam's holy book, the Qur'an, that must be made clear. Gregory M. Davis has produced a detailed piece entitled "Islam 101," which explains Islam to the Western mind in a clear way. In that piece, he explains an important aspect of the Qur'an known as the "Law of Abrogation":

> The principle of abrogation—al-naskh wa al-mansukh (the abrogating and the abrogated)—directs that verses revealed later in Muhammad's career "abrogate"—i.e., cancel and replace—earlier ones whose instructions they may contradict. Thus, passages revealed later in Muhammad's career, in Medina, overrule passages revealed earlier, in Mecca. The Quran itself lays out the principle of abrogation:
>
>> 2:106. Whatever a Verse [revelation] do We [Allah] abrogate or cause to be forgotten, We bring a better one or similar to it. Know you not that Allah is able to do all things?...
>
> The Quran's commandments to Muslims to wage war in the name of Allah against non-Muslims are unmistakable. They are, furthermore, authoritative as they were revealed late in the Prophet's career and so cancel and replace earlier instructions to act peaceably. Without knowledge of the principle of abrogation, Westerners will continue to misread the Qur'an and misdiagnose Islam as a "religion of peace."[10]

Islam expert Bat Ye'or points to the law of abrogation in *Eurabia: The Euro-Arab Axis*:

> The principle of abrogation—mentioned twice in the *Qur'an*—adds an additional difficulty for interpretation:

> Some earlier verses mentioning Jews and Christians are thus believed to have been abrogated and replaced later by others, without specifying which verses were in fact abrogated.[11]

Islam also encourages Muslims to practice deception, letting countries and people groups believe in a truce of sorts known as *hudna,* as long as they—the Muslims involved—are in a minority position. They are allowed to practice *taqiyya*, or religious deception, to gain acceptance, control, and ultimate power.

Taqiyya and *hudna* go hand in hand in the attempt to fulfill an agenda of deception toward total control. Once one is in a position of apparent truce, trust is established (at least from the infidel's perspective) and maintained. Because deception is validated in the Qur'an for the purpose of leading infidels to Islam, *taqiyya* is considered acceptable by Muslims.

One last aspect of Islam that cannot be overlooked is the concept of *dhimmis*. According to Islam, the *dhimma*, or "treaty of protection," may be granted to non-Muslim subjects (read: infidels) who submit to Islam and Qur'anic law and pay the *jizya* (tax). This practice goes back centuries and has financially helped the propagation of Islam.

Modern-day *dhimmis* do exist and are under many restrictions. However, we also are witnessing a self-imposed status of *dhimmi* in the West that Bat Ye'or rightfully coined *dhimmitude.* Ye'or defines *dhimmis* as "subjugated non-Muslim individuals or people that accept the restrictive and humiliating subordination to an ascendant Islamic power to avoid enslavement or death."[12]

All of this should make it very clear to us that some within Islam are using the law of abrogation, *taqiyya, hudna,* and *dhimma* to further Islam's grip on the whole planet.

These principles are all integral parts of Islam and cannot be ignored if one is a practicing Muslim. This requires Muslims to make a choice about whether to adhere to the teachings of the Qur'an. At any time, Muslims could become radicalized simply by taking their religion more literally.

At this point, some might say that over the centuries, Christianity has also succumbed to radicalism that resulted in unnecessary bloodshed. This is especially true of much of the "Christian" treatment of the Jewish people over the past 2,000 years. The key difference, however, is that "Christian" persecution done "in the name of Jesus Christ" was always an abuse of power based on faulty interpretations of the Bible. But in the case of Islam, the Qur'an has always taught normatively that Islam alone is the true religion and that infidels should convert, submit as *dhimmis*, or be killed.

I don't believe that a Muslim can truly be a practicing Muslim unless they adhere to the teachings found in the Qur'an. I am *not* saying that I agree with the teachings found in the Qur'an, but simply that a Muslim cannot pick and choose what fits their agenda or personal convictions of the moment. It is no different for Jewish people who are bound by the 613 *mitzvot* (commandments) found in the Torah. No one within Judaism who still is bound by the Mosaic law can decide to be "some kosher" and not all kosher, or go to synagogue every Shabbat except when they are away or on vacation. These are examples of what I would call religious inconsistency or hypocrisy. To be sure, Christians are not exempt either. We see plenty of modern-day disciples of Yeshua who arbitrarily decide what applies to them and what applies to others within the law of Yeshua the Messiah.

The root of the problem is with the Qur'an, which is not the word of God, just as Allah isn't just another name for Jehovah. The Qur'an teaches that those who do not convert, or at least submit, to Islam should be killed. The fact that the vast majority of modern-day Muslims do not go around killing people who do not follow the Qur'an doesn't take that principle away from the book.

So, this leaves us with the unavoidable fact that the West is faced with up to 240,000,000 potential radical Muslims who are on an ambitious campaign to enroll others to join their ranks. The days of conventional warfare are long gone! We can no longer know when, where, or how the enemy will strike. I think part of the problem is that many in the West simply do not understand the enemy, nor are they able to properly identify him. Many of our political leaders outright refuse to speak the words *radical Islam* when talking about terrorism.

This war that the West is fighting against global Islamists is going to require an increasingly delicate balance between ensuring our safety and maintaining our privacy and individualism. Political correctness and postmodern tolerance vehemently militate against stricter profiling, border control, and information-gathering because they all infringe on the individual.

Given the Islamic indoctrination of hatred against Israel and the Jews, it shouldn't come as a surprise to see the number of antisemitic acts perpetrated by Muslims against Jewish people globally. In a sense, the West has grown somewhat used to it. "Arab-Jewish conflict fatigue" has crept in around the world. Yet speaking of an Arab-Jewish conflict is a misnomer. We need to recognize that not all the Islamic terrorist acts against Jews are done by Arabs. We would be better off speaking of a Jewish-Muslim conflict at the very least. Or, we might as well describe this as an Islamist-West conflict.

In 2002, Jeff Jacoby wrote almost prophetically:

> Jews, it is often said, are the canary in the coal mine of civilization. When they become the objects of savagery and hate, it means the air has been poisoned and an explosion is soon to come. If Europeans don't rise up and turn against the Jew-haters, it is only a matter of time until the Jew-haters rise up and turn against them.[13]

It has become clear, at least during the last decade, that radical Islamists will stop at nothing until they have succeeded in their barbaric subjugation of the rest of the world. For a while now, we have seen many terrorists groups—such as the Taliban, Al-Qaeda, ISIS, Hezbollah, and Hamas—spewing their violence. In many cases, one group takes over the previous one with promises of change, but at the end of the day, they all promote the exact same ideology. They all worship death while the rest of the world values life.

To be sure, the jihadist agenda has always focused on Israel and Jewish people. Yet Islamic extremism is no longer targeting only the Jews and Israel. It has now graduated to conflicts against the whole world, with no relief in sight.

I also want to point out that bowing to Islamic threats, Palestinian social justice demands, and Boycott, Divestment and Sanctions (BDS) rulings against Israel will not stop the enemy. Instead, such actions only encourage further aggression against Israel *and* the West. Political correctness leads to appeasement, and radical Islamists always interpret appeasement as weakness.

King David once fell into a dilemma where he could choose to be judged either by men or by God (1 Chronicles 21:13). He chose God, because he said that even though God is just, He is also merciful. In contrast, David did not trust the justice of men. One of the great legacies of the Bible is that it teaches that we are all one family, that we are all sinful, and that we are all in need of God's healing and grace.

While the greatest commandment is to love God, the second one is to love one another (Matthew 22:36-40). Yeshua took this one step higher, saying that we are to love even our enemies (Matthew 5:44). In Yeshua, we see the example of obeying the authorities, overcoming evil with good, standing for justice, and healing for the helpless. These ethics have long been a strong foundation for Western civilization, even though the freedoms they have rested on have recently been eroding.

In January 2015, on the Monday following the *Charlie Hebdo* and Jewish supermarket massacres carried out in the name of ISIS, French President François Hollande spoke in front of the French Congress in a room in Versailles that hadn't been used since 1955. The speech and its location were historic, and Hollande opened by declaring, "France is at war!" He had the attention of Congress, and he had mine as well. Mr. Hollande's statement contradicted then-US President Obama's sentiments one day before the attack that the Islamic State was "contained."[14] Obama went on to declare that what happened in Paris was a setback. We must ask, "A setback to what? The Middle Ages?"

Mr. Hollande, on the other hand, affirmed that ISIS had to be destroyed—not slowed down, not stopped, not talked to, but destroyed! I couldn't agree more. He spoke one day after having sent fighter jets to bomb strategic ISIS locations in Syria. He followed up by sending the *Charles de Gaulle* aircraft carrier into the Mediterranean Sea. More attacks on ISIS followed. Was that strategic move a military response to a declaration of war, or was it more of a symbolic, political response? Hard to say, but the war against ISIS had just started, and it could last for decades. And looking at the bigger picture, we might win many battles yet never come out fully victorious in the war against Islamic terrorism.

In 2015, France was at a critical crossroads. Many more terrorist attacks have occurred since. How many more will it take, in France or anywhere else, for the West to take radical Islam more seriously? Too many innocent lives have been destroyed by people who glorify death. Unfortunately, most people in the West are still afraid to connect these terrorist attacks to anything even remotely related to Islam.

Things will even get tougher for Jewish people as this hatred intensifies. Beyond radical Muslims, many people around the world hate the Jewish people with every fiber of their being even though they have never met a Jewish person. People who have nothing in common ideologically are joining forces against Israel and the Jewish people simply because, as an old proverb says, "The enemy of my enemy is my friend." The tie that binds these enemies together is a deep hatred of the Jews!

Liberalism

Etymologically speaking, words like *liberalism* or *liberal* come from the Latin word *liber*, meaning "free." Liberalism goes back several centuries as a political philosophy emphasizing values such as freedom of the press, freedom of religion, civil rights, and democratic elections. These are values that Western civilization has been taking for granted, yet at best, they are absent or corrupted in many countries of the world. Liberalism was a reaction from oppressed people trying to overthrow tyrannical rulers. The French Revolution of 1789 is a good example of the positive results coming out of a "liberal" mindset.

The French Revolution is now more than 230 years old, and liberalism has had plenty of opportunity to morph into what it is today. Today we speak of liberals in contradistinction to conservatives. Yet we must understand that both liberalism and conservatism have certain elements in common at the foundational level—namely, freedom and a democratic system of government, as opposed to repressive types of governments such as Communism, fascism, or radical Islam, under which individuals have little freedom. Yet the liberals of today are a far cry from the founders of liberalism.

Overall, liberals have often identified themselves with the oppressed minority, fighting against oppressive rulers. That is one of the reasons why, during the American civil rights movement of the 1950s and 1960s, many Jews and Blacks were found holding hands against white supremacists in the South. Jewish scholar Howard Sachar recognized this when he wrote, "Nowhere did Jews identify themselves more forthrightly with the liberal avant-garde than in the Civil Rights movement of the 1960s."[15]

To this day, most Jewish people lean toward a more liberal philosophy of life, which leads most American Jews to identify with Democrats.[16] This made sense during the American civil right movement but is becoming more nonsensical as today's Democrats turn more and more against Israel.[17] The Democratic Party in America has moved more and more to the left. It supports progressive and woke perspectives on multiculturalism, social justice, women's rights, and gay rights, among other things. It has also become virulently anti-Israel and anti-Zionist (just another way to say antisemitic in most cases). Ironically, only one country in the Middle East supports the same issues as Democrats—Israel. Yet in spite of the antisemitic bent of the Democratic Party, American Jews still vote mostly Democrat (79 percent during the 2024 presidential campaign voted for Kamala Harris[18]).

A few years ago, Michael Curtis presented some interesting statistics about American Democrats and Israel and drew this conclusion: "If it is true that not all Democrats are anti-Israeli, it is also true that most anti-Israelis are Democrats."[19]

Yet it appears that the vast majority of the Jewish people who are not religious today identify as Democrats first and as Jewish second. This is mostly because Jewish people identify with minorities, having been an oppressed and abused minority themselves for their entire existence. In the words of Ben Shapiro, "The vast majority of Jews don't care about Judaism or Israel, they care about secular Leftism which is their actual religion."[20]

In addition, there are some who believe that Jewish people lean toward liberalism and the Democratic Party because the Republican Party is perceived to be connected to or influenced by evangelical Christians.[21] As pointed out in the beginning chapters of this book, over the centuries, many Jewish people have experienced antisemitism from Christians. Whether or not this is true, they identify the Democratic Party as more secular and the Republican Party as more religious or even bigoted or white supremacist.

While liberals and secular Jews (85 percent of all Jews) do share many of the same values, the reality is that Republicans and conservatives are much more likely to love and support Israel and the Jewish people than the liberals, Democrats, and leftists would. This is easily proven by how the Left is currently treating Israel and the Jews. It is no longer a secret that the neo-Dems since the Obama administration have been far from friendly to Israel. The Jewish nation occasionally heard lip service from the White House for appeasement purposes, but the kind of support that would be offered to a true ally was lacking.

President Obama didn't seem to have a good understanding of the Middle East region. In May 2011, he declared in a speech at the State Department that the only viable solution for both Israel and "Palestine" was to return to pre-1967 borders:

> The United States believes that negotiations should result in two states, with permanent Palestinian borders with Israel, Jordan, and Egypt, and permanent Israeli borders with Palestine. The borders of Israel and Palestine should be based on the 1967 lines with mutually agreed swaps, so that secure and recognized borders are established for both states.[22]

Apparently, Obama's cabinet was hoping to appease the Palestinians and convince them to no longer try for unilateral recognition. But one of the problems with the pre-1967 borders is that they would place Israel in an extremely vulnerable position, giving the Jewish people anything but secure borders. In fact, the pre-1967 borders, also known as the Green Line, were described by Israeli ambassador and diplomat Abba Eban as "a memory of Auschwitz" because of how indefensible Israel would become:

> We have openly said that the map will never again be the same as on June 4, 1967. For us, this is a matter of security

> and of principles. The June map is for us equivalent to insecurity and danger. I do not exaggerate when I say that it has for us something of a memory of Auschwitz. We shudder when we think of what would have awaited us in the circumstances of June, 1967, if we had been defeated; with Syrians on the mountain and we in the valley, with the Jordanian army in sight of the sea, with the Egyptians who hold our throat in their hands in Gaza. This is a situation which will never be repeated in history.[23]

If Israel were to go back to the pre-1967 borders, in some areas it would be reduced to a narrow, nine-mile strip of land, virtually impossible to defend. When we recall the enormous damage done by Hamas in the small area known as the Gaza Strip since they have been in charge—including during the summer months of 2014 when the Gaza Conflict occurred as well as when Hamas attacked Israel on October 7, 2023—one can only imagine the carnage that would take place under the proposed, indefensible borders.

Another legacy of the Obama administration is Iran's empowerment. Obama struck a deal that would allow Iran to continue to move forward on a path that would enable it to develop a nuclear arsenal. For Obama to do this while knowing that Iran had Israel (the Little Satan) in its immediate crosshairs and the United States (the Great Satan) as a secondary target was simply bewildering. Does the fact Obama was in favor of a nuclear Iran mean he was also in favor of making it possible for Iran to destroy Israel? A blunt question like that will most certainly garner criticism from some. Unfortunately, Obama represented an ideology that has moved far to the left politically since the days of John Fitzgerald Kennedy, who, although a Democrat, embraced the US instead of embracing foreign cultures more.

It didn't help that earlier, a former Democratic president took a stand against Israel, accusing the Jewish nation of occupation and apartheid. In 2002, Jimmy Carter was awarded the Nobel Peace Prize for his role in mediating the 1978 peace treaty between Israel and Egypt. Carter went on to become a vocal enemy of Israel. In his book entitled *Palestine: Peace Not Apartheid,* Carter defended the Palestinians and accused Israelis of the "worst human rights deprivation" in modern history.[24] Liberals are hungry for social justice. Social justice is not necessarily bad, but we must be careful not to seek it at the expense of truth and before determining the facts. I do not believe Mr. Carter was considering the facts when he wrote, "It will be a tragedy—for the Israelis, the Palestinians and the world—if peace is rejected and a system of oppression, apartheid, and sustained violence is permitted to prevail."[25]

The blindness of liberals with regard to false narratives about Palestine is hard to understand. Their approach to Israel and the Middle East is plagued by a severe case of double standards. There is no other country on the planet that is under the same intense scrutiny as Israel. But being under scrutiny isn't the issue. The problem is that liberals have gone along with the Palestinian accusations of occupation and bloody violence by Israel. They have bought the lies that portray Israelis as perpetrators and Palestinians as victims. And in doing so, they have become co-conspirators in this latest war against the Jews.

Then Israel was plagued with the Biden administration, which put its disdain for Israel on display by constantly asking Prime Minister Netanyahu to show restraint in response to Hamas's murderous attack on October 7, 2023. Accusations of occupation and colonization came regularly from various factions within the Democratic Party. In contrast, Trump has shown Israel a level of support that is extraordinary compared to that of other presidents.[26]

Besides presidents and former presidents, there are other leftist culprits. The next generation of anti-Israel activists is being shaped on college campuses in America, Europe, and other parts of the world. And when a government supports Palestinian statehood and calls Israel an occupier, it doesn't take much for younger people who already have a propensity for Jew-hatred to instigate a new wave of antisemitism, as we'll see next.

CHAPTER 9

THE NEW PLAYERS IN ESCHATOLOGICAL ANTISEMITISM, PART 2

THE CAMPUS INTIFADA AND BDS

In 1968, during a visit to Harvard University, Dr. Martin Luther King Jr. is said to have stated, "When people criticize Zionists, they mean Jews. You're talking anti-Semitism."[1]

There is a movement on American university campuses that has been labeled by some as the Campus Intifada. This involves the dangerous antisemitic indoctrination of college students all across the United States.[2] Up to 70 percent of Jewish students on university campuses in the US have experienced antisemitism at some level, but since October 7, 2023, those numbers have increased by 700 percent.[3]

THE CAMPUS INTIFADA

Dr. King's statement could be used today to describe what takes place on American campuses, but it would most likely be received with fierce criticism from both students and faculty members. And the problem continues to worsen. As a result of the postmodern worldview propagated at educational institutions, students and faculty portray Palestinians and Hamas terrorists as victims—as heroes, martyrs, and freedom fighters. All of this happens at the expense of innocent Jewish students who are said to be guilty of oppression, occupation, and crimes against humanity—simply because they are Jewish.

It is no secret that the vast majority of US campuses are dominated by liberals who lean to the Far Left. While leftists hold to views that are opposed by a variety of pro-Hamas and pro-Palestinian groups, the one bond that holds them tightly together is their opposition to Israel.

We can look to University of California, Irvine (UCI) as one example of what is happening on college campuses. Each year, the Muslim Student Union at UCI organizes a springtime event that has come to be known as Hate Fest. In 2009, the theme of the fest was "The Politics of Genocide."[4] The guests invited to this particular event were anti-Israel to the core and determined to spew their antisemitic venom in whichever direction they could.[5] In *Front Page Magazine*, Gary Fouse reported on the nauseating bias evident at the 2009 event.[6]

In 2013, Students for Justice in Palestine (SJP) at UCI invited Qatari activist Omar Barghouti to visit the campus. The discussion was supposed to be about Boycott, Divestment and Sanctions (BDS). Barghouti—who resides in Israel—was a founding committee member of the Palestinian Campaign for the Academic and Cultural Boycott of Israel (PACBI). He is an advocate for the intellectual and academic boycott of Israeli and Jewish works, yet ironically, he received a PhD degree from Tel Aviv University (TAU).

The one-sided hypocrisy of those who promote the Campus Intifada and BDS movement is so obvious that it is embarrassing. Yet that hypocrisy doesn't stop students or faculty from blindly promoting the Palestinian narrative. It has become the campus cause to emulate, although many students may not realize they are being inculcated with racial hatred.

UCI has long been a hotbed of campus antisemitism. It is there that, in 2010, several members of the Muslim Student Union repeatedly disrupted a speech by Israel's then-ambassador to the US, Michael Oren.[7]

University of California, Davis (UCD)—another well-known school—was in the news in February 2015 for an anti-Israel attack. Jewish students at a fraternity house were in shock when they discovered swastikas spray-painted on the walls of their building.[8] This took place just days after the Associated Students group had voted in favor of BDS. The resolution was sponsored by Students for Justice in Palestine (SJP), the same group that had invited Barghouti to UCI.

SJP, a second-degree offshoot of the Muslim Brotherhood (a terrorist group), used to be known as the General Union of Palestinian Students and is a member of the Muslim Student Union (MSA), which is directly connected to the Muslim Brotherhood.[9] SJP wishes to appear more inclined toward social justice and not as radicalized as the Muslim Brotherhood. It all boils down to the same source with a virulently antisemitic agenda across the globe, and that is indeed the Muslim Brotherhood. They are the backbone of US campus activities against Israel.

In June 2024, a Saudi journalist wrote an article that, according to the Middle East Media Research Institute, explained that "behind the pro-Palestinian student protests taking place on campuses across the U.S. stands a years-long alliance between the American liberal left and movements of political Islam, chief of them the Muslim Brotherhood."[10]

Schools like UCI, UCD, and University of California, Berkeley (UCB) seem to be networked with the common goal of demonizing Israel. All of these establishments invite strongly antisemitic speakers such as Amir Abdel Malik Ali, who believes that Jewish people are behind the tragedy of 9/11. He has openly promoted the idea of jihad in America and insists on telling people that Israel doesn't have a right to exist.[11] If you file a complaint against him, you are immediately accused of Islamophobia, while his xenophobic venom is described as a protected First Amendment right. While promoting global jihad in 2001 might have seemed extreme, it is much more accepted by people these days. The successful spread of propaganda always requires repetition and patience.

Yet you cannot honestly compare antisemitism to Islamophobia. Antisemitism is the hatred of the Jewish people for whoever they are, wherever they are, and whatever they believe. Islamophobia, on the other hand, is a fear of or aversion to Islam, which is an ideology, not a people group. One targets a people, while the other targets a worldview. A person can choose their worldview, but not their ethnicity.

The protest events organized on American campuses are always one-sided in favor of the Palestinian cause when it comes to promoting Hamas' agenda of genocide as far back as 2014, and much more since the 2023 Israel-Gaza War.[12, 13] These protests were on the rise by 50 percent in 2017, from a total of 105 incidents in 2015 to 150 in 2016. That was seven years before October 7, 2023. Jewish students are increasingly feeling unsafe on campuses in America.[14]

In addition to SJP, there is another major Muslim organization present and active on American campuses: the Muslim Student Association (MSA). MSA, also known as the Muslim Student Union (MSU), is a national religious organization with more than 600 chapters. Under a façade of peace activism and multicultural tolerance, the

MSA actually pursues a much different agenda. According to their *Starters Guide*, they claim,

> It should be the long-term goal of every MSA to Islamicize the politics of their respective university...the politicization of the MSA means to make the MSA more of a force on internal campus politics. The MSA needs to be a more "In-your-face" association.[15]

The Muslim Brotherhood itself was founded in 1928 in Egypt by Hassan al-Banna, who happened to be a devout admirer of Adolf Hitler. The Muslim Brotherhood has, as one of its main goals, the establishment of a caliphate. While it might not be as bloody and violent as ISIS, the goal remains identical. The end might justify different means, but it remains the same end![16]

According to the website *The Clarion Project,* the Muslim Brotherhood is an umbrella organization for Islamic radicalization:

> A 1991 U.S. Muslim Brotherhood memo, which describes its "work in America as a kind of grand jihad in eliminating and destroying the Western civilization from within," lists the MSA as "one of our organizations and the organizations of our friends." Most groups affiliated with the U.S. Muslim Brotherhood grew out of MSA. It is currently listed as a "constituent organization" of the Islamic Society of North America.[17]

From the Muslim Brotherhood comes these chilling words, which form part of their mission statement: "Allah is our objective. The Prophet is our leader. Qur'an is our law. Jihad is our way. Dying in the way of Allah is our highest hope."[18]

The same Muslim Brotherhood is sponsoring and funding American

MSAs on campuses. Because the Muslim Brotherhood's agenda is global jihad by any means, we should not be surprised when we witness the antisemitic vitriol thrown at Jewish students and those who support Israel's right to exist.

What changed after October 7 was the involvement of faculty on various US campuses. Many professors are now openly stating their disdain for Israel and the Jewish people, and Ivy League school presidents have also come out of the shadows to support the Palestinian cause and Hamas. This shows a progression that renders Jewish life on campus extremely uncomfortable, if not dangerous.

In December 2023, the presidents of Harvard, University of Pennsylvania, and MIT appeared before the US House Committee on Education and the Workforce to answer some questions about the alarming rise in campus antisemitism. All three presidents couldn't find it in themselves to condemn Hamas for its murders of Jews.

On that topic, former Harvard Law School professor Alan Dershowitz wrote, "The recent spate of rabid anti-Semitism on so many campuses has posed enormous challenges to this new breed of university presidents. For the most part, they have failed miserably to meet these challenges, as reflected by the big three who testified so ineptly."[19]

Following in the trail of some Harvard students who couldn't find any valid reason to condemn Hamas for raping, maiming, burning, and beheading innocent Israeli civilians, president Claudia Gay couldn't condemn Hamas when confronted with a question by House Republican Elise Stefanik, who called Claudine Gay's response a case of "pathetic moral depravity."[20] Gay was asked if calling for the genocide of Jewish people violated Harvard school's code of conduct, to which she answered, "It depends on the context."[21] Seriously, what kind of context could possibly warrant the genocide of *any* people group?

Gay's answer brought chills to my spine. If this is not proof that the beast we call antisemitism is completely out in the open, I don't know what else needs to happen to convince people. After receiving serious backlash for her testimony, Gay released a statement saying, "Calls for violence or genocide against the Jewish community, or any religious or ethnic group are vile, they have no place at Harvard, and those who threaten our Jewish students will be held to account."[22] Too little, too late! She eventually had to step down as president but remained on Harvard's payroll.

THE BOYCOTT, DIVESTMENTS AND SANCTIONS MOVEMENT (BDS)

It should come as no surprise to anyone that US college campuses have become the incubators of the BDS movement against Israel. The liberal left finds BDS to be the perfect weapon in the attempt to cripple Israel's economy via boycott. Unfortunately, the BDS platform (started by the Palestinian Authority in 2005) is just another iteration of the agenda of end-times antisemitism. It follows a pattern identified by Natan Sharansky, which he called the "3D Test of Anti-Semitism: Demonization, Double Standards, Delegitimization."[23]

The main thrust of BDS is to cripple the Israeli economy by boycotting certain products, people, and places. The reason given is the allegation that Israel is an illegal occupier. Most BDS proponents and supporters attempt to compare Israel to apartheid South Africa. They point to the security walls and fences that separate Israel from Palestinian regions as proof that Israel is an apartheid state. Once more, a false premise is used to justify BDS, which is antisemitism cloaked in what is supposedly social justice. That's why BDS proponents get excited about BDS: because they feel like they are making the world a better place by singling out Israel.

The Israeli walls and fences are real, and they are definitely dividers. But there is a difference: South African apartheid was racially motivated, while the Israeli walls and fences aren't. To call Israel an apartheid state is a misnomer because the walls and fences weren't built based on feelings about racial superiority, but on a very real need for the security of Israeli citizens. Many Israelis would rather live without the walls and fences, but the reality is that successful acts of terrorism have plummeted since the walls and fences were put into place.

Israel isn't alone in building walls for protective purposes. To name just a few countries, Kuwait built a wall on its northern border for security from Iraq, Egypt has a wall on its border with Gaza, and France built a wall in the northern town of Calais for protection against out-of-control illegal migration. None of these countries are criticized like Israel is. Again, Israel falls into the category defined by Sharansky as "double standards."

Boycott, Divestment and Sanctions proponents are not interested in the facts. They will stop at nothing to demonize and delegitimize Israel, as was the case when they recently tried to link the *Charlie Hebdo* tragedy of January 2015 to the Jewish secret service Mossad.[24] These groups are continually driven by the same agenda of hatred toward Israel to such an extreme that in the midst of the 2016 Black Lives Matter police shootings and deaths in Minnesota and Louisiana, some members of the New York University SJP used their Facebook page to accuse the Jewish people of being behind the deaths of Black people.[25]

Boycott, Divestment and Sanctions relies on the ignorance of the people it is trying to indoctrinate against Israel and the Jewish people. It pushes all the attractive buttons for college students and liberals: multiculturalism, tolerance, and social justice, when in reality, it is a most intolerant movement.

The level of hypocrisy found among BDS proponents is mind-boggling. The very people who adamantly promote the boycott of all things Israel do not think twice when they use products and service invented, created, and manufactured by and in Israel. It certainly would be inconvenient for them to stop using cell phones, thumb drives, and some critical parts of computers simply to be consistent with their desire to boycott Israel. BDS does not boycott with integrity; convenience should never be a criterion.[26]

Many websites that promote BDS list products, services, and companies that have Israeli connections and advise their viewers not to conduct business with them. However, their methodology can easily be used against them by people who want to support Israel and the Jewish people—the latter can visit sites such as bdsmovement.net and use the list to purchase the very items recommended for boycott.[27]

BDS is not hard to fight with education and common sense, two things that seem to be lacking among pro-Palestinian and pro-Hamas advocates.

But there are other new players of antisemitism that are much more difficult to battle—either because of their political clout or the way they attempt to disguise their antisemitism. They include the next categories of new players we'll survey.

CHAPTER 10

THE NEW PLAYERS IN ESCHATOLOGICAL ANTISEMITISM, PART 3

POLITICAL GROUPS AND PARTIES

In the early decades of the twentieth century, fascist governments could be found in countries like Germany, Italy, Spain, and France. Totalitarian regimes usually don't have room for people who do not fit their ideological mold. While not all iterations of fascism are identical, fascism itself was borne out of the chaos of World War I as a reaction against liberalism, Marxism, and socialism. Benito Mussolini, who came to power in Italy in 1922, is said to be the first leader to formulate and develop fascism. In his own mind, he hoped to save Western civilization from corruption and ultimate self-destruction by having the state control the people. It wasn't long before Mussolini started to promote the idea that fascism was the only genuine path to an ethical state. The leap from an ethical state to a racially pure state isn't necessarily a big one and would be attempted by Adolf Hitler and his dictatorial National Socialist (Nazi) Party.

THE POPULIST AND NEO-NAZI PARTIES

Germany's defeat in World War I and the humiliating results of the Treaty of Versailles in 1919 left that country in ruins both economically and ideologically. This provided fertile ground for Adolf Hitler to appear on the scene and promise to raise the German phoenix, a glorious resurgence of German culture and power, from its ashes. The Nazi Party claimed that based on the science of eugenics, the Germanic race—later known as the Aryan race—was a superior one.

Germany was also the birthplace of Marxism, which promoted race and class equality. The concept of equality would be attractive to many people, including the Jewish people, who had known much of the opposite for close to 2,000 years.

While not all Jews were Marxists at that time, the leftist ideologies were far more attractive to them, and as a result, they found themselves on the other side of the political spectrum from the Nazis. Thus it is not hard to understand why antisemitism has been linked to the racist and supremacist agendas of fascist regimes that existed in such countries as Italy, Germany, or Spain. Yet it remains difficult to define the Nazi and neo-Nazi parties simply by placing them somewhere on a left-to-right spectrum. The terms *Left* and *Right* were developed during the 1789 French Revolution and were based on where members of the government sat in their chambers. Revolution-minded groups sat on the left, while supporters of the monarchy sat on the right. Even this categorization can be too simplistic, but it helps us realize that political parties cannot truly be defined solely by their place on a left-right spectrum.

People have gotten used to the idea that if a party is not on the

Right, it must be on the Left. Hitler's Nazi Party can be identified as being fascist, but even he saw major flaws on both ends of the spectrum, as he said in *Mein Kampf*:

> Today our left-wing politicians in particular are constantly insisting that their craven-hearted and obsequious foreign policy necessarily results from the disarmament of Germany, whereas the truth is that this is the policy of traitors... But the politicians of the Right deserve exactly the same reproach. It was through their miserable cowardice that those ruffians of Jews who came into power in 1918 were able to rob the nation of its arms.[1]

The full name of Hitler's party was Nationalsozialistische Deutsche Arbeiterpartei (National Socialist German Workers' Party, or NSDAP). So when we read the word *Socialist* in the title, it's easy to assume that his party was on the Left. But today, Nazis and neo-Nazis are considered to be on the extreme Right. The Nazi Party was indeed socialist, but only for its people—that is, the Germans. Thus, the word *National* in its name.

So, what was Hitler's leaning: Right or Left? It would be more appropriate to see Hitler's party as a totalitarian or authoritarian party. Hitler was a radical who didn't neatly fit either on the Left or the Right, even though originally, his party would belong more on the Left.

Eventually, the Nazi Party's driving agenda became one of establishing racial superiority as seen in the erroneous Aryan race elitism over all other races, with a special emphasis on eliminating the Jewish people. Elitism and nationalism continue to be the driving forces in the neo-Nazi and populist parties across the globe.

Many European populist parties are on the rise as a reaction to the ongoing migrant crisis and influx of foreigners into Europe. The main ones are listed on the following pages.

Germany: The Homeland, Previously Known as the National Democratic Party

Of all the European countries involved in World War II, Germany was left with the stigma of its association with Nazi ideology. Nazism became taboo overnight as the Jewish people simultaneously declared "Never again" to a global audience very willing to expose the cruelty of Nazism.

Within a couple of decades, even though Nazi ideology had been relegated to the outer fringes of the political arena, the old ideology began to re-emerge on the scene. Unable or more likely unwilling to call its followers Nazis, the term *neo-Nazi* was adopted. This continued to be a fringe movement for a while, to the point of often being ignored by the rest of the world.

While Holocaust denial is punishable by law in Germany, neo-Nazi groups like the National Democratic Party (NDP), founded in 1964 as a successor to the German Reich Party,[2] are allowed under the German constitution,[3] but not without challenges, as they are not able to receive funding because of their racist and antisemitic ideology.[4] Several attempts have been made to ban the NDP.[5] While the NDP was a fringe party in the 1960s, it has continued to grow and has carried the torch of Nazism into the twenty-first century. While neo-Nazis are still a minority, they exist, are increasing in numbers, and advocate an openly antisemitic agenda.

France: The National Rally, Previously Known as the National Front

Started by Jean-Marie Le Pen in 1972 to be the unified voice of anti-immigration, nationalism, and economic protectionism, the National Front (Front National or FN) Party finds its roots in the anti-French Revolution, pro-monarchy France of the late 1700s. It has recently been renamed Rassemblement National, or National Rally, in an attempt to make it sound less radicalized.

Jean-Marie Le Pen was the leader of the party for nearly 40 years until he retired and was replaced by his daughter and current party president, Marine Le Pen. Eventually—and to repair a highly xenophobic reputation—Marine Le Pen ousted her father from the party altogether.

Under Jean-Marie Le Pen, the FN carried a very controversial antisemitic and racist agenda. It has been daughter Marine Le Pen's desire to remove the tarnish from the party's image in recent years. She is very careful to stay away from making xenophobic remarks.[6]

While there is no doubt that many members of the FN Party hold antisemitic views, Marine Le Pen has been working hard to garner French Jewish votes and has somewhat succeeded, with 17.9 percent of the vote in France's 2012 presidential election, 21.3 percent in 2017, and 41.5 percent in 2022.[7] The two terrorist attacks on French soil in 2015 put her in a position of strength, which continues to grow in light of the many immigration issues France has had to deal with. She is the only French political voice that recognizes the need for much stricter immigration laws.

Marine has replaced the antisemitism of her father's party with modern Islamophobia, and due to the rise of the Islamic threat in France, as well as the lack of Muslim assimilation and numerous terrorist attacks, Marine has the attention of many French people. Surprisingly, there are even some in the Jewish community who see her program as valid for the future of France.

What some people fear is that Marine Le Pen's program might become more damaging to the Jewish people if she were in a position of greater power, such as the presidency. While it appears that she isn't as abrasive and toxic as her father, that could change.

Denmark: The Danish People's Party (DPP)

In the June 2015 elections, the Danish People's Party (DPP), a nationalistic and protectionist leaning party, gained 37 seats (21 percent of the votes).[8] The European extreme-right's anti-immigration laws had become attractive enough to the Danes that they voted for the DPP and helped to bring the European extreme-right party to victory. The votes garnered by the DPP helped to shift Denmark from its inclination toward open borders to a position favoring restrictions on immigration. Subsequent elections saw the party lose seats and influence, yet the ideology persists in a Europe that is seeing its more native populations overwhelmed by uncontrolled and often illegal immigration.

This nationalistic trend is also evident in Finland, Sweden, the UK, and several other European countries.[9] While these ascending parties range from right to extreme right on the political spectrum and could create a danger for Jewish communities all over Europe, they are not as extreme as Hungary's Jobbik Party.

Hungary: The Jobbik Party

In 2015, The Jobbik Party won its first by-election[10] in a historic victory.[11] Jobbik has a reputation for being very antisemitic. They are a paramilitary wing reminiscent of World War II fascist groups, but they are attractive to young people to whom they can relate very well. Their leaders are eloquent and polished, separating them from the image people have of skinheads and less-erudite white supremacist, neo-Nazi groups. While situated much more to the Right, the party presents itself as conservative.

Jobbik's ultranationalistic and at times antisemitic views are seen by some as a safety net for Hungary at a time when large numbers of migrants from the Middle East are flowing into many countries in Eastern and Western Europe. The Jobbik Party is also inspiring like-minded Poles to organize into similar groups, apparently to help protect the fabric of Poland.[12]

A GROWING EXTREMISM

There are many more extreme-right groups across Europe and other parts of the world. The list is too long to include here and goes beyond the scope of this book. But we cannot ignore the resurgence of extreme-right ideologies over the last 20 years in Europe. As taboo as the labels *Nazi* or even *neo-Nazi* were after the Holocaust, it has now become more acceptable for people to affiliate with fascist-leaning ideologies, especially when anti-immigration views are shared by many. We even see some Jewish people supporting the Far Right. The problem with this shift is that the vast majority of Far-Right parties don't do much to differentiate between the people groups that they consider being not "us" but "them."

As a result, Blacks, Arabs, and Jews are often grouped in a "them" category, putting them all at risk of being ostracized. While I believe that we live in an era when immigration laws should be a lot tighter around the world, it is not my intention to appear in support of fascist political views because I strongly oppose them. I do believe that it is imperative to perpetuate the freedoms of democracy in Western civilization, which requires standing up for its principles. Bowing to extremes does not promise a solution, neither does appeasing. Adopting shortcuts to security that embrace the abrogation of democratic freedoms within Western civilization is as fatal as caving to ideologies that oppose the constitutional rule of law.

Another co-perpetrator against Israel and the Jews is one that we wouldn't have expected just a couple of decades ago: the Christian church. The term *church* includes many Christian denominations, including those in the evangelical branch. It fits under a wider banner known as Christendom, which includes the Roman Catholic Church.

The shift that has been happening within evangelicalism didn't happen in a vacuum, but is closely linked to what is known as replacement theology, or supersessionism. That's what we'll look at in the next chapter, as well as other ways that today's church opposes Israel.

CHAPTER 11

THE NEW PLAYERS IN ESCHATOLOGICAL ANTISEMITISM, PART 4

THE CHURCH

One of the most tragic realities of antisemitism is that it is alive and well in the church, the body of Christ, which follows a Jewish Messiah and had its beginning in Jerusalem, with Jewish apostles and many initial converts being Jews who became Christians, including the apostle Paul, who wrote much of the New Testament. This antisemitism is manifest both theologically and through a variety of organizations and ministries affiliated with the church. We'll start with a review of a specific kind of theology, then move on to various perspectives, groups, and individuals, some of which are well known, and others lesser so.

REPLACEMENT THEOLOGY

Replacement theology advocates a faulty allegorical approach to the interpretation of the Bible, transferring all of God's promises and covenants away from Israel and to the church. It is a major component of modern antisemitism within the church today.

David L. Cooper (1886–1965), one of the greatest conservative theologians and Bible scholars who ever lived, left a legacy of Bible teaching that to this day is helping many understand and apply God's Word to their lives. In his attempt to understand Scripture the way it was meant to be understood, Cooper concluded that in light of past prophecies fulfilled, only a literal approach to interpreting the Bible would be appropriate to gain a right understanding of God and His plan for mankind. He eventually came up with a rule of interpretation still used by many Bible scholars today, known as the golden rule of interpretation:

> When the plain sense of Scripture makes common sense, seek no other sense; therefore, take every word at its primary, ordinary, usual, literal meaning unless the facts of the immediate context, studied in the light of related passages and axiomatic and fundamental truths, indicate clearly otherwise...A text apart from its context is a pretext.[1]

With this rule in mind, we need to understand the danger of not applying it when we interpret God's Word. If we do not look at Scripture from a literal perspective, and instead, we interpret it figuratively or allegorically, we open the door to whatever meanings people want to ascribe to the texts in the Bible. Theologian Paul Benware points out that to follow the allegorical approach is "to treat the literal sense of a Scripture text as secondary to a deeper, more spiritual meaning."[2]

One system of theology that uses the literal approach to interpreting

Scripture is known as dispensationalism and is defined as follows by theologian Charles Ryrie:

> A dispensationalist keeps the Church and Israel distinct... [Secondly,] the distinction between Israel and the Church is born out of a system of hermeneutics that is usually called literal interpretation...A third aspect of the sine qua non of dispensationalism...concerns the underlying purpose of God in the world...namely the glory of God. The essence of dispensationalism then, is the distinction between Israel and the Church. This grows out of the dispensationalist's consistent employment of normal or plain or historical-grammatical interpretation, and it reflects an understanding of the basic purpose of God in all His dealings with mankind as that of glorifying Himself through salvation and other purposes as well.[3]

If one rejects the dispensationalist[4] view of Scripture, the door is then opened to accommodate a variety of views regarding Israel and the last days. All three major views of the end-times—postmillennialism, amillennialism, and premillennialism—approach the prophecies about God's final plan for mankind from differing vantage points about the timing and nature of the millennium or the millennial kingdom. Only premillennialism stems from a dispensationalist view of God's Word.

To preface further discussion, two terms used by theologians need to be defined:

- *Millennium* is the word used to describe 1,000 years, and it comes from two Latin words *mille* ("a thousand") and *annus* ("year"). When not taken literally, it often refers to a very long period of time, not necessarily 1,000 years long.

- The *tribulation* (also known as "the time of Jacob's trouble," Jeremiah 30:7 NKJV) is an upcoming period of seven years described in Revelation chapters 6 through 19. According to dispensationalists, the tribulation follows the rapture and precedes the millennium. During the tribulation, God will pour His judgment on unbelieving Gentiles and disobedient Israel, who will remain on the earth after the rapture.[5]

As mentioned earlier, the allegorical approach to the interpretation of Scripture takes all the Bible prophecies that speak of blessings for Israel and applies them to the church instead. It is interesting to note that those who apply Israel's blessings to the church do not correspondingly apply Israel's curses to the church, resulting in a rather selective theological position.

In response to replacement theology, we must remember that the Bible tells us God does not change (Malachi 3:6). A careful study of Scripture shows that God's promises to Israel have not been voided. God's promises to Israel still stand (Jeremiah 33:25-26), and the apostle Paul made it clear that God "has not rejected His people" (Romans 11:1). Furthermore, we must be consistent in the way we expound Scripture if we hope to discover the riches God has for us. The allegorical approach to interpretation opens up the possibility of all kinds of inconsistencies. By literally following God's biblical map whenever contextually possible, we will discover His clear plan for humankind in general and Israel in particular.

To all teachers of God's Word, David L. Cooper posted this warning: "A text without a context is only a pretext." This helps us to recognize where other approaches to Bible interpretation can lead. Adherents to replacement theology, who claim that Israel has now been replaced by the church and that all promises from God to Israel are now transferred to Christians, are guilty of just that—taking God's Word out of context. When the words of Scripture are studied literally in their grammatical and historical context, the Bible is very clear about God's relationship with Israel.

As a starting point, here is a simple exercise to remove any doubts about the identity of Israel today. Simply read through the New Testament, and every time you encounter the word *Israel* (more than 70 times), replace it with the word *church*. And after honestly keeping with the context of the verse, chapter, and book where you find each instance, decide whether it makes any sense that Israel would be synonymous with church. This handily demonstrates that only a literal approach to interpretation makes sense.

According to nonliteral interpreters, as soon as a verse mentions Israel in a slightly different and possibly broader context, then it *must* refer to the church. A good example of a passage they use to impose this distorted thinking on Scripture is Galatians 6:16: "Those who will walk by this rule, peace and mercy be upon them, and upon the Israel of God."

Here, replacement theology would have "Israel" mean the church, but the surrounding context of this passage describes Jewish believers in Messiah who, while still being part of Israel proper, are now part of the Israel of God, or the branch of the body of Messiah that is made up of Jewish people.

As we respond to replacement theology, we must remember Genesis 12:1-3, where we read God's divine decree that He has chosen the Jewish people for a special purpose. This decree is known as the Abrahamic covenant.

> Now the LORD said to Abram, "Go forth from your country, and from your relatives and from your father's house, to the land which I will show you; and I will make you a great nation, and I will bless you, and make your name great; and so you shall be a blessing; and I will bless those who bless you, and the one who curses you I will curse.

> And in you all the families of the earth will be blessed" (Genesis 12:1-3).

God proposes the terms, seals them, and faithfully adheres to them independent of any promises or actions on the part of the recipients. *The Abrahamic covenant is unconditional.* The only response God requested of Abraham was to go forth from his country, and Abraham complied. A unique aspect of the Abrahamic covenant is that when it was ratified, God alone passed through the animal sacrifices[6] set on the ground; He took on Himself the responsibility for both parties in His act of ratifying the covenant (Genesis 15:17-18). Because this covenant rests on the immutability and faithfulness of God alone (Malachi 3:6), it is eternal. God's relationship to Israel, as established by the Abrahamic covenant, was to be an example to the world.

When the Shekinah glory of the Lord passed through the animals to ratify the covenant, Abraham was in a deep sleep. Being unconscious, he could not be a partner in ratifying the covenant. God alone passed through the animals, thus taking on the full weight of keeping the terms of the covenant He made with Abraham. In this way, God unilaterally ensured that the Abrahamic covenant could not be broken, because God never changes. If we question the durability of God's covenant with Abraham in light of the disobedience of the Jewish people, then we open the door to questioning the durability of God's salvation through Yeshua given the sinfulness of all mankind. It is necessary that we apply a consistent standard to how we view both covenants.

If we claim that God has replaced Israel with the church, we are, in effect, making God a liar and a covenant breaker. We are saying that God changed His mind regarding His unconditional promises to Abraham. If this were true, none of God's promises to Israel—or for that matter, to the church—would stand.

Does replacement theology lead believers in Yeshua to an antisemitic view of Israel and the Jewish people? Or is it instead the influence of centuries of unaddressed antisemitism in the church that has led to a theological approach that replaces Israel with the church? The answer is both!

Replacement theology and antisemitism are connected. Human nature is such that when a believer hears teaching about Israel not being the people of God anymore, it is only logical to feel a disconnect with the Jewish people, and perhaps even resentment. The result of replacement theology is that it leads people to say, "If God is done with Israel, shouldn't I be done as well?"

From a premillennial eschatological standpoint, replacement theology plays into Satan's desire to keep the Jews out of God's plan. It leads people in the church to look the other way as Satan does whatever he can to destroy the Jews.

After Satan fell from heaven to earth (Isaiah 14:12-14; Ezekiel 28:16-17), he became "the accuser" who now spends his time pointing out the sins of believers to God (Revelation 12:10). Satan's first project was to tempt Eve to eat from the fruit of the tree of the knowledge of good and evil in the garden of Eden. The result was the first sin, which brought the whole human race under the condemnation of sin (Genesis 3:1-19).

But instigating the downfall of the human race was not enough for the enemy. He has also made a point of counterfeiting for bad all that God does for good. What God loves, Satan hates; what God hates, Satan loves.

While God uses people to be the vessels that carry out His plan and further His kingdom, Satan attempts to use people to further his destructive agenda. The examples through the ages abound, but here are two famous ones. In the book of Esther, set during the time of the captivity of Israel in Babylon, Satan used Haman to try to destroy the Jews, but did not succeed. In the twentieth century,

Satan used the Nazis and Hitler to attempt to destroy God's chosen people. But even though Hitler succeeded in murdering six million European ethnic Jews, ultimately, Satan's genocidal plan was defeated.

Satan will not stop trying to destroy Israel for one simple reason: Yeshua will return when Israel repents as a nation and corporately calls upon Him to come, saying, "Blessed is He who comes in the name of the Lord" (Matthew 21:9; see also Psalm 118:26). When Yeshua returns, He will set up His kingdom on earth, leaving Satan without a job, and he doesn't like his retirement plan!

To fully understand why Satan, despite having powerful allies and unwitting recruits, keeps failing in his mission to annihilate the Jews, we must understand what is at stake from God's perspective. While most Bible scholars agree that God has a plan to restore the world to Himself, few recognize the important role that God has reserved for the Jews in the end times.

The apostle Paul (Rabbi Saul of Tarsus) tells us there will come a day when all Israel will corporately put her trust in Messiah Yeshua (Romans 11:25-26). That day will come in the future, at the end of a seven-year tribulation period, when all surviving Jewish people will realize they missed Messiah at His first coming and will call upon Him, saying, "*Baruch haba Bashem Adonai*" (Hebrew for "Blessed is He who comes in the name of the Lord"). This cry of recognition and repentance will be a direct fulfillment of the prophecy of Zechariah 12:10.

By then, "all Israel will be saved" (Romans 11:26) as they all recognize Yeshua for who He is. This reference to "all Israel" does not include all Jews of all times, but only the Jews who survive the tribulation. Unfortunately, according to Zechariah 13:8-9, two-thirds of the Jewish people living during the tribulation will perish.

At this point, it is important to look closely at God's breakdown of the Jewish people who will perish and those who will survive. God clearly tells us that "two parts in it will be cut off and perish," and that He will "bring the third part through the fire, refine them as silver is refined, and test them as gold is tested" (Zechariah 13:8-9). If we were to look at today's Jewish demographics, about ten million Jews would perish, while five million would survive and become the "all Israel" of Romans 11:25-26. This is a number greater than the six million murdered during the Holocaust. This would be an unprecedented tragedy. Yet, as much as we want to ignore this passage, it is part of God's Word, and it will be fulfilled. So how do we live with it?

It is helpful to understand that God never gives us an exact count of how many Jewish people will perish. Rather, He gives us a percentage of the total number of Jewish people who will still be alive at the end of the tribulation. In other words, all the Jewish followers of Yeshua would have already been raptured prior to the seven-year tribulation.

It remains the responsibility of disciples of Yeshua to share the message of hope with the Jewish people prior to the rapture so that while the percentages in Zechariah 13:8-9 will never change, the final count of those who will perish will diminish with every soul that turns to Yeshua prior to the tribulation. This should serve as a great incentive for presenting the gospel to Jewish people. God is clearly not finished with Israel and the Jewish people, and replacement theology has no place in the church because it is not supported in the Bible.

While many believers hold to this faulty view based on ignorance, we must not miss the fact that it is taught by seasoned preachers and theologians alike. These men and women responsible for teaching biblical truths are held to a higher standard by God (James 3:1), and ultimately, they will be held accountable for being instrumental in hurting the people whom God calls "the apple of His eye" (Zechariah 2:8). In spite of teachings and strategies to the contrary, God has promised in Jeremiah 31:35-37 that He will never abandon the Jews or Israel. In the same way that the heavenly bodies are of a "fixed order" that will not change, so will God's commitment to Israel never change.

So, according to Jeremiah 31:35-37, there is a way to destroy Israel. If one can destroy the fixed order of the moon and the stars, then it's possible for "the offspring of Israel [to] cease." But from God's perspective—and it is His perspective alone that matters—Israel was, is, and continues to be in His plan. A right understanding of God's Word will lead to a right understanding of Israel's place in His program and to denouncing antisemitism on biblical grounds. It will also give us clarity as to the dangers of replacement theology.

CHRISTIAN PALESTINIANISM

The Teachings

In recent years, and way beyond the theological error of replacement theology, there has been a shift in Christian theology away from traditional biblical teachings. We could call it replacement theology on steroids. When faced with conflict in the Middle East that has arisen since Israel became a nation again in 1948, a growing number of Bible believers appear to have made it their personal duty to act as theological referees between Jews and Arabs (redefined as Palestinians by Arafat and his disciples).

Those who second-guess the Bible appear to be hoping and praying that Yeshua will truly become the reconciling person between the two groups, making them into the one new man as described in Ephesians 2:13-16.

One of the key words heard over and over is *reconciliation*, and it often punctuates the various programs and projects aimed at bringing both Jews and Palestinians to Yeshua. It seems to be the ultimate goal of evangelicals who are involved in such programs.

Reconciliation should be the act of getting two people or people groups—the Jewish people and the Palestinians—to agree through dialogue and compromise as they find a spiritual common ground in Yeshua and His message of salvation. As a two-way street, reconciliation needs to include forgiveness, mutual acceptance, and a desire to press on together toward a common goal.

In recent years, a new way of thinking has emerged within the evangelical community at large, known as Christian Palestinianism. Simply put, Christian Palestinianism offers a new way to look at the Middle East. It is almost like a new worldview. It has ramifications politically, historically, geographically, archaeologically, culturally, and even spiritually.

In his book *For Zion's Sake,* Dr. Paul Wilkinson defines Christian Palestinianism by contrasting it with Christian Zionism. He writes:

> Christian Palestinianism is an inverted mirror image of Christian Zionism. All the basic elements of a Christian Zionist eschatology are reversed, so that the Bible is seen to be Christian, not Jewish, the land of the Bible is Palestine not Israel, the son of God is a Palestinian not a Jew, the Holocaust is resented not remembered, 1948 is a catastrophe not a miracle, the Jewish people are illegal occupiers not rightful owners, and biblical prophecy is a moral manifesto and not a signpost to the Second Coming.[7]

Christian Palestinianism seems to be reinterpreting the biblical record to allow for the inclusion of a Palestinian narrative including a Palestinian Jesus.[8] But is this accurate? What about the biblical account of Israel, its land, and its people? Have Christian Palestinians and their sympathizers ignored the Jewish nature of the biblical narrative? After all, the modern concept of Palestine did not emerge until the mid-1960s. Before that, the term *Palestine* was simply a descriptive name of a geographical area populated by diverse people going back to the days following the destruction of Herod's temple and the dispersion of the Jews from their homeland. On what basis has this label for the Holy Land gone from simply being the name of a geographical area to describing a people group named the Palestinians?

In a 1977 interview, Zahir Muhsein, a member of the PLO executive committee, clearly stated,

> Only for political and tactical reasons do we speak today about the existence of a Palestinian people, since Arab national interests demand that we posit the existence of a distinct Palestinian people to oppose Zionism.[9]

Christian Palestinianism continues to spread and influence evangelicals and even Catholics around the world. During the 2024 Christmas season, Pope Francis received a gift from Palestinian artists from Bethlehem. It was an olive wood nativity scene, and baby Jesus was laying in His manger atop a keffiyeh (the Palestinian head scarf popularized by Yasser Arafat).[10]

According to Dr. Wilkinson, Christian Palestinianism became a reality in 1994 through the work of Naim Ateek at the time that he started the Palestinian Ecumenical Liberation Theology Center known as Sabeel.[11] At one time, their motto was "Working for Justice, Peace and Reconciliation in Palestine-Israel, " and evidently the motto has since changed.[12] Sabeel is established in Jerusalem and across the world as Friends of Sabeel.[13] Christian Palestinianism has increased in popularity with the help of key international proponents, such as Archbishop Desmond Tutu of South Africa, Vicar of Christ Church; Reverend Stephen Sizer; Mark Ellis (Baylor University); and Gary Burge (Calvin Theological Seminary).

Those who promote Christian Palestinianism portray Israelis as occupiers, colonizers, and adherents of apartheid. It is not uncommon for proponents of Christian Palestinianism to compare the struggle of Palestinians to that of African Americans during the civil rights movement, as in the movie *Little Town of Bethlehem*.[14]

As a result, Christian Palestinianism appears on the other side of the spectrum from Christian Zionism, which, according to Stephen Sizer, is a "devious heresy" and "an erroneous interpretation of the Bible which is subservient to the political agenda of the modern State of Israel."[15]

The Proponents

To better understand the current agenda of Christian Palestinianism, we need to identify its major proponents and the words they choose to promote their views.

Naim Ateek (Born 1937)

In a 2014 interview with Rabbi Brant Rosen, Naim Ateek agreed that he believed in replacement theology, which is also known as supersessionism:

> Well, I would say it is true that if you read the New Testament, there is Supersessionism. There is. And that's how the early church, I think, understood it—that they are really the "New Israel..." But I don't have to stick to it today—today I have a different way of interpreting this.[16]

Ateek compares the Israeli treatment of the Palestinians today to the Nazis' treatment of the Jews in the 1930s and 1940s. He also claims that Israel was built on Palestinian ashes.[17]

Elias Chacour (Born 1939)

Elias Chacour was the Archbishop of Akko, Haifa, and All Galilee for the Melkite Greek Catholic Church (2006–2014). He is the author of *Blood Brothers* and *We Belong to the Land*, in which he claims to be a seeker of reconciliation between Israelis and Palestinians, but also compares the Israelis of today to the Nazis of yesterday.[18] Furthermore,

Chacour claims that corporate guilt over the Holocaust caused the West to seek reparations for the Jews, but in the wrong places:

> After World War II, because of what had happened in Europe and mainly in Germany, Jews started streaming to Palestine with this nightmare they had lived through, which was the Jewish Holocaust. And we never imagined that soon we would become the Jews of the Jews, the victims of the victims of the Second World War.[19]

There is a real danger when history is revised to fit an agenda, especially when that agenda aims at demonizing a people group. It is the dehumanizing and demonizing of the Jews that led many people to participate in the deaths of six million during World War II without giving it a second thought.

An even greater danger is created when supposedly mainstream Christians bring their support to any cause that endangers or demonizes any side of a conflict. Unfortunately, this is what we are facing today. The threat of Christian Palestinianism spreading among mainstream evangelicals is very real. Some of its key proponents are doing much damage to Christianity and driving a wedge in Judeo-Christian relationships.

Christian Individuals Who Speak Against Israel

Stephen Sizer is, without a doubt, one of the most outspoken enemies of Israel among modern evangelicals. He is the poster boy for anti-Zionism—so much so that he says Christian Zionists are engaged in "Christian Jihad."[20] He even recently accused the Jewish people of being behind the terrorist attacks of 9/11.[21] He is part of the Church of England, and because of his antisemitic activity, a disciplinary tribunal has forbidden him from practicing any priestly roles until 2030.[22]

Gary Burge, a professor at Calvin Theological Seminary, is another proponent of Christian Palestinianism. In his book *Jesus and the Land,* he relabels replacement theology as fulfillment theology, claiming that all was fulfilled at Yeshua's death and resurrection 2,000 years ago, leaving no room for Israel in God's plan today.[23]

Lynne Hybels, the wife of former senior pastor Bill Hybels of Willow Creek Community Church in the Chicago area, has joined forces with Sami Awad over the last few years, speaking together on a tour of US cities in various churches to speak about injustices against Palestinian Christians in the Middle East.[24] They have been successful in drawing audiences from Lutheran and Presbyterian Church USA groups.

Together, Awad and Hybels heavily promoted the 2010 movie *Little Town of Bethlehem,* hiding their anti-Zionism while appearing to promote conflict resolution and reconciliation. In the advertising for the movie, only English and Arabic is found in the promotional materials. Hebrew is nowhere to be seen, which makes one wonder from the start what they really meant by reconciliation.

Hank Hanegraaff is another of the key Christian players who opposes Israel through replacement theology. He has been known as the "Bible Answer Man" since 1989, when he replaced Walter Martin at the head of the Christian Research Institute. He has gone so far as to accuse the Jewish people of Palestinian ethnic cleansing in his book *The Apocalypse Code.*[25] He has participated in anti-Zionist conferences such as Christ at the Checkpoint, and he joined the Eastern Orthodox Church in 2017.

Christ at the Checkpoint

Christ at the Checkpoint (CATC) is a biennial conference that started in 2010 and takes place at the Bethlehem Bible College in the Bethlehem "disputed territories." On the Bethlehem Bible College website, CATC says, "The mission of 'Christ at the Checkpoint' is to challenge Evangelicals to take responsibility to help resolve the conflicts in Israel/Palestine by engaging with the teaching of Jesus on the Kingdom of God."[26]

This sounds commendable at a time when the whole Middle East seems to be sitting on a powder keg with a very short fuse. Biblically speaking, anything done in the name of Yeshua and following His teachings should lead to reconciliation and peace. Furthermore, the leadership of CATC claims, "We deeply mourn the death and suffering of all people because it is our firm conviction that all humans are made in God's image. We are also profoundly troubled when the name of God is invoked to promote violence and religious national ideologies."[27]

Their mission appears to deal with any form of extremism within Christianity, Judaism, and Islam, but the problem is that CATC conferences that take place every two years build on the work accomplished by the previous conferences, and consequently, CATC has gained a reputation that increasingly lacks ethical stability. [28] The first three conferences were all advertised under the banner of reconciliation, but ultimately, each one resembled more of a witch hunt against Israel than a dialogue to encourage healthy compromise. Unfortunately, many evangelicals have been blinded by Palestinian victimhood rhetoric.

Much about the CATC is revealed in their manifesto. I recognize that it includes some truthful statements; however, it offers a theologically dangerous mixed bag of views, as seen below:

> **CATC:** "The Kingdom of God has come. Evangelicals must reclaim the prophetic role in bringing peace, justice and reconciliation in Palestine and Israel."
>
> **The error**: Kingdom Now theology claims, among other things, that Yeshua's kingdom was inaugurated at His first coming, while Scripture states that He will reign as messianic king on the throne of David from Jerusalem

in a yet-to-come millennial kingdom (Psalm 72:8, 11, 17; Isaiah 9:7; 11:6-11; Jeremiah 23:6; Zechariah 3:10).

CATC: "Racial ethnicity alone does not guarantee the benefits of the Abrahamic Covenant."

The error: The benefits of the Abrahamic covenant are multifaceted. They include God's promises to both the Jewish people and the nations (non-Jews) through Abraham, yet the physical land is promised *only* to the Jewish people—the ethnic descendants of Abraham, Isaac, and Jacob (Genesis 12:1-3, 7; 13:15; 17:7-8, 19; 25:5-6; 26:3; 28:3-4; 35:9-15).

CATC: "Any exclusive claim to the land of the Bible in the name of God is not in line with the teaching of Scripture."

The error: The land of Israel belongs to God Himself (Leviticus 25:23). He chose to make a covenant with Abraham that would include the giving of that land as an eternal *and* unconditional part of that covenant. In addition, God's gifts are irrevocable (Romans 11:29).[29]

For the honest person who respects the Word of God, the veneer of reconciliation and fight against extremism isn't very hard to peel. Once that is done, it is easy to see that Christ at the Checkpoint is indeed interested in reconciliation, as long as that means Israel's unilateral apology for its "crimes" against Palestinians, along with Israel relinquishing the "occupied" land of Palestine and further submitting to the regional demands made by its Arab neighbors. Such a one-way street has nothing to do with true reconciliation and is not inspired by biblical principles.

The Movie *With God on Our Side*[30]

This movie, released in 2010 and directed by Porter Speakman Jr., claims to offer a balanced view on the Middle East crisis that presents "God's side" of the issue. Speakman claims he is not taking a Palestinian or Israeli perspective, but rather, a human approach. The synopsis of the movie seems to indicate it does clearly take sides, however:

> *With God On Our Side* takes a look at the theology of Christian Zionism, which teaches that because the Jews are God's chosen people, they have a divine right to the land of Israel. Aspects of this belief system lead some Christians in the West to give uncritical support to Israeli government policies, even those that privilege Jews at the expense of Palestinians, leading to great suffering among Muslim and Christian Palestinians alike and threatening Israel's security as a whole.
>
> This film demonstrates that there is a biblical alternative for Christians who want to love and support the people of Israel, a theology that doesn't favor one people group over another but instead promotes peace and reconciliation for both Jews and Palestinians.[31]

The movie was endorsed by a few influential evangelicals, which helped to promote it at the time of its release. However, when you watch it, you will quickly recognize the biased narrative, which ignores a proper interpretation of the biblical text.

The Movie *Little Town of Bethlehem*[32]

The destructive ideology of "Christian" anti-Zionism is featured in this antisemitic propaganda piece in the name of reconciliation. The movie *Little Town of Bethlehem* paints the portrait of three men who wanted peace and reconciliation in the region: an Arab Muslim, an Israeli Jew, and a Palestinian Christian. They promote their views of reconciliation against all odds. Who would disagree with that?

The issue does not lie in the validity of such aspirations, but in how the different sides were portrayed. Palestinians were compared to African Americans during the civil rights movement under the leadership of Martin Luther King Jr. and fighting the National Guard for their freedom. And Israelis were painted as oppressors and invaders of "Palestine." It is a shame to see that many evangelicals are buying into these kinds of distortions.

Kairos Palestine Document

The Kairos Palestine Document was penned by "Palestinian Christians" wanting to solve the Middle East crisis with impartiality. Their understanding of fairness and justice seems a little lopsided as they claim the following on their site:[33]

> We are a Christian Palestinian movement, born out of the Kairos Document, which advocates for ending the Israeli occupation and achieving a just solution to the conflict. The Kairos Document is the word of Christian Palestinians to the world about what is happening in Palestine.
>
> Our word is a cry of hope, with love, prayer and faith in God. We address it first of all to ourselves and then to all the churches and Christians in the world, asking them to stand against injustice and apartheid, urging them to work for a just peace.

The Dangers

The projects and people we have reviewed pose a real danger to Israel and the Jewish people as they legitimize the demonization of the people and the land.

A closer look reveals that Christian Palestinianism holds a distorted view of God's Word and is hiding a political agenda behind reformed theology, resulting in the presentation of Christian Zionism as heretical. The Bible is slowly getting "de-judaized."

When the Jewish roots of Christianity are disregarded and eradicated, Israel and the Jewish people will be treated as irrelevant. Evangelicals who make the move from Christian Zionism to Christian Palestinianism are putting Israel and the Jewish people at risk. This shift in the Christian psyche from Israel to Palestine is a slap in God's face and a grave altering of His Word.[34]

At the core of Christian Palestinianism is a distortion of the Bible. It wasn't too long ago that we could find ourselves arguing Israel's position in God's plan against people who were promoting replacement theology. And the long-held dichotomy between dispensationalists and Reformed theologians didn't always lead to contempt for Israel and the Jewish people, let alone antisemitism. This has changed. [35]

Postmodernism's thirst for a secular social justice and tolerance has positioned many evangelicals on the other side of the spectrum from Christian Zionism, bringing them to rally for the perspectives held by Christian Palestinianism. To be against Israel is "in," and to stand with Israel is to be a "hater." It could be argued that Christian Palestinianism is replacement theology amplified.

The promise God made to Abraham and the Jewish people in Genesis 12:1-3 still stands. God never changed the land boundaries promised to Abraham in Genesis 15:18-21; and although these promises have never been changed, they have yet to be fully fulfilled. Unfortunately, biblical illiteracy is running rampant within the evangelical church, and that creates a shaky foundation upon which historical revisionism can be built with very little challenge, if any.

Christian Palestinianists excel at biblical revisionism. They will go as far as painting Yeshua as the first Palestinian. This far-fetched revisionist approach to Yeshua's origins has been heavily promoted by the Palestinian Authority.[36] Back in 2014, the president of Palestinian Authority, Mahmoud Abbas, went as far as celebrating Christmas to validate Yeshua's connection with Palestine. Christians shouldn't line up with men such as Mahmoud Abbas, who, under a veneer of desire for world peace and Israeli-Palestinian entente (understanding or diplomacy), remains a promoter of hatred, a supporter of terrorism, and a Holocaust denier (a position he defended in his PhD dissertation).[37]

In both cases of the distortion and rejection of God's Word, the authority of the Bible is put in question. The God of the Bible, who is the God of Israel—as well as the God of Abraham, Isaac, and Jacob—is made into a different god. This allows for the insertion of a revised agenda favoring the Palestinian people at the expense of Israel and the Jewish people.

Christian Palestinianism changes God from a covenant maker and keeper to a covenant breaker. While this next point might not be clear to many evangelicals yet, for Christian Palestinianism to exist, Israel has to cease to exist.

What better way to postulate that Israel has become irrelevant than to say that God's covenants with the Jewish people have been changed, or even done away with? If God were to renege on His covenant or change the original recipients of His covenantal blessings, it would become obvious that He is done with Israel and the Jews.

But God never changed His mind after He said the following to Abraham:

> I will establish My covenant between Me and you and your descendants after you throughout their generations for an everlasting covenant, to be God to you and to your descendants after you. I will give to you and to your descendants after you, the land of your sojournings, all the land of Canaan, for an everlasting possession; and I will be their God (Genesis 17:7-8).

If God were a covenant breaker, that would make Him a liar. First Samuel 15:29 tells us otherwise: "The Glory of Israel will not lie or change His mind; for He is not a man that He should change His mind."

Once a person is convinced that God is finished with Israel and the Jews, it becomes easier to extrapolate the generalization that Israel is the cause of evil against the Palestinians. French author Pierre-André Taguieff develops this thought further in his recent book *Israel et la Question Juive* (*The Jewish Question*) when he writes, "Intellectual and political conformism moves alongside radical anti-Zionism, having nothing to do with a critique of Israel's politics but rather aiming at the final destruction of the Jewish State."[38]

In *Eurabia: The Euro-Arab Axis,* Jewish author and activist, Bat Ye'or describes Christian Palestinianism as "Palestinian Marcionism":

> The Christian policy that would eliminate the Jewish source of Christianity by suppressing the link between the Hebrew Bible and the Gospels represents an old and lingering trend, always opposed by the Church. Today, Palestinian Marcionism (Palestinianism) paves the way for the Islamization of the Church as it prepares mentalities for an Islamic replacement theology…and encompasses the whole paraphernalia of traditional anti-Semitism.[39]

Bat Ye'or's assessment has tragically proven true. Christian Palestinianism is well on its way to de-judaizing Yeshua—a job that the Gentile branch of Christianity generously contributed to, sometimes out of ignorance and other times out of pure hatred of the Jews. Christian Palestinianism will also continue to invalidate much of the Jewish Scriptures as history gets rewritten and Jewish references get replaced to accommodate the Islamization of the Bible.

The Christian Palestinianists' general stance of painting Israel as an apartheid state and other aspects of their platform that distort history are representative of key components of the latest trends in end-times antisemitism.

The Allies

Reminding ourselves of the fact that antisemitism is the irrational hatred of the Jewish people, we can see the obvious converging of many unlikely allies against Israel. Muslims, liberals, and evangelicals have many reasons to disagree ideologically and spiritually, yet they find it acceptable to go against Israel in one accord. All these groups are different but provide arrows in Satan's quiver of hate, and the target remains the same in all cases: Israel and the Jews.

An errant evangelical might not be as determined to destroy Israel as a radical Muslim is, but they have become co-conspirators and co-perpetrators by accepting and promoting unbiblical perspectives. As such, they could become guilty of the same hatred in the eyes of the God of Israel. According to His Word, He is not done with the Jewish people or the land of Israel.

In the unholy, irrational alliances of unlikely partners against Israel's existence, the common denominator is eschatological antisemitism. I see it as Satan's newest weapon against Israel and the global Jewish community.

The Biblical Response

We can all agree that we haven't seen the worst yet from the enemy of the apple of God's eye (Zechariah 2:8). We must continue to teach and promote a biblical approach to Israel as well as a biblical approach to mankind's need for a Savior. Jews and Palestinians need an encounter with the Jewish Messiah and Savior of the world.

John Metzger has written an excellent book on God's final chapter for fulfilling the salvation of the Jews during the end times, traced through the writings of Moses and the prophets of the Old Testament.

In *Israel's Only Hope: The New Covenant,*[40] Metzger calls attention to Yeshua's first-coming intent of initiating the new covenant, and His intention to fulfill it during the end times in association with His second coming. This book is eye-opening even for well-taught Christians and provides a strong counter to the erroneous and dangerous teachings of replacement theology.

Part of the solution for regaining clarity might be in our responsibility to teach other believers to be like the Bereans and thrive for biblical accuracy (Acts 17:11). Then we might be able to return to the Bible's original meanings and recover the rapidly dying Jewish perspective so crucial to a proper understanding of the whole of God's counsel.

God was the first Zionist, but He also gave His only begotten Son for both Jews and Arabs. I am obviously pro-God, and thus I am pro-Israel; but being pro-Israel doesn't mean that one is anti-Palestinian. Sadly, the opposite is seldom true—rarely do we see someone who is pro-Palestinian also be pro-Israel. As in many of the "tolerance wars" of today, tolerance is expected by those who oppose Judeo-Christian teachings, but unfortunately, that tolerance is not returned.

BOYCOTT, DIVESTMENT AND SANCTION (BDS)

Another area in which the evangelical church is guilty of jumping on the bandwagon of biased accusations against Israel is Boycott, Divestment and Sanction (BDS). While BDS isn't an invention of the church, it has become increasingly attractive to many evangelicals, with some believing that it is a valid and peaceful way to protest against Israel. There are several problems with that train of thought, but first, let's look at the origin of the BDS movement. Though I presented a lot of information about BDS earlier, there's more I'll share here that Christians often find to be surprising.

It is ironic that most of the people who take a political stand with BDS have very little knowledge of how it began and by whom. This movement was started on July 9, 2005,[41] by the Palestinian civil society and orchestrated by the current leader of the Palestinian Authority, Mahmoud Abbas, and the Palestinian BDS National Committee.[42]

Omar Barghouti is cofounder of and main spokesperson for BDS.[43] His organization claims that Israel must meet three obligations for BDS to stop:

1. Ending its occupation and colonization of all Arab lands occupied in June 1967 and dismantling the wall
2. Recognizing the fundamental rights of the Arab-Palestinian citizens of Israel to full equality
3. Respecting, protecting, and promoting the rights of Palestinian refugees to return to their homes and properties as stipulated in UN Resolution 194[44]

Too often, there is an unspoken expectation from the Palestinian side. Much of the not-so-hidden agenda of the Palestinian Authority is focused on the destruction of Israel and the Jews. At the time that the Palestinian people were invented in the mid-1960s, the problem of refugees didn't exist. The Jewish people abandoned the use of the term *Palestine* when Israel was declared a state in 1948. The word became exclusively descriptive of the Arab side and was adopted and repurposed by Arafat when he created the PLO.

The creation of a Palestinian narrative that has promoted 60 years of historical fabrications has helped the world to turn on Israel. But the Palestinian Authority doesn't really care about the well-being of even their own "citizens." If they did, they would never use their own people as human shields when doing battle or use schools and hospitals to store weapons and explosives.

The Palestinian Authority takes great pains to misinform, or simply not inform, the people they are trying to influence with regard to their standoff against Israel. The proper word for this is *propaganda*, and that is the mechanism by which BDS functions.

BDS was born out of a Palestinian desire to enroll otherwise unengaged and apathetic people in the fight against Israel. The Palestinian Authority and Hamas's goal is the total destruction of Israel. What if they could get support from different groups of people? This would greatly help their cause, wouldn't it? BDS does just that, and it does it well—in the entertainment industry, the government, academia and the universities,[45] and even some Christian denominations such as The Presbyterian Church USA (PCUSA), whose General Assembly voted in the spring of 2014 to divest from three companies engaged in business with Israel (Caterpillar Inc., Hewlett Packard, and Motorola Solutions). This is the same PCUSA that unsuccessfully tried to blot out the word *Israel* from their prayer and hymn books in 2014,[46] leading to a split within the denomination. They continue to dig in their heels in 2024.[47]

Originators of BDS count on the altruistic feelings people feel in association with boycotting for a social justice issue. Of course, BDS supporters are plagued with decisions that force them to be very inconsistent, at best, when they apply their boycott efforts. Divestment is usually a matter of reinvesting your funds elsewhere, and there are plenty of opportunities for such a move. When it comes to boycotting, however, it is a bit trickier, especially if you want to be consistent and do it with integrity. It is easy to stop buying Jaffa oranges or Osem cookies from Israel, but not so much to stop using the Intel chip in personal computers or mobile phones (both originated from Israeli ingenuity).

BDS proponents often nip the pro-Israel narrative in the bud by loudly condemning Israel, which has become the hip, liberal mantra du jour, even though their own narrative is flawed and biased. Most Christians do not want to be called haters, and so may be easily motivated to avoid that label by relaxing their convictions or by adopting a popular cause without biblical insight.

The BDS movement justifies its actions by resorting to false accusations about Israeli occupation and apartheid policies. It is our responsibility to expose those lies and educate those who don't know the origins of BDS or its flawed perspectives.

BDS proponents are inconsistent in their boycotting activity and need to be made aware of their hypocrisy or ignorance about Israel's contributions to the modern world (and the list of those contributions keeps growing every day),[48] which include everyday products used by millions.[49]

BDS counts on people's ignorance and natural desire for justice to sell their falsified agenda of Palestinian victimhood.

While not many are willing to admit it, the Boycott, Divestment and Sanction movement could possibly lead to what took place during and after *Kristallnacht.* We must never forget the many simultaneous violent attacks on Jewish businesses, synagogues, and properties that occurred all over Germany on the night of November 9-10, 1938. *Kristallnacht*, or the "Night of Broken Glass."[50] Hitler had taken the first openly violent steps against European Jewry; *Kristallnacht* is recognized as the official start date for the Holocaust.

Kristallnacht was a pogrom (government-sponsored riot against the Jews) connected to one of the most famous boycott attempts in the history of the Jewish people, and it ultimately resulted in the murder of six million Jews as Hitler conquered country after country in Europe. Many of those who bought into the boycott and the destructive pogroms organized by Hitler never foresaw where they were going. Is it possible that some of the current non-Palestinian proponents of BDS are unaware of the underlying agenda of destruction that drives the Boycott, Divestment and Sanctions movement?

BDS isn't going to stop now and will most likely spread to other Christian denominations. So what are believers who still see Israel at the center of God's program to do? Should we remain silent and just pray? Should we do our own boycotting of those who are proponents of BDS?

Some are coming to grips with the destructive nature of BDS toward our Middle East ally, Israel. A third of the states in the US have passed anti-boycott laws to punish the businesses supporting BDS, and the list is growing.[51]

Another great resource for fighting BDS can be found at the Stop BDS website.[52] Even though it is meant to equip students, most of the information here is helpful for those who are eager to learn the truth and apply real fairness and justice. In addition, an organization known as the Canary Mission[53] is keeping tabs on BDS and its proponents.

Yet another thing we can do is to make sure that we do our best to buy Israeli products in the US to beat the BDS proponents at their own game. The endnote citation at the end of this sentence will take you to a website that offers a partial list of what BDS wants you to boycott.[54] My mention of this list doesn't mean that I endorse all of the products on it, but my guess is you will find plenty of brands that you already support. Review them, keep at it, and tell others. This would be a strong application of Genesis 50:20, when Joseph proved to his brothers that what some want to use for evil, God can turn around and use for good: "As for you, you meant evil against me, but God meant it for good in order to bring about this present result, to preserve many people alive."

What BDS proponents, by commission and omission, too often have in common is a lack of a biblical approach to Israel and the Jewish people. Biblical truth provides a solid foundation for Israel. It describes a people created by God through Abraham, Isaac, and Jacob and the 12 tribes of Israel, as well as the precise land boundaries starting early in Genesis 12 and continuing through chapters 15, 17, and following. Knowing what Scripture says about Israel and the Jewish people is vital. Without a biblical backbone, Zionism lacks the strength to fight the hypocrisy, hatred, and double standards of the BDS campaigns around the world. BDS relies on the **B**ullying, **D**elegitimizing and **S**landering of Israel and does it on a foundation of lies that can be debunked. If truth really matters, let us speak up! As believers, we can all **B**uy, **D**efend and **S**upport Israel in our own ways.

CHRISTIANS UNITED FOR ISRAEL

Christians United for Israel (CUFI), led by John Hagee of Cornerstone Church in San Antonio, Texas, positions itself under the umbrella of evangelical Christianity and is popular among Christians and Jews alike. CUFI receives most of its funding from evangelical Christians who love Israel and the Jewish people. So far, so good! Israel is desperately in need of friends within the Christian community in this age of BDS and Christian Palestinianism. But is there a catch to receiving support and friendship from CUFI?

Jewish people generally feel safe with CUFI because the organization will almost never proselytize. This doesn't mean that every single supporter of CUFI refrains from personally sharing the gospel with Jewish people. But if an evangelical Christian who isn't vocal about sharing the good news with his Jewish friends decides to pledge financial support to CUFI in the hopes that CUFI would share the gospel with Jewish people, they might be gravely mistaken. This might have something to do with Hagee's theological position on Israel. He is convinced that the Jewish people don't need to believe in Yeshua the Messiah to be saved. This came as a shock to me the first time I read of this. While everybody else in the world needs Yeshua to be saved, Hagee claims that Jewish people do not have to believe that Yeshua is the Messiah to be in good standing with God:

> The law of Moses is sufficient enough to bring a person into the knowledge of God until God gives him a greater

> revelation...Everyone else, whether Buddhist or Baha'i, needs to believe in Jesus, but not Jews.[55]

This view of Israel in God's plan is known as dual-covenant theology. This view was first formulated in the early 1900s by Franz Rosenzweig in his volume *The Star of Redemption.*[56] It claims that Israel is in a relationship with God through the Abrahamic covenant, while Gentiles need Yeshua's sacrifice on the cross to redeem them from their sins. According to dual-covenant theology, nothing more than a connection to the Abrahamic covenant—by virtue of being Jewish—is necessary to be saved. Hagee is a promoter of dual-covenant theology.[57]

In the first edition of his book *In Defense of Israel*, published in 2007, Hagee was clear about his position regarding Israel's relationship with God having no connection to Yeshua's atonement.[58] Hagee brings up five points, and the first three had to do with the death of Yeshua. He claims that Yeshua had to live to be the Messiah. While this is a partially true statement, it lacks clarity. Hagee seems to ignore the Jewish understanding of two appearances of Messiah: *Mashiach ben Yoseph*, who will come and suffer humiliation and pain unto the point of death for His people Israel (Isaiah 52:13–53:12), and *Mashiach ben David*, who will come, conquer the world, and reign on David's throne in Jerusalem. Evangelicals can easily accept that Yeshua fulfilled the office of *Mashiach ben Yoseph* at His first coming and that He will return in the future to fulfill the office of *Mashiach ben David.*

The fourth and fifth points that Hagee makes are also problematic because he rather dogmatically asserts that Yeshua never claimed to be the Messiah by words or deeds. Evidently Hagee seriously lacks a Jewish perspective on the Bible, which would help him to recognize that Yeshua claimed to be the Messiah in John chapters 7 and 8.

In John 7:37-38, Yeshua is in Jerusalem during the Feast of

Tabernacles, one of the three Jewish feasts requiring a presence in Jerusalem at the temple. Note His words:

> Now on the last day, the great day of the feast, Jesus stood and cried out, saying, "If anyone is thirsty, let him come to Me and drink. He who believes in Me, as the Scripture said, 'From his innermost being will flow rivers of living water.'"

Yeshua claims to be a source of living water at the very time when the Levites were performing the ceremony of the water libations by pouring water on the altar. That ceremony was meant to indicate that just like the water is poured all over, one day the whole world will know God through His Messiah.

Furthermore, in John 8:12, Yeshua claims to be "the Light of the world" as the Levites are performing what was known as the "torch ceremony"—forming a procession all the way to the temple and carrying lights. That ceremony was meant to show Israel that one day, the Messiah would come to be the Light of the world. Jesus said, "I am the Light of the world; he who follows Me will not walk in the darkness, but will have the Light of life."

In both cases, by His very words, Yeshua claims to be the Messiah. He may not have said, "I am the Messiah," but His Jewish audience knew very well that only the Messiah could make such claims.

Hagee received a lot of criticism for his ambiguous approach to the gospel message. So much so that in 2009, he decided to publish a revised version of *In Defense of Israel*, in which he made changes to chapter 10. The controversial passage on the Jews not needing to believe in Yeshua to be saved is no longer in the book.

I take no pleasure in bringing up these concerns about Hagee, but I continue to believe strongly that the best thing that could be offered to a Jewish person is the news that they can have eternal life in God's presence by accepting Yeshua's death and resurrection as a free gift unto salvation. By refraining from sharing that gift, I am convinced that Hagee and those who follow his teaching are committing an act of "soft" antisemitism. Their humanitarian efforts on behalf of the Jewish people are to be commended, but in the scope of eternity, they fall short.

It has been said that refraining from sharing the gospel with Jewish people when we do humanitarian work in their midst is akin to sending someone to hell on a full stomach. Let's make sure we never find ourselves in that predicament.

JEWISH VOICE FOR PEACE

Jewish Voice for Peace's vision statement includes these words: "We picture Palestinians—from the Jordan River to the Mediterranean Sea—living with their inalienable rights respected, building schools and hospitals and planting olive groves with the resources they need."[59] While that sounds very positive and peaceful, the world has discovered since October 2023 that the phrase "from the Jordan River to the Mediterranean Sea" has a very different meaning—that is, the complete destruction of Israel.

JVP is yet another group of liberal Jews (and some non-Jews) who, under the guise of a pro-peace organization, are doing everything they can to demonize and delegitimize Israel, as demonstrated by the propaganda in one of their "educational videos" they claim to be "historically accurate."[60] Their primary platform is the university campuses in the US, where they can aggressively promote BDS and the pro-Palestinian narrative. At times, they also team up with the women-led grassroots organization known as CODEPINK.[61]

CODEPINK seems to be more concerned about people profiling Muslims and displaying signs of Islamophobia than the fact that by far, the majority of the terrorism in today's world is committed by Muslims. While it is true that not all Muslims are terrorists, it is challenging not to be profiling Muslims when there is documented evidence that, at the time of this writing, nearly 48,000 terrorist acts have been carried out in the name of Islam since 9/11, per the website thereligionofpeace.com.[62]

NETUREI KARTA

To the untrained Christian eye, the group Neturei Karta (NK) appears as if they are just another sect of Orthodox Judaism. They look the same, sound the same, and many of them reside in Jerusalem and Beit Shemesh, Israel. But they are not just another sect! This fringe group has about 5,000 members worldwide and is a minor player on the team of end-times antisemites. But they hold to views that shouldn't be ignored.

Neturei Karta is Aramaic for "Guardians of the City." The group was founded in 1938 in British Mandate Palestine (pre-1948 Israel). Most of the original members immigrated to Israel during the nineteenth century from Hungary and Lithuania. They consider themselves to be "the real Jews" or "Jews true to the Torah" and promote radical anti-Zionist views. In appearance, they dress like Orthodox Jews, with the men wearing black outfits with hats, *peyot* (side curls), and *tzitzit* (fringes or tassels). At the core of their belief system—originally based on Orthodox Judaism—is their conviction that the "retaking" of the land of Eretz Yisrael before the coming of the *Mashiach* (Messiah) is forbidden.

The Neturei Karta used to simply ignore Israel's existence even though they live there, but in recent years, they have become much more vocal. Their international website features the statement, "Despite being the opposite of what Judaism represents, the Zionist entity calls itself a Jewish state. Since they are using our identity to violate Judaism, we, as true followers of the Jewish religion, are required to stand up and clarify that Judaism and Zionism are diametric opposites. Jewish opposition to Zionism is as old as Zionism itself."[63]

Taking their claim down the eschatological road, we can easily see a group like Neturei Karta buying into the claims of the end-times Antichrist, who will one day come on the scene and, among all of his feats, will reconcile Jews and Arabs so that the tribulation-era temple can be built.

In the Q&A section of the Neturei Karta website, the group answers several questions about themselves. Some of their responses are puzzling at best and antisemitic at worst. For instance, to the question "What is the current alternative to the state of Israel according to the Torah view?," they say, "Jews will be able to live in peace in the Holy Land under Palestinian rule once Zionism is abolished."[64]

Many members of Neturei Karta have close ties with Iran and often visit, attend conferences, and even speak from the platform. In a recent visit to Iran, one of the NK members spoke to a large group of Muslims and ended his speech with a series of shouts of "Allahu Akbar!" ("God is greater!").[65]

As oxymoronic as this might sound, Neturei Karta is comprised of self-hating Jews who actually deserve the title of anti-Zionist Jews,[66] if not antisemitic! They are a fringe group and definitely not the norm. Though they are small in numbers, they are not only a thorn to the Jewish people and to the West but also a potential danger. They are Jews who fight Zionism, try their hardest to discredit the establishment of the modern State of Israel, and have met with the ayatollahs of Iran—Ahmadinejad, Rouhani, and Hezbollah.[67]

Howard Sachar, in his book *A History of Israel,* calls Neturei Karta "an almost surrealistically Orthodox splinter group."[68] By nature of their loathing of Zionism, their promotion of an unconditional Palestinian State in all of Eretz Yisrael, the Jew haters they support, and how abrasive they (Neturei Karta) are, they cannot be dismissed and are—albeit small—a part of eschatological antisemitism.

A CUMULATIVE WAVE OF HATRED

So many groups and organizations—non-Jewish and Jewish, religious and atheistic, political from all across the spectrum, church denominations, and even professedly evangelical Christians—are taking part in end-times antisemitism. This is the wave of hatred that will well up and enable the terrible atrocities of the tribulation. Some of these people fan the flames of hatred by commission, and others by omission. Satan is desperate because time is running out for him, so he will use every weapon at his disposal. He has a lot of experience in the area of antisemitism. He invented it, he perfected it, and he is constantly fine-tuning it to fit the times and his destructive agenda.

CHAPTER 12

TAKING A STAND AGAINST END-TIMES ANTISEMITISM

After hearing about how Israel and the Jews are treated by much of the world, our first reaction can often be silence. After all, what can one person do to push back? As Leo Tolstoy said in his book *A Confession*, "Wrong does not cease to be wrong because the majority share in it."

But silence can be generated by different feelings. People can keep quiet out of indifference. Sometimes they are confronted with issues, even ethical issues, that would normally merit a position being taken, but none is because they are simply not feeling concerned.

RESPONSES WE WANT TO AVOID

Silence

How many of us hear of a war, famine, or crisis on the other side of the world, and within seconds, go back to our daily routines? But when a particular crisis strikes a chord within us or it hits close to home, we give it our attention.

Frankly, I admit that an earthquake on the other side of the planet isn't going to affect me equally as a street riot in a community that is minutes from where I live. That isn't because I do not care about distant crises. Rather, I am being honest about the fact different crises elicit different levels of concern in us.

Indifference is one of the worst responses we can give to a problem. When it comes to racism, as well as antisemitism, we know what indifference can lead to. We need only to look back 75 years to see what can happen. Sir Ian Kershaw said it best: "The road to Auschwitz was built by hate but paved with indifference."[1]

What we don't dare fail to understand is that in the twenty-first century, the silence of indifference is much more dangerous than it was during World War II. I absolutely do not wish to minimize the Holocaust in saying that. But the reality of today's antisemitism is that it's coming from so many different directions all over the globe. Which makes it more all-encompassing than ever.

Radical Islam is probably the most vocal and active enemy faced by the Jewish State and the Jewish people worldwide, and IT WILL NOT STOP AT ISRAEL. We are seeing this unfold on our smartphones and TVs. While they have Israel and all Jews in their crosshairs, they are expanding, and the West is next.

We cannot afford to be silent because of indifference, period. But what about fear? Fear is also a reason why people don't speak up. Fear of reprisals, fear of ostracism, or fear of legal action by their own government.

In a day and age when Israel is painted as the enemy of world peace and the occupier of Palestinian land committing human rights violations every other day, it takes courage to speak up for Israel. We don't have to agree blindly with everything that the Israeli government says or does, but it is time to side with the victim and expose the perpetrator, not the other way around.

Yet understandably, we fear speaking up in public because we risk facing verbal abuse from those who hate Israel. Or even physical violence. We don't want to be singled out because of our support of Israel. But anytime we stay silent, antisemitism gains ground.

Speaking up against radical Islam is also difficult in this day of political correctness. We are told that if we point a negative finger at anything connected to Islam, we are Islamophobes—the worst possible kind of racists. But let us remember that Islam is an ideology (comprising a religion, a political structure, a banking system, and much more), and not a race. Thus, one can be critical of Islam's ideology and not be a racist.

While I strongly disagree with the teachings of the Qur'an, I am not and never will be an Arabophobe. Too many people are quick to connect Arabs with Islam and Islam with Arabs. Indonesia, for instance, accounts for nearly 13 percent of all Muslims in the world. Pakistan is 11 percent Muslim, and so is India. These are just three very large countries where many Muslims can be found, yet they are *not* Arabs. In fact, more than 60 percent of all Muslims live in the Asia-Pacific region.[2] Countries such as Bangladesh, Nigeria, Iran, and Turkey are not Arabic countries, yet they represented 22 percent of the global Muslim population in 2010.[3] We must make that critical distinction, and we must explain it to others as well.

When it comes to protecting the innocent, silence is never an option in a free society. Today, our voices are the means for assuring our survival, as well as the survival of Western civilization. We must speak up against racism in general and antisemitism in particular, whatever the cost. In an acceptance speech at the 1986 Nobel Peace Prize awards ceremony, Holocaust survivor, writer, and activist Elie Wiesel said,

> I swore never to be silent whenever and wherever human beings endure suffering and humiliation. We must always take sides. Neutrality helps the oppressor, never the victim. Silence encourages the tormentor, never the tormented.[4]

Appeasement

When we do speak up, there is another danger we face. We must recognize that evil cannot be reasoned with through appeasement. This is even more dangerous than silence because it makes one feel as though they are actually participating in the solution to the problem when, in fact, they are aggravating the problem.

While silence from indifference or even from fear could possibly be explained with logic, appeasement, on the other hand, defies logic. Because appeasement is not the same as negotiations, it is bound for failure.

One particularly noteworthy example of a common type of failed appeasement is the Munich Agreement, which was signed by France, Great Britain, Italy, and Germany on September 30, 1938.[5] In this pact, Germany was pretty much given western Czechoslovakia for peace purposes. In other words, within months before the start of World War II, because Hitler had already become a force to be reckoned with, he was appeased by being granted part of Czechoslovakia. British Prime Minister Neville Chamberlain went home, proud of his group's achievement, telling all that as a result of it, they had achieved peace in their time. The rest is history, and suffice it to say, Chamberlain and the Allies were proven wrong about 50 million times over,[6] once for each life lost in the war.

The same mistake can be seen in the Russia-Ukraine conflict that started in 2022. Up to the time of this writing, all attempts at resolving the war through dialogue with Putin have failed. Any political, geographical, or economic reward is sure to fall short of the Russian dictator's delusion of grandeur. The only response that he will understand is a taste of his own medicine, and that is strength!

Another example can be found in how the US and the European Union (EU) have handled Iran's race to nuclear power since 2002. Instead of demanding restraint and open doors to Iran's nuclear facilities, billions of dollars have been sent to Iran in the hopes of obtaining cooperation. Through appeasement, the West is financing and helping to build the very weapons that could eradicate us all.

Appeasement, as good as it looks sometimes, is a one-way street that is taken when two-way negotiations end up not working and the party being appeased appears to be a danger. It is akin to rewarding a guilty party for acts of treachery, abuse, or even destruction.

There should be no dialogue with those who want to replace or eliminate Western civilization. One of the postmodern West's greatest weaknesses is its frequent use of appeasement to resolve conflict, which could eventually lead to its demise. This is born out of a desire to remain within the boundaries of what is considered acceptable by political correctness. Yet both political correctness and appeasement are clearly seen by our enemies for exactly what they are: weaknesses. And today, the principal recipient of the "blessing" of appeasement is the main protagonist on the scene of end times antisemitism.

Among other modern enemies, Islamic ideology is behind the reshaping of Europe, the United States, and of course, most of the Middle East and Asia. Islam has become the main benefactor of Western appeasement. It has slowly infiltrated large corporations, government agencies, schools and universities, and even financial institutions over the last 50 years to reshape the West in what can be called "the stealth jihad." It is obviously behind the Palestinian agenda as well.

Appeasement shows weakness and even desperation, which is exactly what we are seeing all over the world when it comes to everything people do to avoid offending Muslims. We can have no mention of Jesus in American public schools, no wearing of *kippot* (Jewish skullcap) in French public schools, and we are told we must take down crosses in some public places because they offend Muslims. In one case, there were so many crosses in a Catholic (that's right, Catholic!) University that a complaint was filed by Muslim students who said they were uncomfortable praying there.[7] This is a Catholic school, for goodness's sake. What do they expect? Why can't they choose to pray in a room without crosses, or some other place?

This hatred against the Christian cross is becoming more widespread, especially in Europe.[8] Muslims have a great aversion for the cross, and we're expected to appease them by taking down or covering crosses. I would understand their objection if we tried to erect crosses in Muslim countries like Iran, Afghanistan, or Saudi Arabia. But in Western Europe? It is looking more and more like the Eurabia spoken of by Bat Ye'or in her 2005 book *Eurabia: The Euro-Arab Axis*.

Why appease Muslims and erase the symbol of Christianity in what have traditionally been Christian countries? Keep in mind that the cross is also offensive to Jewish people because of all the carnage and persecution done in its name against the Jewish people for the last 2,000 years. But you don't see Jews suing for being offended by the cross or protesting its public display. They simply walk away or do not enter buildings with a cross—end of story!

Any type of appeasement is simply an act of postponement. In the name of tolerance, political correctness, multiculturalism, or even out of fear, appeasement is a time bomb connected to a powder keg sitting under Western civilization. We as Christians must stand firmly—in love, but firmly—on our biblical convictions.

Appeasement should make us upset and cause us to speak against it, but it shouldn't lead us to hate the people who attempt to appease. The danger is that in the process of disagreeing with appeasers, we can easily become hateful toward those whom they are trying to appease, all because we want to prove to them (the appeasers) that they are playing with fire and eventually will get burned. While it is important for us to identify the enemies—including ISIS, Al-Qaeda, Hamas, Boko Haram, Hezbollah, Iran, and others—we don't want to fall into hating those who are behind the surge of end-times antisemitism. We don't want to become to them what they have been to Israel and the Jewish people. Humanly speaking, it can be hard for us to refrain from expressing a racist and hateful kind of anger, but xenophobia can *never* be the answer.

Xenophobia

According to the Merriam-Webster dictionary, *xenophobia* is "fear and hatred of strangers or foreigners or of anything that is strange or foreign." Xenophobia includes racism, but is broader. It can be evident in our responses to cultural or religious differences and should have no place in modern society. Unfortunately, we tend to define people by our own standards based on what we believe should be the norm: ourselves! It is all too easy for us to ostracize or profile people who are different from us because of their race, creed, skin color, and other factors.

Also, tragically, incorrect interpretations of the Bible have led to much unnecessary bloodshed over the centuries. God's perfect, inerrant Word has suffered in the hands of both friends and foes who have misinterpreted it to say things that God hasn't said.

It has also been man's propensity to fight people in "the name of Jesus" in ways that are not taught by Jesus. The Jewish people know this too well! Nowhere in the New Testament do we find Jesus teaching us to kill those who refuse to follow Him. The key here is that God's Old Testament instructions to conquer land and kill people (when He didn't do it Himself) is historical, not normative. It was needed then, but not now. This is especially true in light of what He has done for the whole world through Christ's death and resurrection.

The Bible is clear. God told the children of Israel to conquer a specific region, known back then as the land of Canaan. But He gave them strict boundaries in Genesis 15:18-21—boundaries that will be fulfilled during the millennial kingdom of Yeshua and not before. In addition, God clearly instructed Israel not to take even an inch of land not prescribed. He said this with regard to the sons of Esau (Deuteronomy 2:4-5) and the Moabites (Deuteronomy 2:17-18).

Land grabs were descriptive and not prescriptive, which is the opposite of what Islam teaches.

Islam has long taught that the killing and maiming of infidels is central to the Qur'an. Not all Muslims buy into this, yet it continues to be taught by many from the Qur'an because it is normative. Who, then, is genocidal? Certainly not Israel!

This is probably the most important difference we need to grasp between the Bible and the Qur'an, outside of the fact only the Bible is the inspired Word of God. I say this not to foment hatred against Muslims, but to affirm truth and provide a simple reality check. Radical Islam is a root of antisemitic hatred. Yet we cannot succumb to xenophobia. While we can all differ on ideologies, it is never appropriate to hate people for any reason. Yet radical Muslims do not hesitate to do so.

What kind of message is radical Islam sending to the world when it says those who do not bend to sharia[9] will be killed? A recent detailed Pew Research Center[10] survey shows that the desire for sharia is much more prevalent among Muslims than one might expect.

Sharia law is based on the teachings of Islam's most holy book, the Qur'an. Sharia is, by definition, an inflexible ideology because it teaches the ideal of excluding all people who do not comply with the Qur'an. It is critical that the rest of the civilized world not fall into doing what the Islamists are. But how do you interact with a group that worships death and martyrdom when you adhere to values like freedom, dignity, and the sanctity of life? Is it even possible?

Sharia is bad news for anyone who is not a Muslim. Women have no rights, homosexuals get killed, and Christians cannot freely worship, while Muslims are always free to build mosques and worship Allah anywhere in the world. This is what Qur'anic Islam looks like—it's the brand of Islam that abides by the teachings of the Qur'an. Qur'anic Islam is radical, exclusive, and lethal to infidels.

We must differentiate between those who blindly and indiscriminately behead, burn, or crucify "infidels" and those who want to be part of Islam without its bloody, radical ideology. This has nothing to do with xenophobia because the civilized world is at war against Islamic radicalism, not Islam as a whole.[11] War is unfortunate, but it is war, and it always includes casualties. When war occurs, our distinguishing between sharia proponents and more nominal or cultural Muslims will help to reduce the number of casualties and collateral damage. And anyone who still believes that we are not at war against radical or Qur'anic Islam and that the world can become a better place through appeasement should be ready to submit to Islam and become a twenty-first century *dhimmi*.[12]

RESPONSES THAT ARE HELPFUL AND EFFECTIVE

Go on a Fact-Finding Mission

While I understand that not all my readers will agree with me theologically with regard to eschatology, we can all agree that we are seeing an increase in antisemitism that shows no sign of stopping.

Our fight is not over, and it will not be easy. The foundation to an effective fight about anything is to be armed with factual truth. There are past historical truths as well as contemporary truths about the events happening around us today.

With the advent of the internet, anybody can claim to be an expert or a scholar. That's why it is vital that we make sure the "facts" we read are actual facts and not fabrications. Within cyberspace, there are many websites that can be trusted to deliver factual truth, sometimes with a slant due to a political agenda, and other times in a more nonpartisan way.

When you search for factual truth, it is always good to look at as many sources as possible. Looking at several perspectives is helpful, and reading printed books written and published by reliable sources is also recommended.

But there is a catch. Going on a fact-finding mission will require a tremendous amount of time, patience, and discernment. This is what keeps most people from making the effort. This is also why I wrote this book: to bring together in one volume all that a reader needs on this topic. The endnotes that I included in this book will help you to do further research for the purpose of knowing how to factually defend Israel and the Jewish people against any kind of antisemitism. I have given you a start with this book, but it is up to you to look further.

In addition, at my website at shalominmessiah.com, you will find a list of additional helpful resources. This list is regularly updated.

Become an Advocate for Israel

An expected result of equipping yourself with factual truth about Israel and the Jewish people is that you will develop a deeper appreciation for the people, their customs, and their land. You will eventually become an advocate for Israel. Let me clarify at this point that being a Zionist, an advocate for Israel, or a philosemite (respecter and lover of the Jewish people), doesn't mean that you have contempt for Arabs or Palestinians. Being pro-Israel doesn't mean that one is anti-Palestinian. Sadly, the opposite is seldom true.

When you are equipped with factual truth, you are able to dialogue with those who hold a different view of Israel and the Jewish people. You have arguments and data that can help vindicate your bold position of support.

As you become an advocate for Israel, you should consider visiting the only democracy in today's oppressed Middle East. One of the best ways to show your support for Israel is by having your feet on the ground there. Take a tour to discover the geography, history, and archaeology of the land. Many tours also offer humanitarian options for visitors to get involved with local organizations and bless Israelis. Such help has been needed for decades, but since the terrorist attack of October 7, 2023, it is needed more than ever.

Boycott BDS

There is absolutely nothing wrong with the concept of boycotting anything. This is a valid, nonviolent way to express one's opinion and position against a person, product, organization, policy, or country.

For instance, a movie about Jesus came out in 1988. It bothered me, to the point that I thought it was extremely blasphemous. Even though it was directed by one of my favorite directors, I chose to boycott his subsequent films, including those I knew to be masterpieces of cinematography.

Now, the most important part of boycotting is consistency. Boycotts can quickly become inconvenient, but if you follow your convictions, you will be able to stay strong. Integrity is foundational to a proper boycott. As we saw earlier, proponents of BDS are sometimes inconsistent in their efforts.

As a friend of Israel and the Jewish people, you can boycott the boycotters. Why not find out who is behind the boycott of Israel, and turn around and boycott them? Beat them at their own game.

A partial list of who is boycotting Israel[13] can be helpful to see who you want to boycott. However, before you commit, make sure you can be consistent. You might be surprised about what you find out when you choose to boycott the boycotters!

Buying Israeli products made in Israel or produced by companies with offices in Israel is a tangible way to show your support for the nation and contribute to the economy. Do your research and check the labels. You can also use lists created by BDS boycotters and do the opposite of what they are doing by *supporting* those companies and products.[14]

Expose Those Who Demonize the Jews

Another way to support Israel and the Jewish people is to expose those who demonize the Jews. We need to be bold enough to expose the lies and liars—whether to those in our immediate circle of influence, our social media posts, our friends, fellow churchgoers, community, local government officials, or the media. When you become aware of an anti-Israel, anti-Zionist, or pro-Palestinian event, make sure you share with others about the real motives behind these gatherings.

If you see individuals or groups engaging in antisemitic speech or actions, you can report such activity to the local authorities, who, by law, have to treat these as hate crimes and prosecute the perpetrators to the fullest extent possible. At the same time, you should also go to the press or media if you feel that what you have witnessed needs further exposure.

Be aware that oftentimes, local authorities and the media are less than enthusiastic about helping deal with or covering antisemitic incidents. So do not get discouraged, because that is exactly what Satan wants. He wants us to feel helpless, give up, and become silent bystanders. We cannot afford to let that happen. As long as we as Americans still have the freedoms that our forefathers fought so hard for, we must expose the antisemites around us.

Reach Out to Your Jewish Community

As Jewish people around the world continue to face rising antisemitism, it is vital that we reach out and help our respective Jewish communities. For evangelical Christians to do this can help set the record straight that not all Christians are antisemitic, which is an ingrained Jewish oversimplification that, unfortunately, is based on 2,000 years of real Christian antisemitism.

As you are made aware of news about your local Jewish community—especially when vandalism occurs at a synagogue or Jewish community center or private residence—reach out. It is definitely appropriate for us to call as concerned citizens and local neighbors. Be sure to let the Jewish people you connect with know that you are a Christian, and as such, you love Israel and the Jewish people. Let them know that you want to do whatever you can to help.

You can call, email, send cards, or even pay a visit to a synagogue or Jewish community center to express your love, concern, and availability to help in any way needed. It is possible that your offer to help will be turned down, and if so, that is perfectly fine. Just remember that no matter what the outcome, your kind intention will not go unnoticed.

If you pastor a church, you can also become a part of our No Synagogue Left Behind grassroots movement. Many evangelical churches have heightened security during services, usually on Sunday mornings. You can call your local rabbi and offer to meet for coffee, then offer the Jewish congregation free security during Shabbat services on Friday nights or Saturday mornings when Christians don't meet for church. This kind of support will go a long way toward rebuilding the bridge between Jews and Christians that has been destroyed by 2,000 years of Christian antisemitism.

For a list of helpful ways to minister to a synagogue or Jewish people, please visit us at resources.shalominmessiah.com. The list is regularly updated.

CHAPTER 13

WHY WE SHOULD FIGHT END-TIMES ANTISEMITISM

As Christians, it is our responsibility to denounce antisemitism and fight it in any way we can. We are to love our neighbors and stand hand in hand against any injustice committed against them. We might run into government or bureaucratic deadlocks, but we cannot stop trying—especially at this time in our history, when things are heating up for the Jewish people and for Israel. End-times antisemitism is Satan's latest iteration of his hateful agenda against the Jews, and because time is short for him, he is going full force.

HUMAN DECENCY ALWAYS WINS

Human decency isn't the norm in a world where, early on, we are taught to fend for ourselves and not worry about the fate of others. Despite society's prevailing opposition to Judeo-Christian biblical morality, we live in a world with God-given moral absolutes. As much as a new generation of postmodern thinkers and leaders want to make us believe that there are no moral absolutes, we know deep down that isn't true. Our consciences tell us what is right and wrong, even when our culture denies such.

Human decency always wins even though it might not make you the most popular person in the eyes of some. By human decency, I do not mean the blind tolerance that has been displayed by many in the hopes of a better world in which multiculturalism can somehow thrive. Tolerance is a wonderful virtue, but it must be established on a firm foundation of moral values. Otherwise, it becomes an invitation for people to do whatever they want in the name of what they believe is right for them.

Morality will always lead to moral decency, which should be our goal as a human race. Simply put, the golden rule and reverence for God, or one's ability to grasp the absolute goodness and righteousness of God, are foundational to civilization. Isn't it part of our biblical mandate to reach out to those who don't know Yeshua and show them His love? Some call it a higher purpose. Allow me to elaborate.

OUR ULTIMATE MODEL OF LOVE IS YESHUA THE MESSIAH

Biblically speaking, followers of Yeshua have an obligation to bless Israel and the Jewish people. We have a beneficial vested interest in doing this.

First Peter 2:21 guides us toward that, saying, "You have been called for this purpose, since Christ also suffered for you, leaving you an example for you to follow in His steps."

Yeshua loved unconditionally, and so should we. Don't attach conditions to whatever you can say or do to encourage or help others, and don't expect anything in return.

Yeshua loved us sacrificially and died for us: "God demonstrates His own love toward us, in that while we were yet sinners, Christ died for us" (Romans 5:8; see also 1 John 3:1, 16). Yeshua is God and God is love: "The one who does not love does not know God, for God is love" (1 John 4:8).

Based on God's promise in Genesis 12:3—in which God said He would bless those who bless Abraham's descendants—loving Israel and the Jewish people is the biblical thing for us to do as Christians.

The state of our own relationship with God will have an effect on how we respond to Genesis 12:3. It is my conviction that not only is a proper relationship with the living God critical to our future, it also leads us to love the Jewish people.

What's more, when believers understand and honor God's relationship to the Jewish people, they will come to better understand Yeshua Himself, who took on human form, as a Jewish man, to bring salvation to the world.

How is it possible to hate the Jews when one claims to be a Christian, a disciple of Yeshua, who is our Jewish Messiah? While some people might become children of God (John 1:12) yet still hold resentment against the Jews based on their human nature and upbringing, God can and will perform a change of heart in those who desire to be in His will. This kind of transformation is real and life-changing.

Having an eternal relationship with the God of Abraham, Isaac, and Jacob is not only the key to real peace, it is also the only real hope for the world, no matter what a person's background or birthright. A personal relationship with the God of Abraham, Isaac, and Jacob is available to all who desire it. The Bible clearly states that God is patient and does not want any soul to perish (2 Peter 3:9).

If you are not yet a Christian, you need to understand that the way to the Almighty, while simple, requires you to assess yourself and recognize your shortcomings. Simply put, every person needs salvation, and the Hebrew Scriptures tell us what we need to know about our need for a redeemer, and God's solution for meeting that need. To find out more, see the appendix.

NOW WHAT?

When I started conducting my research for my first book on the new antisemitism in 1999, little did I know that antisemitism would grow so quickly in frequency and intensity on such a global scale.

I watched as the oldest hatred—which was racially motivated—morphed into a quest for social justice, a quest driven by the Palestinian narrative. At the time, only 25 years ago, the Palestinian cause was picking up steam, but it was still questioned by many, especially within evangelical Christian circles.

As all this happened, evangelicals were either positioning or repositioning themselves on the broad spectrum that runs from unconditional support of Israel and philosemitism (brotherly love of the Jewish people) to replacement theology and even antisemitism. Christians have become increasingly polarized at opposite ends of the spectrum.

At the same time, the Jewish people are being ostracized and demonized more and more by "Christian Zionists" who have been converted to Christian Palestinianism. Biblical facts are no longer a factor in the neo-Christian assessment of Israel and the Jewish people's place in God's plan.

It is such a shame that we are fighting about Israel within the body of Messiah. In a sense, Satan has us exactly where he wants us. He is pleased that we are arguing about Israel's claim to self-determination and refraining from telling Jewish people about the Jewish Messiah, His coming kingdom, and how to get in.

It gets much worse when you venture outside of the evangelical community to see how Israel and the Jewish people are regarded by the rest of the world. The media, the entertainment industry, the New Left, the Old Right, and apocalyptic Islam are joining forces in an eerie affirmation of the adage "The enemy of my enemy is my friend."

As happened during the Holocaust era of the 1930s and 1940s, we are seeing antisemitism become more normalized everywhere. With that in mind, I hope that Messianic Jews like me and Jews who do not believe on Yeshua as the Messiah of Israel can agree on one thing: No matter what our level of religiosity, our degree of Jewish ethnicity, or our support of Israel, as Jews, we are all prospective victims of antisemitism. This is becoming even more of a reality under the threat of end-times antisemitism.

We as Jews might be divided by our allegiance to Yeshua or lack of, but we cannot be divided about the need to oppose the evil of antisemitism. For this, we must stand together.

For the most part, the rest of the world continues to be in denial about our fate as a global village. But today, the radical elements seeking to destroy the Jewish people will stop at nothing, including the complete destruction of Israel. Israel remains, in Islamist theology, "the Little Satan" to be eradicated before "the Great Satan" (America); and other groups have been willingly or blindly co-opted as unlikely supporters of that agenda.

End-times antisemitism is here to stay. It is very damaging, and I am afraid that we haven't seen the worst yet. It will eventually be superseded by one more iteration of the oldest hatred before the return of Yeshua the Messiah, and that is tribulation antisemitism.

As a result of the rise in antisemitism, we have seen many Western European Jews leaving for Israel in unprecedented numbers. If Bible-believing disciples of Yeshua the Messiah would take a stand against this antisemitism and tangibly support Israel and the Jewish people, that would help this rise to be less damaging to my people.

As much as Satan tries to eliminate the Jewish people, they will never cease to be the chosen people of God. It is time, though, for many Christians to take their Bible more seriously and be more active for the winning team. The Jews are going back to Eretz Yisrael in a fulfillment of prophecy happening in real time in front of our very eyes, just as Ezekiel predicted, for their final regathering:

> Therefore say to the house of Israel, "Thus says the Lord God, 'It is not for your sake, O house of Israel, that I am about to act, but for My holy name, which you have profaned among the nations where you went. I will vindicate the holiness of My great name which has been profaned among the nations, which you have profaned in their midst. Then the nations will know that I am the LORD,' declares the Lord God, 'when I prove Myself holy among you in their sight. For I will take you from the nations, gather you from all the lands and bring you into your own land. Then I will sprinkle clean water on you, and you will be clean; I will cleanse you from all your filthiness and from all your idols. Moreover, I will give you a new heart and put a new spirit within you; and I will remove the heart of stone from your flesh and give you a heart of flesh. I will put My Spirit within you and cause you to walk in My statutes, and you will be careful to observe My ordinances. You will live in the land that I gave to your forefathers; so you will be My people, and I will be your God'" (Ezekiel 36:22-28).

Satan's newest war is raging, and the Jews are again in grave danger for their lives. According to an Anti-Defamation League Global 100 survey, "2.02 billion people in the world harbor anti-Semitic attitudes."[1] Nevertheless, God remains faithful. Just as Satan has used many people, groups, organizations, and even countries to fulfill his nefarious agenda, God can use *you* to spread His love and light and to be a part of the final chapter about the Jews. The time is now, as the clock is ticking, and as things are getting much worse for the global Jewish village.

AND THEN THERE WAS OCTOBER 7, 2023!

As we are inching closer to the tribulation and return of Yeshua, things are becoming increasingly shaky for Jewish people worldwide. This is what prompted me in 2019 to start a network of like-minded believers who are willing to open their homes to rescue and shelter Jews in case of need.[2]

Then came October 7, 2023. Hamas terrorists and Palestinian civilians invaded southern Israel from the Gaza Strip and brutally murdered 1,200 innocent people. Jewish people have always been careful not to compare any historical event to the Holocaust, but October 7 has been described as Holocaust 2.0, with good reason. It saw the largest killing of Jews in one day since the Holocaust.

October 7 changed everything. Antisemitism is out of the box for good. It is almost as if it has now become trendy to be against Israel. We've witnessed this on university campuses, in the media, in politics, through organizations like BDS, and more. At a time when the world should come to the rescue of Israel, it has turned its back on the Jewish state.

As it pertains to the Jewish people and Israel, today's society has reached the point of no return. Antisemitism will continue to worsen until Yeshua returns and inaugurates His 1,000-year kingdom. Yet now is not the time to throw in the towel.

The battle is real, and it is against Satan, his posse, and the people and groups he has subcontracted his hatred to. As believers, we are on God's side as long as we come to the rescue of Israel and the Jewish people. This is a very basic but profound understanding of Genesis 12:3, which says, "I will bless those who bless you, and the one who curses you I will curse."

As Christians, we cannot afford to be silenced. We must speak up anytime we have the chance to. And we need to commit to more than words and prayers; now is the time for action. If not now, when? And if not us, who?

With us or without us, God's plan will come to fruition, and the Jewish people will play a key role in the final chapter of mankind. As those who are on God's team, we should desire to be actively on the side of God's chosen people all the way to the end, looking forward to the day when all things will be reversed for the Jews, as promised by the prophet Zechariah:

> Thus says the LORD of hosts, "In those days ten men from all the nations will grasp the garment of a Jew, saying, 'Let us go with you, for we have heard that God is with you'" (Zechariah 8:23).

APPENDIX

OUR ONLY HOPE OF SALVATION IS YESHUA THE MESSIAH

God loves mankind and wants to bless all. It is not and never was God's intention for us to be separated from Him. God is a God of relationships, and He wants nothing more than to enjoy this relationship with His creation:

> You will make known to me the path of life; in Your presence is fullness of joy; in Your right hand there are pleasures forever (Psalm 16:11).

> How precious is Your lovingkindness, O God! And the children of men take refuge in the shadow of Your wings. They drink their fill of the abundance of Your house; and You give them to drink of the river of Your delights. For with You is the fountain of life; in Your light we see light.
>
> O continue Your lovingkindness to those who know You, and Your righteousness to the upright in heart (Psalm 36:7-10).

However, mankind is separated from God because of sin, which results in spiritual death—and later, physical death.

> From the tree of the knowledge of good and evil you shall not eat, for in the day that you eat from it you shall surely die (Genesis 2:17).

Despite this separation, God still desires to have a relationship with man. Being the perfect and just God that He is, He is separated from us by our sin. And humanly speaking, the chasm is insurmountable.

The Bible makes clear the fact our sin nature—which is the result of Adam and Eve's sin in the garden—has separated us from a relationship with God. The Bible also explains the punishment for our sins—that is, our trespasses. This punishment is the same for all, Jews and Gentiles alike, if they remain separated from God:

> Indeed, there is not a righteous man on earth who continually does good and who never sins (Ecclesiastes 7:20).

> The heart is more deceitful than all else and is desperately sick; who can understand it? (Jeremiah 17:9).

> All of us have become like one who is unclean, and all our righteous deeds are like a filthy garment; and all of us wither like a leaf, and our iniquities, like the wind, take us away (Isaiah 64:6).

> Behold, all souls are Mine; the soul of the father as well as the soul of the son is Mine, The soul who sins will die (Ezekiel 18:4).

> Everyone will die for his own iniquity; each man who eats the sour grapes, his teeth will be set on edge (Jeremiah 31:30).

> Your iniquities have made a separation between you and your God, And your sins have hidden His face from you so, that He does not hear (Isaiah 59:2).

THERE IS NOTHING MAN CAN DO HIMSELF TO BE RECONCILED TO GOD

The Bible is very clear on this point as well; there is nothing we can do to save ourselves. And there is nothing that any man can do for us to reconcile us to God.

> "Although you wash yourself with lye and use much soap, the stain of your iniquity is before Me," declares the Lord God (Jeremiah 2:22).

> No man can by any means redeem his brother, or give to God a ransom for him (Psalm 49:7).

But do not be discouraged. Because God loves us, He provided us with a solution to a humanly unsolvable problem. God sent Yeshua the Messiah to be the ultimate sacrifice for our sins. Messiah, whom the Scriptures teach is God, died on our behalf and atoned for our sins.

We should pay special attention to the following words from the prophet Isaiah who predicted the humiliation, suffering, death by crucifixion, resurrection, and exaltation of the Messiah in Isaiah 52:13 through 53:12. Following is a part of that section of the Hebrew Scriptures, along with two other passages:

> He was despised and forsaken of men,
> a man of sorrows and acquainted with grief;
> and like one from whom men hide their face,
> He was despised, and we did not esteem Him.

Surely our griefs He Himself bore,
and our sorrows He carried;
yet we ourselves esteemed Him stricken,
smitten of God, and afflicted.
But He was pierced through for our transgressions,
He was crushed for our iniquities;
the chastening for our well-being fell upon Him,
and by His scourging we are healed.
All of us like sheep have gone astray,
each of us has turned to his own way;
but the LORD has caused the iniquity of us all
to fall on Him.

He was oppressed and He was afflicted,
yet He did not open His mouth;
like a lamb that is led to slaughter,
and like a sheep that is silent before its shearers,
so He did not open His mouth.
By oppression and judgment He was taken away;
and as for His generation, who considered
that He was cut off out of the land of the living
for the transgression of my people, to whom the stroke
was due?
His grave was assigned with wicked men,
yet He was with a rich man in His death,
because He had done no violence,
nor was there any deceit in His mouth.

But the LORD was pleased
to crush Him, putting Him to grief;
if He would render Himself as a guilt offering,
He will see His offspring,

> He will prolong His days,
> and the good pleasure of the Lord will prosper in His hand.
> As a result of the anguish of His soul,
> He will see it and be satisfied;
> by His knowledge the Righteous One,
> My Servant, will justify the many,
> as He will bear their iniquities.
> Therefore, I will allot Him a portion with the great,
> and He will divide the booty with the strong;
> because He poured out Himself to death,
> and was numbered with the transgressors;
> yet He Himself bore the sin of many,
> and interceded for the transgressors (Isaiah 53:2-13).

> The life of the flesh is in the blood, and I have given it to you on the altar to make atonement for your souls; for it is the blood by reason of the life that makes atonement (Leviticus 17:11).

> I, even I, am the Lord,
> and there is no savior besides Me (Isaiah 43:11).

YESHUA'S ATONING DEATH FOR OUR SINS GIVES US SALVATION

The problem barrier that sin created between God and us has been knocked down by Messiah's selfless sacrifice on our behalf. It is our choice to accept this free gift by faith.

> He believed in the Lord; and He reckoned it to him as righteousness (Genesis 15:6).

> Behold, as for the proud one,
> his soul is not right within him;
> but the righteous will live by his faith (Habakkuk 2:4).

Only by repenting of our sins and accepting Yeshua's death on our behalf can we be saved and reconciled to God.

The solution is here and readily available for those who desire an eternal relationship with God. Only by repentance, as we voluntarily admit and turn away from our sins, can we be saved. Our faith, and only our faith in the atoning death of Yeshua the Messiah, can reconcile us to God. Yeshua bridged the gap between God and us. Our faith is our response to His gift, which is salvation for those who put their trust in Him.

> How blessed is he whose transgression is forgiven,
> whose sin is covered!
> How blessed is the man to whom the Lord does not impute iniquity,
> and in whose spirit there is no deceit!
>
> When I kept silent about my sin, my body wasted away
> through my groaning all day long.
> For day and night Your hand was heavy upon me;
> my vitality was drained away as with the fever heat of summer.
> I acknowledged my sin to You,
> and my iniquity I did not hide;
> I said, "I will confess my transgressions to the Lord";
> and You forgave the guilt of my sin (Psalm 32:1-5).
>
> He who conceals his transgressions will not prosper, but he who confesses and forsakes them will find compassion (Proverbs 28:13).

Contrary to all man-made religions, our biblical faith in God is rather simple. We realize nothing we can do will reconcile us to God except to believe by faith in the atoning death of Yeshua the Messiah.

DO YOU WANT TO BECOME A CHILD OF GOD?

If you do not currently have this relationship with the living God and desire to establish it, you are only a prayer away from becoming a child of God. Just as you are right now, wherever you may be, whatever your identity, you can stop for a moment and invite God into your heart. He is waiting! Why don't you pray right now to invite Him to be the Lord of your life and change you into a new person?

> *Dear God, I agree that I am a sinner, and that I fall short. I desire a relationship with You, but cannot do it on my own. I thank You for sending Yeshua the Messiah to die for me, and I accept His death as my atonement. By faith, I invite You into my heart, and ask You to be my Lord and Redeemer.*

YOU'RE IN!

Congratulations! If you just prayed this prayer from the bottom of your heart, you are now a child of God and can have the eternal assurance of your salvation. Nothing and nobody can ever snatch you away from His loving embrace. Accepting God's free gift of salvation is the most important decision of a lifetime. If you have accepted this gift, go tell someone, and find a good Bible-teaching church!

NOTES

LOOKING FOR ANSWERS: WHY IS HATRED GROWING?

1. Mark Hitchcock, *The End: A Complete Overview of Bible Prophecy and the End of Days* (Carol Stream, IL: Tyndale House, 2012), 300.
2. According to *Britannica*, "eugenics is the selection of desired heritable characteristics in order to improve future generations, typically in reference to humans." See at https://www.britannica.com/science/eugenics-genetics. Accessed March 8, 2025.
3. Antisemitic cartoons have flooded magazines, books, and the internet, and continue to do so on various platforms. Ian Black, "Cartoon symbols of the Israeli-Palestinian conflict," *The Guardian*, December 19, 2008, https://www.theguardian.com/world/2008/dec/18/israelandthepalestinians-pressandpublishing. See also "Antisemitism Policy Trust," https://antisemitism.org.uk/wp-content/uploads/2020/07/Antisemitic-imagery-May-2020.pdf. Accessed March 8, 2025.
4. "Queers for Palestine," Instagram, https://www.instagram.com/queers.for.palestine/?hl=en. Accessed March 8, 2025.

PART I: A SURVEY OF DEFINITIONS, FACTS, AND MYTHS

CHAPTER 1—TOWARD A CLEAR UNDERSTANDING OF ANTISEMITISM

1. Olivier J. Melnick, *They Have Conspired Against You: Responding to the New Anti-Semitism* (Huntington Beach, CA; JHousePublishing, Purple Raiment, 2007), 9.
2. Yeshua is the transliteration of the Hebrew word ישוע, which means salvation. It is Jesus' name in Hebrew.
3. Richard S. Levy, ed., *Antisemitism: A Historical Encyclopedia of Prejudice and Persecution* (Santa Barbara, CA: ABC Clio, 2005), 24-25.

4. "Wilhelm Marr," *Jewish Virtual Library*, https://www.jewishvirtuallibrary.org/wilhelm-marr. Accessed March 8, 2025.
5. Wilhelm Marr, *The Victory of the Jewish Spirit over the Germanic Spirit: Observed from a non-religious perspective,* a political tract translated by Gerhard Rohringer, 2009, 13; now available online at https://www.theoccidentalobserver.net/2010/01/06/wilhelm-marr%e2%80%99s-the-victory-of-judaism-over-germanism-viewed-from-a-nonreligious-point-of-view/.
6. Marr, *The Victory of the Jewish Spirit*, 19.
7. Wilhelm Marr, *The Way to Victory of Germanicism over Judaism, 1879,* a political tract discussed on Coordination Forum for Countering Anti-Semitism (CFCA), https://archive.org/details/marr-wilhelm-the-victory-of-judaism-over-germanism_202312/page/9/mode/2up. Accessed March 17, 2025.
8. Much of the content written here about Wilhelm Marr is from an article I wrote that appeared in *The Times of Israel*, June 15, 2016.
9. Edward Flannery, *The Anguish of the Jews* (Mahwah, NJ: Paulist Press, 1985), 33.
10. Dan Cohn-Sherbok, *The Crucified Jew* (New York: HarperCollins, 1992), xi.
11. Benjamin Netanyahu, "Millions of Children Are Taught that Jews Are Apes and Pigs," *The Jerusalem Post,* updated May 23, 2016, https://www.jpost.com/annual-conference/netanyahu-at-jpost-conference-pa-inciting-to-kill-jews-454669. Accessed March 8, 2025.
12. Adolf Hitler, *Mein Kampf*, trans. James Murphy, https://greatwar.nl/books/meinkampf/meinkampf.pdf. PDF file. Accessed August 22, 2024.
13. Arnold G. Fruchtenbaum, *The Remnant of Israel: The History, Theology and Philosophy of the Messianic Jewish Community* (San Antonio, TX: Ariel Press, 2011), 1-20.
14. Fruchtenbaum, *The Remnant of Israel*, 8.
15. Olivier J. Melnick, *They Have Conspired Against You: Responding to the New Anti-Semitism* (Huntington Beach, CA: JHousePublishing, 2007), 58-64.
16. For further study on Israel's right to the land, the boundaries, and the eternal and unconditional Abrahamic covenant, I recommend reading the following Scripture passages: Genesis 12:1-7; 17:7-8, 19; 25:5-6; 28:3-4; 35:9-15; Exodus 2:24; 3:8; Deuteronomy 1:8; 3:27-28; Leviticus 26:44-45; Ezekiel 37:11-12; Jeremiah 31:31-34. The following books also provide good insight: David Hocking, *What the Bible Says About Israel and Its Land* (Orange, CA: Promise Publications, 1983); J. Dwight Pentecost, *Things to Come: A Study in Biblical Eschatology* (Grand Rapids, MI: Zondervan, 1958), 65-94; Arnold G. Fruchtenbaum, *Israelology: The Missing Link in Systematic Theology* (San Antonio, TX: Ariel Press, 1989).

CHAPTER 2—FACTS AND MYTHS ABOUT THE PALESTINIANS, ZIONISM, AND THE ISRAELI HOMELAND

1. "Ancient Jewish History: The Bar-Kokhba Revolt," *Jewish Virtual Library*, https://www.jewishvirtuallibrary.org/the-bar-kokhba-revolt-132-135-ce. Accessed March 8, 2025.
2. "British Palestine Mandate: Text of the Mandate," *Jewish Virtual Library*, https://www.jewishvirtuallibrary.org/text-of-the-british-mandate-for-palestine. Accessed March 8, 2025.
3. "British Palestine Mandate: Text of the Mandate," *Jewish Virtual Library.*
4. Mitchell Bard, *Myths and Facts: A Guide to the Arab-Israeli Conflict* (Chevy Chase, MD: American-Israeli Cooperative Enterprise, 2001), 26.

5. Daniel Pipes, "Claiming Jerusalem is in the Koran," *Middle East Forum*, February 29, 2012, https://www.danielpipes.org/blog/2012/02/claiming-jerusalem-is-in-the-koran. Accessed March 8, 2025.
6. Bard, *Myths and Facts: A Guide to the Arab-Israeli Conflict*, 44-45.
7. Ernst Pawel, *The Labyrinth of Exile: A Life of Theodor Herzl* (New York: Farrar, Strauss & Giroux, 1989), 271.
8. "Zionism: A Definition of Zionism," *Jewish Virtual Library*, https://www.jewishvirtuallibrary.org/a-definition-of-zionism. Accessed March 8, 2025.
9. Blood libel can be broadly defined as an accusation that Jews kidnapped and murdered the children of Christians to use their blood as part of their religious rituals during Jewish holidays. More than 150 claims of blood libel were recorded throughout history resulting in the deaths of many Jewish people, mostly during the Middle Ages. More on blood libel can be read in Joshua Trachtenberg's book *The Devil and the Jews, The Medieval Conception of the Jew and Its Relation to Modern Antisemitism* (New Haven, CT: Yale University Press, 1983), 140-155.
10. "Texts Concerning Zionism: Excerpts from 'The Jewish State,'" *Jewish Virtual Library*, https://www.jewishvirtuallibrary.org/excerpts-from-quot-the-jewish-state-quot. Accessed March 8, 2025.
11. Theodor Herzl, as cited in Howard M. Sachar, *A History of Israel from Zionism to Our Time* (New York: Knopf, 1996), 40.
12. Ernst Pawel, *The Labyrinth of Exile: A Life of Theodor Herzl* (New York: Farrar, Strauss & Giroux, 1989), 3.
13. "Zionist Congress: First Zionist Congress & Basel Program," *Jewish Virtual Library*, https://www.jewishvirtuallibrary.org/first-zionist-congress-and-basel-program-1897. Accessed March 8, 2025.
14. Abba Eban, *My People: The Story of the Jews* (New York: Random House, 1968), 335-337.
15. *Aliyah* is Hebrew for "ascent." It is used to describe the specific move that a Jewish person makes to the pulpit (*bema*) where the Torah is opened for Shabbat reading in a synagogue. It is also used to describe the process of immigration to Israel from the worldwide dispersion (Diaspora). It describes the various waves of immigration that officially started in 1882. For more details, see "Jewish Immigration to Historical Palestine," *CJPME*, www.cjpme.org/fs_181. In modern times, "making Aliyah" refers to Jews moving to Israel under the law of return.
16. Ahad Ha'am, "Texts Concerning Zionism: 'The Jewish State and Jewish Problem,'" *Jewish Virtual Library*, https://www.jewishvirtuallibrary.org/quot-the-jewish-state-and-jewish-problem-quot-ahad-ha-am. Accessed March 8, 2025.
17. Abram Leon Sachar, *A History of the Jews* (New York: Knopf, 1965), 360-361.
18. The First Aliyah of 1881–1903 was one of several consecutive mass returns of Jews in the late nineteenth and early twentieth centuries, usually due to persecution. It took place as a result of the intense Eastern European pogroms. The Second Aliyah of 1904–1914 was a result of the Kishniev pogrom. Both mostly consisted of Orthodox Jews, including those in the Second Aliyah who started the kibbutz movement.
19. Hebrew has continued to exist as an ancient, written language, pure in form and applied to the accurate preservation of the Jewish Scriptures. However, Hebrew as a spoken, conversational language was no longer practical in modern times. Ben-Yehuda's contribution was to revitalize Hebrew with written and spoken expression, bringing it into common usage. Traditional Hebrew was not replaced or changed. Ben-Yehuda believed that having a common

tongue would prove to be a unifying factor in bringing together the great diversity of Jewish people dispersed throughout the nations.

20. Robert St. John, *Tongue of the Prophets* (North Hollywood, CA: Wilshire Book, 1952), 266.
21. Eban, *My People: The Story of the Jews*, 341.
22. Eban, *My People: The Story of the Jews*, 357.
23. M.E. Yapp, *The Making of the Modern Near East 1792–1923* (Harlow, UK: Longman, 1987), 290.
24. Said Edward, *Question of Palestine* (Vintage Books Edition, 1992), 16.
25. Eban, *My People: The Story of the Jews*, 359.
26. Lucy S. Dawidowicz, *The War Against the Jews: 1933–1945* (New York: Holt, Rinehart and Winston, 1975).
27. *Yeshua* is the Hebrew name for Jesus. It means "salvation."
28. Abba Eban, "Zionism and the U.N.," *The New York Times*, November 3, 1975, https://www.nytimes.com/1975/11/03/archives/zionism-and-the-un.html. Accessed March 8, 2025.

PART 2: A TIMELINE OF HATRED

CHAPTER 3—ANTISEMITISM FROM THE CHURCH FATHERS TO THE EARLY MIDDLE AGES

1. For additional study in the field of eschatology, please refer to the following resources: J. Dwight Pentecost, *Things to Come* (Grand Rapids, MI: Zondervan, 1958); Mark Hitchcock, *The End* (Carol Stream, IL: Tyndale, 2012); and Arnold G. Fruchtenbaum, *Footsteps of the Messiah* (San Antonio, TX: Ariel Press, 1982).
2. *Exegesis* refers to the explanation or interpretation of a text.
3. Replacement theology teaches that all the blessings promised by God to Israel (Abraham, Isaac, Jacob, his 12 sons and their descendants) have been transferred to the church because of Israel's constant disobedience against God. It is also known as supersessionism.
4. "Epistle to the Magnesians," chapter 6, *Apostolic Fathers*, 99, as quoted by Edward Flannery, *The Anguish of the Jews* (Mahwah, NJ: Paulist Press, 1985), 303.
5. David P. Efroymson, *Tertullian's Anti-Judaism and Its Role in His Theology* (Ann Arbor, MI: University Microfilms International, 1980), 226.
6. "Contra Celsus," *New Advent*, Book IV, Chapter 22, https://www.newadvent.org/fathers/04164.htm. Accessed March 18, 2025.
7. John Chrysostom, *Against the Jews,* excerpts from Homilies 1-5, https://www.tertullian.org/fathers/index.htm#Chrysostom_Against_the_Jews. Accessed March 8, 2025.
8. Augustine, "A Sermon on Catechumens on the Creed," *New Advent*, https://www.newadvent.org/fathers/1307.htm. Accessed March 8, 2025.
9. Theodosiani Libri XVI, https://archive.org/details/theodosianilibri02code/page/n5/mode/2up. Accessed March 8, 2025. There is also an online edition of the Codex Theodosianus at http://ancientrome.ru/ius/library/codex/theod/.
10. Codex Theodosianus, 16.9.2.
11. S. Hilarii, *Episcopi Pictaviensis Tractatus super psalmos*, https://archive.org/details/shilariiepiscopi22hilauoft/page/n15/mode/2up. Accessed March 8, 2025.

12. Jerome, *The Dialogue Against the Luciferians,* paragraph 22, *New Advent,* https://www.newadvent.org/fathers/3005.htm. Accessed March 8, 2025.
13. Edward Flannery, *The Anguish of the Jews* (Mahwah, NJ: Paulist Press, 1985), 61-62.
14. Aloysius Ziegler, *Church and State in Visigothic Spain* (Washington, DC: The Catholic University of America, 1930).
15. David Zaklikowski, "Maimonides: His Life and Works," *Chabad.org,* https://www.chabad.org/library/article_cdo/aid/75991/jewish/Maimonides-His-Life-and-Works.htm. Accessed March 8, 2025.
16. Nissan Mindel, "Who Was Rashi?," *Chabad.org,* https://www.chabad.org/library/article_cdo/aid/111831/jewish/Rabbi-Shlomo-Yitzchaki-Rashi.htm. Accessed March 8, 2025.
17. Rashi's commentaries have been included in every edition of the Talmud since 1520.

CHAPTER 4—ANTISEMITISM FROM THE CRUSADES TO THE SPANISH INQUISITION

1. "The Council of Clermont (1095)," *The Latin Library,* http://www.thelatinlibrary.com/imperialism/notes/clermont.html. Accessed March 8, 2025.
2. Guibert de Nogent, *De Vita Sua,* III, 5 (PL, 156:903).
3. A guild was an association of merchants or laborers that provided help and resources to a specific community. Guilds were an early form of workers' unions.
4. "St. William of Norwich," *Catholic Encyclopedia* (New York: Robert Appleton, 1913).
5. Ariel Toaff, *Pasqua di sangue,* https://www.scribd.com/document/600075779/Pasqua-Di-Sangue. Accessed March 8, 2025.
6. Cyrus Adler, Joseph Jacobs, "The Badge," *Jewish Encyclopedia,* https://www.jewishencyclopedia.com/articles/2317-badge. Accessed March 8, 2025.
7. *The Protocols of the Learned Elders of Zion* was a written hoax first published by Russian mystic Sergei Nilus. He claimed that the text came from the minutes from the First Zionist Congress, compiled by Jewish leaders who wanted to take over the whole world. This work first came out in 1903, and continued to be published well into the twenty-first century, even though it was officially debunked in 1920–1921.
8. "Black Death," *Britannica,* updated January 17, 2025, https://www.britannica.com/event/Black-Death/Cause-and-outbreak. Accessed March 9, 2025.
9. The first Jewish ghettos were formed in the fifteenth and sixteenth centuries. They were walled-off areas where Jews were forced to live under terrible conditions. The word came to describe the many areas of Eastern Europe where Jews were confined before they were sent to death camps.
10. *Converso,* meaning "converted," from the Latin *conversus,* "converted, turned around," and its feminine form, *conversa,* referred to Jews or Muslims or the descendants of Jews or Muslims who converted to Catholicism in Spain and Portugal, particularly during the fourteenth and fifteenth centuries. "Converso," *Encyclopedia Britannica,* https://www.britannica.com/topic/converso. Accessed March 9, 2025.

CHAPTER 5—ANTISEMITISM FROM THE REFORMATION TO THE FIRST WORLD WAR

1. Christian Hebraists were scholars interested in the original Hebrew text of Scripture and exegeting it.

2. Johannes Gutenberg had come up with the essential elements for his press by 1440, but not until the 1450s did he have a working press.
3. "Indulgences," *New Advent*, https://www.newadvent.org/cathen/07783a.htm. Accessed March 9, 2025.
4. These words from *Jesus Christ Was Born a Jew* were sourced from "Primary Texts on History of Relations," *Council of Centers on Jewish-Christian Relations*, https://ccjr.us/dialogika-resources/primary-texts-from-the-history-of-the-relationship/luther-1523, and "What Luther Thought of Jews," *Zwinglius Redivivus*, November 4, 2012, https://zwingliusredivivus.wordpress.com/2012/11/04/what-luther-thought-of-the-jews/. Accessed March 9, 2025.
5. Excerpted from Martin Luther, *On the Jews and Their Lies, Part XI*, jdstone.org, https://jdstone.org/cr/files/martin_luther/onthejewsandtheirlies11.html. Accessed March 9, 2025.
6. Gerhard Falk, *The Jew in Christian Theology: Martin Luther's Anti-Jewish* Vom Schem Hamphoras, *Previously Unpublished in English, and Other Milestones in Church Doctrine Concerning Judaism* (Jefferson, NC: McFarland, 1992).
7. Lucy Dawidowicz, as cited in *Encyclopedia Judaica*, Vol. 8 (Jerusalem: Keter Publishing, 1972), 693.
8. David Nirenberg, *Anti-Judaism: The Western Tradition* (New York: W.W. Norton, 2013), 4.
9. "Bogdan Chmielnicki," *Jewish Virtual Library*, https://www.jewishvirtuallibrary.org/chmielnicki-khmelnitski-bogdan-x00b0. Accessed March 9, 2025.
10. "Tatar," *Britannica*, https://www.britannica.com/topic/Tatar. Accessed March 9, 2025.
11. "Modern Jewish History: The Pale of Settlement," *Jewish Virtual Library*, https://www.jewishvirtuallibrary.org/the-pale-of-settlement. Accessed March 9, 2025.
12. Paul R. Mendes-Flohr and Jehuda Reinharz, eds., "The Jew in the Modern World: A Documentary History," *ldorvdor.net*, https://www.ldorvdor.net/laws.html. Accessed March 9, 2025.
13. Herman Rosenthal, "May Laws," *Jewish Encyclopedia*, https://www.jewishencyclopedia.com/articles/10508-may-laws. Accessed March 9, 2025.
14. Charles Y. Glock and Harold E. Quinley, *Anti-Semitism in America* (Chicago, IL: Transaction Publishers, 1983), 168.
15. "The International Jew: The World's Foremost Problem," *Holocaust Sources in Context*, https://perspectives.ushmm.org/item/the-international-jew-the-worlds-foremost-problem. Accessed March 9, 2025.
16. Adolf Hitler, *Mein Kampf*, trans. Ralph Mannheim (Boston, MA: Houghton Mifflin, 1943), 307-308.
17. The term *Palestine* is used here simply as a geographical description of a piece of land in the Middle East later to be known as modern Israel (1948). It does not carry the meaning that was assigned to it from the mid-1960s onward, when it became a politically charged term used to speak of Arabs who lived in the land.
18. Said Edward, *Question of Palestine* (New York: Vintage Books, 1992), 16.
19. The San Remo Conference took place in San Remo, Italy, in 1920. At that time, the region in the Middle East that is now known as Israel was split into two parts carved out of the old Ottoman province of Syria: the northern half (Syria and Lebanon) went to France, the southern half (Palestine) to Great Britain. From this point onward until 1948, the British Mandate became known as British Mandate Palestine. During that conference, the biblical land of Israel

(Palestine) was confirmed as sovereign Jewish land. See Howard Grief, *The Legal Foundation and Borders of Israel Under International Law* (Jerusalem: Mazo Publishers, 2008).

CHAPTER 6—ANTISEMITISM FROM THE HOLOCAUST ONWARD

1. Eugenics is the "applied science or the bio-social movement which advocates the use of practices aimed at improving the genetic composition of a population." "History of Eugenics," *University of Washington*, February 6, 2012, https://depts.washington.edu/prehlth/?p=1621. Accessed March 8, 2025.
2. Edward Flannery, *The Anguish of the Jews* (Mahwah, NJ: Paulist Press, 1985), 210.
3. Robert Conot, *Justice at Nuremberg* (New York: Harper and Row, 1983), 164-172.
4. Mitchell Bard, *Myths and Facts: A Guide to the Arab-Israeli Conflict* (Chevy Chase, MD: AICE Publishing, 2001), 26.
5. Bard, *Myths and Facts*.
6. Olivier J. Melnick, *They Have Conspired Against You: Responding to the New Anti-Semitism* (Huntington Beach, CA: JHousePublishing, 2007), 93-160.
7. "Contemporary Global Anti-Semitism: A Report Provided to the United States Congress," *U.S. Department of State*, March 13, 2008, https://2009-2017.state.gov/j/drl/rls/102406.htm#_Toc174854631. Accessed March 8, 2025.
8. Deborah Freund, "The Shocking Murder of Ilan Halimi," *aish*, https://aish.com/the-shocking-murder-of-ilan-halimi/. Accessed March 8, 2025.
9. Simone Rodan-Benzaquen, "Being Jewish in France Today," *Jewish News Syndicate*, https://www.jns.org/being-jewish-in-france-today/#.VKhrdMbNhiE=. Accessed March 8, 2025.
10. Henry Samuel, "Toulouse killer Mohamed Merah was 'traced' to al-Qaeda stronghold," *The Telegraph*, June 2012, https://www.telegraph.co.uk/news/worldnews/europe/france/9312399/Toulouse-killer-Mohamed-Merah-was-traced-to-al-Qaeda-stronghold.html. Accessed March 8, 2025.
11. "France shootings: Teacher 'in gunman tribute suspended,'" *BBC News*, March 23, 2012, https://www.bbc.com/news/world-europe-17491814. Accessed March 8, 2025.
12. Paul Cruickshank and Tim Lister, "How did Mohamed Merah become a jihadist?," *CNN*, https://www.cnn.com/2012/03/26/world/europe/france-shooting-suspect/index.html. Accessed March 8, 2025.
13. Steven Jambot, "Paris suburb reels after 'anti-semitic' robbery, rape," *France24*, December 6, 2014, https://www.france24.com/en/20141205-france-anti-semitic-attack-paris-suburb-creteil-shock-rape-robbery-jewish-community. Accessed March 8, 2025.
14. Dave Bender, "Paris Jewish Community in Shock Over Rape, Home Invasion 'Because You Are Jews,'" *The Algemeiner*, https://www.algemeiner.com/2014/12/02/paris-jewish-community-in-shock-over-rape-home-invasion-because-you-are-jews/. Accessed March 8, 2025.
15. Richard S Levy, ed., *Antisemitism: A Historical Encyclopedia of Prejudice and Persecution* (Santa Barbara, CA: ABC Clio, 2005), 727-729.
16. Oren Dorell, "Leaflet tells Jews to register in East Ukraine," *USA Today*, https://www.usatoday.com/story/news/world/2014/04/17/jews-ordered-to-register-in-east-ukraine/7816951/. Accessed March 8, 2025.
17. Giulio Meotti, "A French Street Named for a Serial Killer—of Jews," *7 Israel National News*,

October 22, 2014, https://www.israelnationalnews.com/news/344431. Accessed March 8, 2025. See also https://forward.com/fast-forward/211773/paris-suburb-honors-jailed-marwan-barghouti/.

18. Dov Lieber, "Belgian lawmakers nominate jailed Palestinian Barghouti for Nobel," May 18, 2016, https://www.timesofisrael.com/belgian-lawmakers-nominate-jailed-palestinian-barghouti-for-nobel/. Accessed March 8, 2025.
19. Joshua Levitt, "ISIS Soldier Behind Brussels Jewish Museum Killings, Says France's Hollande," *The Algemeiner*, June 13, 2014, https://www.algemeiner.com/2014/06/13/france-alleged-brussels-jewish-museum-shooter-was-member-of-isis/. Accessed March 8, 2025.
20. "Charlie Hebdo attack: Three days of terror," *BBC News*, January 14, 2015, https://www.bbc.com/news/world-europe-30708237. Accessed March 8, 2025.
21. David Jolly, "Satirical Magazine Is Firebombed in Paris," *The New York Times*, November 2, 2011, https://www.nytimes.com/2011/11/03/world/europe/charlie-hebdo-magazine-in-paris-is-firebombed.html?_r=0. Accessed March 8, 2025.
22. Vivienne Walt, "Paris March in Solidarity against Terror Attacks Was Largest in French History," *Time*, updated January 11, 2015, https://time.com/3662772/paris-march-solidarity-terrorism/. Accessed March 8, 2025.
23. "Shootings Targeting American Jews," *Jewish Virtual Library*, https://www.jewishvirtuallibrary.org/shootings-targeting-american-jews. Accessed March 8, 2025.
24. Peter Smith, "Mass shooter found guilty of murdering 11 people at Tree of Life synagogue in 2018," *PBS*, updated June 16, 2023, https://www.pbs.org/newshour/nation/mass-shooter-found-guilty-of-murdering-11-people-at-tree-of-life-synagogue-in-2018. Accessed March 8, 2025.
25. Lucy Perkins, "Pittsburgh Synagogues Dramatically Increasing Security Measures After Tree Of Life Attack," *WESA News*, May 8, 2019, https://www.wesa.fm/identity-justice/2019-05-08/pittsburgh-synagogues-dramatically-increasing-security-measures-after-tree-of-life-attack. Accessed March 8, 2025.

PART 3: A NEW AND MORE DANGEROUS AGE OF ANTISEMITISM

CHAPTER 7—ESCHATOLOGICAL ANTISEMITISM: AN EVEN GREATER DANGER

1. The 12 categories are as follows: theology proper—the study of the character of God; bibliology—the study of the Bible; anthropology—the study of the nature of man; hamartiology—the study of sin; Christology—the study of Christ; pneumatology—the study of the Holy Spirit; soteriology—the study of salvation; angelology—the study of angels; demonology—the study of fallen angels (demons); ecclesiology—the study of the church; eschatology—the study of the end days. One more was added as Israelology, or the study of Israel. It was introduced in recent years by Dr. Arnold Fruchtenbaum in his seminal work *Israelology: The Missing Link in Systematic Theology* (San Antonio, TX: Ariel Press, 1989).
2. John Lukacs, "The Coming of the Second World War" *Foreign Affairs*, September 1, 1989, https://www.foreignaffairs.com/europe/coming-second-world-war. Accessed March 8, 2025.
3. "Earthquakes with 1,000 or More Deaths 1900–2014," *USGS*, https://public.tableau.com/views/Earthquakeswith1000orMoreDeaths1900-2014/Dashboard1?%3Aembed=y&%3AshowVizHome=no&%3AshowTabs=y&%3Adisplay_count=y&%3Adisplay_static_image=y. Accessed March 8, 2025.
4. Stephen Devereux, "Ten worst famines of the 20th century," *The Sydney Morning Herald*,

August 15, 2011, https://www.smh.com.au/world/ten-worst-famines-of-the-20th-century-20110815-1iu2w.html. Accessed March 8, 2025.

5. Thomas Ice, "Is Modern Israel Fulfilling Prophecy?," *Scholars Crossing*, May 2009, https://efaidnbmnnnibpcajpcglclefindmkaj/https://digitalcommons.liberty.edu/cgi/viewcontent.cgi?article=1023&context=pretrib_arch. Accessed March 8, 2025.
6. "Six-Day War summary," *Britannica*, https://www.britannica.com/summary/Six-Day-War. Accessed March 8, 2025.
7. "Modern Israel & the Diaspora Timeline," *Jewish Virtual Library*, https://www.jewishvirtuallibrary.org/modern-israel-and-the-diaspora-timeline-table of contents. Accessed March 8, 2025.
8. Harold A. Sevener, *Israel's Glorious Future* (New York: Chosen People Ministries, 1996), 11-12.
9. Arnold G. Fruchtenbaum, *The Sequence of Pretribulational Events*, Messianic Bible Study 038 (San Atonio, TX: Ariel Ministries, 2005).
10. For additional study in the field of eschatology, please refer to these three volumes: J. Dwight Pentecost, *Things to Come* (Grand Rapids, MI: Zondervan, 1958); Mark Hitchcock, *The End* (Carol Stream, IL: Tyndale, 2012); and Arnold G. Fruchtenbaum, *The Footsteps of the Messiah* (Tustin, CA: Ariel Press, 2003).
11. Arnold G. Fruchtenbaum, *Ariel's Bible Commentary: The Book of Genesis* (San Antonio, TX: Ariel Ministries, 2009), 143-155.
12. For a detailed look at how the principle of blessings and cursings has worked through history and continues to affect Gentile nations and individuals, see John B. Metzger's book *Poking God's Eye: A Theological and Historical View of Anti-Semitism Based on the Blessings and Cursings of Genesis 12:3* (Keller, TX: JHousePublishing, 2016).
13. W. Max Muller and Kaufmann Kohler, "Amalek, Amalekites," *Jewish Encyclopedia*, https://www.jewishencyclopedia.com/articles/1351-amalek-amalekite#:~:text=Amalek%20is%20a%20son%20of,or%20clan%2C%20verse%2040). Accessed March 8, 2025.
14. "The ADL Global 100: Index of Antisemitism," *ADL*, https://www.adl.org/adl-global-100-index-antisemitism. Accessed March 8, 2025.
15. Silas, "Do Christians and Muslims Worship the Same God? (Part 1)," *Answering Islam*, https://www.answering-islam.org/authors/silas/same_god1.html. Accessed March 8, 2025.
16. Milo, "This Week in Stupid: 'Queers for Palestine,'" *Breitbart*, https://www.breitbart.com/europe/2014/08/01/this-week-in-stupid-queers-for-palestine/. Accessed March 8, 2025.
17. Joel C. Rosenberg, "Bible prophecy says the world will turn against Israel in the 'last days'—is it happening now?," *All Israel News*, April 9, 2024, https://allisrael.com/bible-prophecy-says-the-world-will-turn-against-israel-in-the-last-days-is-it-happening-now. Accessed March 8, 2025.
18. Madeleine A. Hung and Joyce E. Kim, "Encampment Protesters Briefly Raise 3 Palestinian Flags Over Harvard Yard," *The Harvard Crimson*, April 28, 2024, https://www.thecrimson.com/article/2024/4/28/palestine-flag-harvard-yard/. Accessed March 8, 2025.
19. Lauren Gambino, "US university presidents face firestorm over 'evasive' answers on antisemitism," *The Guardian*, December 7, 2023, https://www.theguardian.com/us-news/2023/dec/07/university-presidents-antisemitism-congress-testimony. Accessed March 8, 2025.
20. "Top UN Aid Official Says Hamas Is Not a Terrorist Group," *Foundation for Defense of Democracies*, February 16, 2024, https://www.fdd.org/analysis/2024/02/16/top-un-aid-official-says-hamas-is-not-a-terrorist-group/. Accessed March 8, 2025.
21. Natan Sharansky, "3D Test of Anti-Semitism: Demonization, Double Standards, Delegitimization,"

Jerusalem Center for Security and Foreign Affairs (JCFA), October 21, 2004, https://jcpa.org/article/3d-test-of-anti-semitism-demonization-double-standards-delegitimization/. Accessed March 8, 2025.

22. Katherine Donlevy, "NYU student admits ripping down Israeli hostage posters," *New York Post*, October 17, 2023, https://nypost.com/account/subscribe?cjdata=MXxOfDB8WXww&cjevent=0773b6cbfca011ef828200d40a1cb82a&g2i_source=CJ&g2i_medium=Online&g2i_campaign=AffiliateHD. Accessed March 8, 2025.
23. Jacob Gurvis, "Us Jewish teens are looking at a new factor in their college search: antisemitism," *The Times of Israel*, February 18, 2024, https://www.timesofisrael.com/us-jewish-teens-are-looking-at-a-new-factor-in-their-college-search-antisemitism/.
24. "Stars of David spray-painted on buildings in Paris, heightening fears among Jews," *The Times of Israel*, October 21, 2023, https://www.timesofisrael.com/stars-of-david-spray-painted-on-buildings-in-paris-continuing-antisemitic-spate/. Accessed March 8, 2025.
25. Stuart Winer, "Fear in Berlin as Star of David scrawled at entrances of buildings where Jews reside," *The Times of Israel*, October 15, 2023, https://www.timesofisrael.com/fear-in-berlin-as-star-of-david-scrawled-at-entrances-of-buildings-where-jews-reside/. Accessed March 8, 2025.
26. Imogen Foulkes, "Swiss antisemitism shock at Davos shop sign saying no skis for Jews," *BBC*, February 13, 2024, https://www.bbc.com/news/world-europe-68283043. Accessed March 8, 2025.
27. "Activist damages painting of Lord Balfour, who played key role in creation of Israel," *ArtForum*, March 11, 2024, https://www.artforum.com/news/activist-damages-painting-of-lord-balfour-who-played-key-role-in-creation-israel-550588/. Accessed March 8, 2025.
28. Lee Harpin, "Israeli Maccabi Tel Aviv fans violently attacked in Amsterdam," *Jewish News*, November 8, 2024, https://www.jewishnews.co.uk/israeli-maccabi-tel-aviv-fans-violently-attacked-in-amsterdam/. Accessed March 8, 2025.

CHAPTER 8—THE NEW PLAYERS IN ESCHATOLOGICAL ANTISEMITISM, PART I

1. Richard S. Levy, ed., *Antisemitism: A Historical Encyclopedia of Prejudice and Persecution* (Santa Barbara, CA: ABC-CLIO, 2005), 195-197.
2. Edward H. Flannery, *The Anguish of the Jews* (New York: Paulist Press, 1985), 263-267.
3. Flannery, *The Anguish of the Jews.*
4. "What does the Palestinian keffiyeh symbolize?," *Hirbawi*, August 9, 2023, https://kufiya.org/what-does-the-palestinian-keffiyeh-symbolize/. Accessed March 9, 2025.
5. Jeffrey Goldberg, "Is It Time for the Jews to Leave Europe?," *The Atlantic*, April 2015, https://www.theatlantic.com/magazine/archive/2015/04/is-it-time-for-the-jews-to-leave-europe/386279/. Accessed March 9, 2025.
6. Drew Desilver and David Masci, "World's Muslim population more widespread than you might think," *Pew Research Center*, January 31, 2017, https://www.pewresearch.org/short-reads/2017/01/31/worlds-muslim-population-more-widespread-than-you-might-think/. Accessed March 9, 2025.
7. "The Future of World Religions: Population Growth Projections, 2010–2050," *Pew Research Center*, April 2, 2015, https://www.pewresearch.org/religion/2015/04/02/religious-projections-2010-2050/#beyond-the-year-2050. Accessed March 9, 2025.

8. Abdullah Yusuf Ali, *The Qur'an: Text, Translation and Commentary* (Elmhurst, NY: Tahrike Tarsile Qur'an, Inc., 2005), 252.
9. Yusuf Ali, *The Qur'an: Text, Translation and Commentary*, 252-253.
10. Gregory M. Davis, "Islam 101," *Jihad Watch*, March 13, 2007, https://jihadwatch.org/2007/03/islam-101_2. Accessed March 9, 2025.
11. Bat Ye'or, *Eurabia: The Euro-Arab Axis* (Cranbury, NJ: Associated University Presses, 2005), 212.
12. Ye'or, *Eurabia*, 9.
13. Jeff Jacoby, "The canary in Europe's mine," *Boston Globe*, April 28, 2002, https://www.jeffjacoby.com/13169/the-canary-in-europe-mine. Accessed March 9, 2025.
14. Alexander Mallin, "Obama Criticized for Claim that ISIS Is 'Contained,'" *ABC News*, November 14, 2015, https://abcnews.go.com/Politics/obama-criticized-claim-isis-contained/story?id=35202328. Accessed March 9, 2025.
15. Howard Sachar, "Jews in the Civil Rights Movement," *My Jewish Learning*, https://www.myjewishlearning.com/article/jews-in-the-civil-rights-movement/. Accessed March 9, 2025.
16. "U.S. Jews' political views," *Pew Research Center*, May 11, 2021, https://www.pewresearch.org/religion/2021/05/11/u-s-jews-political-views/. Accessed March 9, 2025.
17. Jennifer Rubin, "Democrats' Israel problem," *Washington Post*, February 27, 2013, https://www.washingtonpost.com/blogs/right-turn/wp/2013/02/27/democrats-israel-problem/. Accessed March 9, 2025.
18. Philissa Cramer, "79% of US Jews voted for Harris, according to largest preliminary exit poll," *The Times of Israel*, November 6, 2024, https://www.timesofisrael.com/79-of-us-jews-voted-for-harris-according-to-largest-preliminary-exit-poll/. Accessed March 9, 2025.
19. Michael Curtis, "American Democrats and Israel," *American Thinker*, May 30, 2013, https://www.americanthinker.com/articles/2013/05/american_democrats_and_israel.html. Accessed March 9, 2025.
20. Ben Shapiro, "Why Jews Vote Leftist?," *Ben Shapiro's Truth Revolt*, https://secure.piryx.com/donate/MCifZavB/David-Horowitz/0088-021115-tr-video. Accessed March 9, 2025.
21. Evan Sayet, "Another Take On Why Jews Vote Democrat," *Evan Sayet*, July 18, 2014, https://evansayet.com/another-take-jews-vote-democrat/. Accessed March 9, 2025.
22. "Obama Speech Backlash on Call to Reinstate 1967 Mideast Borders," *ABC News*, May 19, 2011, https://abcnews.go.com/Politics/obama-speech-backlash-call-reinstate-1967-mideast-borders/story?id=13639200. Accessed March 9, 2025.
23. Frank Dimant, "The 1967 Lines Are 'Auschwitz Borders,'" *The Algemeiner*, January 20, 2014, https://www.algemeiner.com/2014/01/20/the-1967-lines-are-auschwitz-borders/. Accessed March 9, 2025.
24. "Jimmy Carter unveils truth about Israel," MSNBC interview, YouTube, https://www.youtube.com/watch?v=uvtC_qzHVM4. Accessed March 9, 2025.
25. Jimmy Carter, *Palestine, Peace Not Apartheid* (New York: Simon & Schuster, 2007), 216.
26. Tracy Wilkinson, "Biden vs. Trump: Where they stand on Israel, Palestinians, Middle East," *Los Angeles Times*, June 12, 2024, https://www.latimes.com/politics/story/2024-06-12/biden-trump-on-israel-palestinians-middle-east. Accessed March 9, 2025.

CHAPTER 9—THE NEW PLAYERS IN ESCHATOLOGICAL ANTISEMITISM, PART 2

1. "Black-Jewish Relations: Martin Luther King & Israel," *Virtual Jewish Library*, https://www.jewishvirtuallibrary.org/martin-luther-king-and-israel. Accessed March 9, 2025.
2. Cathryn J. Prince, "Uniting as the Student Intifada, anti-Israel groups plan to further disrupt US campuses," *The Times of Israel*, August 25, 2024, https://www.timesofisrael.com/uniting-as-the-student-intifada-anti-israel-groups-plan-to-further-disrupt-us-campuses/. Accessed March 9, 2025.
3. "Antisemitism on College Campuses: Incident Tracking," *Hillel International*, https://www.hillel.org/antisemitism-on-college-campuses-incident-tracking/. Accessed March 9, 2025.
4. The Muslim Student Union often produces a "promotional video" like this one at youtu.be/gF5u76uMFcQ. For a while now, the Muslim Student Union has gone by the name of Arab Student Union.
5. The general theme was that Israel is an oppressor and deliberately murders innocent Palestinians, aided and abetted by an imperialistic America. California State University, Stanislaus political science professor As'ad Abu Khalil, for example, claimed that civilian casualties by Israel are "never accidental." UCLA history professor Gabriel Piterberg made a macabre remark about Israelis "dancing on the blood of Palestinian children" and called for the prosecution of Israeli "war criminals." David Theo Goldberg, director of the University of California Humanities Research Institute, referred to Jews, and particularly Ashkenazi Jews, as racists. Nubar Hovsepian, associate professor of political science and international studies at Chapman University, described Israeli soldiers as "Israeli terrorist soldiers" and accused the Israel Defense Forces (IDF) of warning civilians to evacuate and then bombing the evacuation routes. Self-described "independent scholar" Norman Finkelstein was by far the most obnoxious, living up to his reputation for arrogance and condescension. He droned on endlessly, going over his allotted time and attacking others with prepared quips designed to evoke laughter. But not everyone was amused. After hogging the microphone to the obvious annoyance of conference moderator and UCI history professor Mark LeVine, Finkelstein began a new topic only to be cut off abruptly and left to sit sullenly with his face in his hands...None of the speakers expressed any support for a two-state solution. In broaching the possibility of a one-state solution in which Jews and Arabs would live together peacefully, no one mentioned the Hamas charter, which explicitly calls for the obliteration of Israel and the Jewish people, as well as the imposition of an Islamic state. No one spoke out against Hamas and Hezbollah or their oppression of fellow Muslims. Most importantly, no one mentioned the 800-pound gorilla in the room: worldwide Islamic terrorism and jihad.
6. Gary Fouse, "Mark Levine Exposed, Denying the connections between the Muslim Brotherhood and MSA doesn't make them go away," *Front Page Magazine*, May 19, 2010, https://www.frontpagemag.com/mark-levine-exposed-gary-fouse/. Accessed March 9, 2025.
7. "Israeli Ambassador's UC-Irvine Speech: Another Episode in Campus Radicalism," *The Investigative Project on Terrorism*, February 9, 2010, https://www.investigativeproject.org/1788/israeli-ambassadors-uc-irvine-speech-another. Accessed March 9, 2025.
8. William Bigelow, "More Swastikas at UC Davis," *Breitbart*, October 14, 2015, https://www.breitbart.com/local/2015/10/14/swastikas-uc-davis/. Accessed March 9, 2025.
9. The Hudson Institute, "The Muslim Brotherhood's U.S. Network," https://www.hudson.org/national-security-defense/the-muslim-brotherhood-s-u-s-network. Accessed March 18, 2025.
10. Abdallah bin Bjad Al-Otaibi, "Saudi Journalist: Behind U.S. Student Protests Stands The Muslim Brotherhood, Which Does Not Have The Palestinians' Interests At Heart," *MEMRI*, June

3, 2024, https://www.memri.org/reports/saudi-journalist-behind-us-student-protests-stands-muslim-brotherhood-which-does-not-have. Accessed March 10, 2025.

11. "Amir Abdul Malik Ali speaks on the evil US and Israel at UC Davis," YouTube, https://www.youtube.com/watch?v=Z5oyLj6AIyw. Accessed March 10, 2025.
12. "Hamas on Campus," https://www.youtube.com/watch?v=00PODH73ylo. Accessed March 10, 2025.
13. "A look at the protests of the war in Gaza that have emerged at US colleges," *Associated Press*, updated April 30, 2024, https://apnews.com/article/gaza-war-campus-protests-966eb531279f8e4381883fc5d79d5466. Accessed March 10, 2025.
14. Center for Antisemitism Research, "Campus Antisemitism: A Study of Campus Climate Before and After the Hamas Terrorist Attacks," *ADL*, November 29, 2023, https://www.adl.org/resources/report/campus-antisemitism-study-campus-climate-and-after-hamas-terrorist-attacks. Accessed March 10, 2025.
15. Jonathan Dowd-Gailey, "Islamism's Campus Club: The Muslim Students' Association," *Middle East Forum*, Spring 2004, https://www.meforum.org/middle-east-quarterly/islamisms-campus-club-the-muslim-students. Accessed March 10, 2025.
16. "Muslim Brotherhood (MB)," *Discover the Networks*, https://www.discoverthenetworks.org/organizations/muslim-brotherhood-mb/. Accessed March 10, 2025.
17. Dr. Talat Sultan, "Interview: From MSA to ICNA to ISNA," *The Message International*, February 16, 2016, https://messageinternational.org/from-msa-to-icna-and-isna/. Accessed March 18, 2025
18. Erick Stackelbeck, *The Brotherhood: America's Next Great Enemy* (Washington, DC: Regnery, 2013), 6.
19. Alan Dershowitz, "Woke Cowardice: Wrong University Presidents at the Wrong Time," *Gatestone Institute*, December 13, 2023, https://www.gatestoneinstitute.org/20216/woke-cowardice-university-presidents. Accessed March 10, 2025.
20. "Elise Stefanik says she was left 'shaken' by university presidents' 'pathetic' answers about antisemitism," *Fox News*, December 6, 2023, https://www.foxnews.com/media/elise-stefanik-says-left-shaken-university-presidents-pathetic-answers-antisemitism. Accessed March 10, 2025.
21. Kyla Guilfoil, "White House condemns university presidents after contentious congressional hearing on antisemitism," *NBC News*, December 6, 2023, https://www.nbcnews.com/politics/white-house/white-house-condemns-university-presidents-contentious-congressional-h-rcna128373. Accessed March 10, 2025.
22. Claudia Gay, "Statement on Congressional Hearing," *Harvard University*, December 7, 2023, https://www.harvard.edu/president/news-gay/2023/statement-on-congressional-hearing/. Accessed March 10, 2025.
23. Natan Sharansky, "3D Test of Anti-Semitism: Demonization, Double Standards, Delegitimization," *Jerusalem Center for Public Affairs*, Fall 2004, https://jcpa.org/article/3d-test-of-anti-semitism-demonization-double-standards-delegitimization/. Accessed March 10, 2025.
24. Ben Cohen, "BDS Leaders Promote Anti-Semitic Conspiracy Theory Linking Mossad to Charlie Hebdo Atrocity," *The Algemiener*, January 8, 2015, https://www.algemeiner.com/2015/01/08/bds-leaders-promote-anti-semitic-conspiracy-theory-linking-mossad-to-charlie-hebdo-atrocity/. Accessed March 10, 2025.
25. NYU Students for Justice in Palestine's Post, Facebook, July 7, 2016, https://www.facebook.com/NYU.SJP/posts/in-the-past-48-hours-another-two-black-men-have-been-lynched-by-the-police-the-t/1109663052432704/. Accessed March 10, 2025.

26. The list of Israeli inventions and innovations is ever-growing. Israeli ingenuity has literally changed the world we live in, from computers to cell phones to drip irrigation and so much more. See "List of Israeli inventions and discoveries," *Wikipedia*, https://en.wikipedia.org/wiki/List_of_Israeli_inventions_and_discoveries. Accessed March 10, 2025.
27. You can find a nonexhaustive list of what to boycott at https://bdsmovement.net/Act-Now-Against-These-Companies-Profiting-From-Genocide. Accessed March 10, 2025.

CHAPTER 10—THE NEW PLAYERS IN ESCHATOLOGICAL ANTISEMITISM, PART 3

1. Adolf Hitler, *Mein Kampf* (Sommerville, TN: Bottom of the Hill Publishing, 2010), 287.
2. "National Democratic Party of Germany," *Counter Extremist Project,* https://www.counterextremism.com/threat/national-democratic-party-germany. Accessed March 10, 2025.
3. "Germany's supreme court decides not to ban the neo-Nazi party," *The Economist*, January 17, 2017, https://www.economist.com/europe/2017/01/17/germanys-supreme-court-decides-not-to-ban-the-neo-nazi-party. Accessed March 10, 2025.
4. Kirsten Grieshaber, "Germany's top court rules a far-right party is ineligible for funding because of its ideology," *Associated Press*, January 23, 2024, https://apnews.com/article/germany-far-right-party-constitutional-court-ruling-funding-64eb91d080a73ff0804f04b5812f3921. Accessed March 10, 2025.
5. Lucian Kim, "Hands Off Germany's Neo-Nazi Party," *The New York Times*, December 18, 2012, https://archive.nytimes.com/latitude.blogs.nytimes.com/2012/12/18/hands-off-germanys-neo-nazi-party/?_r=0. Accessed March 10, 2025.
6. Marine Le Pen, "Marine Le Pen in political attack on her father after he belittles Holocaust," *The Guardian*, April 8, 2015, https://www.theguardian.com/world/2015/apr/08/marine-le-pen-front-national-jean-marie-elections-holocaust. Accessed March 10, 2025.
7. Marine Le Pen presidential elections stats for 2012, 2017, and 2022 are taken from "Marine Le Pen," *Wikipedia*, https://en.wikipedia.org/wiki/Marine_Le_Pen. Accessed March 10, 2025.
8. "Denmark election: Anti-EU Danish People's Party gets big boost," *BBC News*, June 19, 2015, https://www.bbc.com/news/world-europe-33199488. Accessed March 10, 2025.
9. Steve Erlanger, "Rise of Far-Right Party in Denmark Reflects Europe's Unease," *The New York Times*, June 20, 2015, https://www.nytimes.com/2015/06/20/world/europe/rise-of-far-right-party-in-denmark-reflects-europes-unease.html?_r=0. Accessed March 10, 2025.
10. A by-election is used to fill the vacated seat or office of an incumbent who became ineligible to stay in office, resigned, or died.
11. Matthew Day, "Hungary's Far-Right Jobbik party wins first by-election," *The Telegraph*, April 13, 2015, https://www.telegraph.co.uk/news/worldnews/europe/hungary/11532818/Hungarys-far-Right-anti-Semitic-Jobbik-party-wins-its-first-by-election.html. Accessed March 10, 2025.
12. Human Rights First, "The Jobbik Party in Hungary: History and Background," PDF download, https://humanrightsfirst.org/wp-content/uploads/2022/11/Jobbik-Party-Fact-Sheet-final.pdf. Accessed March 10, 2025.

CHAPTER 11—THE NEW PLAYERS IN ESCHATOLOGICAL ANTISEMITISM, PART 4

1. David L. Cooper, "The Golden Rule of Interpretation," *Bible Research Studies Group*, https://www.biblicalresearch.info/page47.html. Accessed March 10, 2025.

2. Paul N. Benware, *Understanding End Times Prophecy* (Chicago, IL: Moody Press, 1995), 321.
3. Charles Ryrie, *Dispensationalism* (Chicago, IL: Moody Press, 1995), 38-41.
4. For a clear understanding of dispensationalism and a literal interpretation of the Bible, read Charles Ryrie's *Dispensationalism* (Chicago, IL: Moody Press, 1995).
5. Benware, *Understanding End Times Prophecy*, 324.
6. Arnold G. Fruchtenbaum, *The Book of Genesis* (San Antonio, TX: Ariel Press, 2009), 276-280.
7. Paul R. Wilkinson, *For Zion's Sake* (Nottingham, UK: Paternoster, 2007), 65.
8. Itamar Marcus and Nan Jacques Zilberdik, "PA: Jesus Was a Palestinian," *Palestinian Media Watch*, December 28, 2014, https://palwatch.org/page/7476. Accessed March 10, 2025.
9. Joseph Farah, "There is no such thing as a Palestinian people—believe it!," *World Net Daily*, August 20, 2024, https://www.wnd.com/2024/08/there-is-no-such-thing-as-a-palestinian-people-believe-it. Accessed March 10, 2025.
10. Olivier Melnick, "Exposing the Palestinian Jesus Syndrome," *Shalom in Messiah* blog, December 18, 2024, https://www.shalominmessiah.com/2024/12/18/exposing-the-palestinian-jesus-syndrome/. Accessed March 10, 2025.
11. Wilkinson, *For Zion's Sake*, 49.
12. Sabeel Ecumenical Liberation Theology Center at https://sabeel.org/. Accessed March 10, 2025.
13. Friends of Sabeel North America at https://www.fosna.org/. Accessed March 10, 2025.
14. "Little Town of Bethlehem," *Culture Unplugged*, https://www.cultureunplugged.com/documentary/watch-online/play/11243/little-town-of-bethlehem. Accessed March 10, 2025.
15. Stephen R. Sizer, *Christian Zionism a British Perspective in Holy Land Hollow Jubilee: God, Justice and the Palestinians,* eds. Naim Ateek and Michael Prior (London: Melisende, 1999), 196.
16. Rabbi Brant Rosen, "Land and Liberation: An Interview with Reverend Naim Ateek," *Shalom Rav*, https://rabbibrant.com/2014/03/24/land-and-liberation-an-interview-with-reverend-naim-ateek/. Accessed March 10, 2025.
17. "Naim Ateek Lets It All Hang Out in…Norway! (Thank You Google!)," *Snapshots*, https://blog.camera.org/archives/2010/10/naim_ateek_lets_it_all_hang_ou.html. Accessed March 10, 2025.
18. Elias Chacour, *We Belong to the Land* (London: Marshall Pickering, 1992), 3.
19. Jonty Langley, "Profile: Elias Chacour," *Premier Christianity*, February 4, 2014, https://www.premierchristianity.com/home/profile-elias-chacour/3246.article. Accessed March 10, 2025.
20. Stephen Sizer, "Christian Jihad: A Biblical Response to the Islamic State," *Stephen Sizer*, https://www.stephensizer.com/2014/10/christian-jihad-a-biblical-response-to-the-islamic-state/. Accessed March 10, 2025.
21. Steve Doughty, "Priest banned from using social media sites for six months after posting 'anti-Semitic' comments claiming Israel was behind 9/11," *Daily Mail*, February 9, 2015, https://www.dailymail.co.uk/news/article-2946831/Priest-banned-using-social-media-sites-six-months-posting-anti-Semitic-comments-claiming-Israel-9-11.html. Accessed March 10, 2025.
22. Harry Farley, "Retired vicar banned over 'virulently antisemitic' posts," *BBC*, January 30, 2023, https://www.bbc.com/news/uk-64460767. Accessed March 10, 2025.
23. Gary Burge, *Jesus and the Land* (Grand Rapids, MI: Baker Academic, 2010), 60-61.
24. David Brog, "The End of Evangelical Support for Israel?," *Middle East Forum*, Spring 2014,

https://www.meforum.org/middle-east-quarterly/israel-evangelical-support. Accessed March 10, 2025.

25. Hank Hanegraaff, *The Apocalypse Code: Find Out What the Bible Really Says About the End Times and Why It Matters Today* (Nashville, TN: Thomas Nelson, 2010), 162, 164, 166, 167, and 189.
26. "Christ at the Checkpoint: CATC 2021," Bethlehem Bible College, https://bethbc.edu/christ-at-the-checkpoint/. Accessed March 10, 2025.
27. "An Open Letter from Palestinian Christians to Western Church Leaders and Theologians," *Change.org*, https://www.change.org/p/an-open-letter-from-palestinian-christians-to-western-church-leaders-and-theologians?recruiter=1319605589&recruited_by_id=a6f6fd10-6e69-11ee-abdf5b152ac3937c&utm_source=share_petition&utm_campaign=share_for_starters_page&utm_medium=copylink. Accessed March 18, 2025.
28. In the same article from their website, the leadership of Christ at the Checkpoint accuses Israel of ethnic cleansing, openly killing innocent civilians, apartheid, and double standards—see at https://www.change.org/p/an-open-letter-from-palestinian-christians-to-western-church-leaders-and-theologians?recruiter=1319605589&recruited_by_id=a6f6fd10-6e69-11ee-abdf5b152ac3937c&utm_source=share_petition&utm_campaign=share_for_starters_page&utm_medium=copylink. Accessed March 18, 2025.
29. Olivier Melnick, "A biblical analysis of the 'Christ at the Checkpoint' manifesto," *The Times of Israel*, March 9, 2014, https://blogs.timesofisrael.com/250708/. Accessed March 10, 2025.
30. With God on Our Side, YouTube, https://www.youtube.com/watch?v=NahTjAsDThs. Accessed March 10, 2025.
31. With God on Our Side (2010), *Films for Action*, https://www.filmsforaction.org/watch/with-god-on-our-side/. Accessed March 10, 2025.
32. *Little Town of Bethlehem* video, EthnoGraphic Media, https://www.amazon.com/Little-Town-Bethlehem-Sami-Awad/dp/B003YCKW5O?tag=usdeexplicits-20. Accessed March 10, 2025.
33. "About Us," *Kairos Palestine*, https://www.kairospalestine.ps/. Accessed March 10, 2025.
34. For a detailed discussion of the land covenant and its enduring implementations according to the Bible, please read John B. Metzger's book *Poking God's Eye: A Theological and Historical View of Anti-Semitism Based on the Blessings and Cursings of Genesis 12:3* (Keller, TX: JHousePublishing, 2016).
35. One of the basic differences between dispensationalists and Reformed theologians is their position on God's plan for Israel and the Jewish people. Dispensationalists believe that ethnic Israel and the church always remain two separate entities, while the Reformed will tend to flock to more of a replacement theology approach that views the church as the new "spiritual Israel."
36. Itamar Marcus and Nan Jacques Zilberdik, "PA: Jesus Was a Palestinian," *Palestinian Media Watch*, December 28, 2014, https://palwatch.org/page/7476. Accessed March 10, 2025.
37. Yair Rosenberg, "Mahmoud Abbas: Still a Holocaust Denier," *Tablet*, April 27, 2014, https://www.tabletmag.com/sections/news/articles/mahmoud-abbas-still-a-holocaust-denier. Accessed March 10, 2025.
38. Pierre-André Taguieff, *Israel et la Question Juive* (Paris: Les Provinciales, 2011), 191-192.
39. Bat Ye'or, *Eurabia: The Euro-Arab Axis* (Teaneck, NJ: Fairleigh Dickinson University Press, 2006), 213.
40. John B. Metzger, *Israel's Only Hope: The New Covenant* (Keller, TX: JHousePublishing, 2015).

41. Palestinian Civil Society, "Palestinian Civil Society Call for BDS," *BDS*, July 8, 2005, https://www.bdsmovement.net/call#Endorsed_by. Accessed March 10, 2025.
42. "Palestinian BDS National Committee," *BDS*, https://www.bdsmovement.net/BNC. Accessed March 10, 2025.
43. "The Many Lies of Omar Barghouti, *Canary Mission*, https://canarymission.org/individual/Omar_Barghouti. Accessed March 10, 2025.
44. To see these stipulations, go to "What Is BDS?," *BDS*, https://www.bdsmovement.net/what-bds. Accessed March 10, 2025.
45. Jerusalem Post Staff, "Northwestern University BDS group narrowly passes divestment measure," *The Jerusalem Post*, February 19, 2015, https://www.jpost.com/Breaking-News/Northwestern-University-BDS-group-narrowly-passes-divestment-measure-391516. Accessed March 10, 2025.
46. "Presbyterian Church Proposal to Wipe 'Israel' off the Map," *United with Israel*, December 25, 2014, https://unitedwithisrael.org/presbyterian-church-tries-to-wipe-israel-off-the-religious-mappresbyterian-church-proposal-to-wipe-israel-off-the-map/. Accessed March 10, 2025.
47. Bethany Daily, "By Slim Margin, Assembly Approves Divestment from Three Companies Doing Business in Israel/Palestine," *PCUSA*, https://old.pcusa.org/news/2014/6/20/slim-margin-assembly-approves-divestment-three-com/. Accessed January 2, 2025.
48. Abagail Klein Leichman, "Israel's Top 45 Greatest Inventions of All Time," *Israel 21c*, updated August 22, 2016, https://www.israel21c.org/israels-top-45-greatest-inventions-of-all-time-2/. Accessed March 10, 2025.
49. Christa Case Bryant, "11 Brands You'll Have to Let Go If You're Boycotting Israel," *Medium*, November 16, 2023, https://medium.com/@theethicalbuyingteam/11-brands-youll-have-to-let-go-if-you-want-to-boycott-israel-84fb3aba9db0. Accessed March 10, 2025.
50. "Kristallnacht" *Holocaust Encyclopedia* (under Learn About the Holocaust tab), https://encyclopedia.ushmm.org/tags/en/tag/kristallnacht. Accessed March 10, 2025.
51. "US: States Use Anti-Boycott Laws to Punish Responsible Businesses," *Human Rights Watch*, https://www.hrw.org/news/2019/04/23/us-states-use-anti-boycott-laws-punish-responsible-businesses?gad_source=1. Accessed March 10, 2025.
52. "How to Confront and Defeat BDS," *Stop BDS*, https://www.stopbds.com/. Accessed March 10, 2025.
53. "Boycott Divestment Sanctions," *Canary Mission*, https://canarymission.org/organization/Boycott_Divestment_Sanctions. Accessed March 10, 2025.
54. "Act Now Against These Companies Profiting from the Genocide of the Palestinian People," *BDS*, January 25, 2023, https://www.bdsmovement.net/Act-Now-Against-These-Companies-Profiting-From-Genocide. Accessed March 10, 2025.
55. Julia Duin, "San Antonio Fundamentalist Battles Anti-Semitism," *The Houston Chronicle*, April 30, 1988, 1.
56. Michael A. Meyer, "The Star of Redemption by Franz Rosensweig," *Commentary.org*, July 1971, https://www.commentary.org/articles/michael-meyer-3/the-star-of-redemption-by-franz-rosenzweig/. Accessed March 18, 2025.
57. David R. Reagan, "Christian Zionism," *Christ in Prophecy*, https://christinprophecy.org/articles/christian-zionism/. Accessed March 10, 2025.
58. John Hagee, *In Defense of Israel* (Lake Mary, FL: Frontline, 2007), 135-136. Hagee claims, "Five

major points must now be made that are crucial to understanding that the Jews did not reject Jesus as Messiah. Jesus had to live to be the Messiah. If it was God's will for Jesus to die from the beginning. If it was Jesus' intention to be obedient unto death. If there is not one verse of Scripture in the New Testament that says Jesus came to be the Messiah. If Jesus refused by His words or actions to claim to be the Messiah to the Jews, then how can the Jews be blamed for rejecting what was never offered?"

59. "Our Vision," *Jewish Voice for Peace*, https://www.jewishvoiceforpeace.org/resource/our-vision/. Accessed March 11, 2025.
60. Jewish Voice for Peace, "Palestinian conflict explained: an animated introduction to Israel and Palestine," YouTube, https://www.youtube.com/watch?v=Y58njT2oXfE. Accessed March 19, 2025.
61. "What is CODEPINK," *CODEPINK*, https://www.codepink.org/about. Accessed March 11, 2025.
62. When you go into the website, you'll find lengthy, detailed lists of Islamic terror attacks going back 25 years. At the time of this writing, the counter on the website shows the total number of attacks since 9/11 to be nearly 48,000.
63. "Mission Statement," *Neturei Karta International*, https://nkusa.org/about-us/mission-statement/. Accessed March 19, 2025.
64. "The Solution," *Neturei Karta International*, https://nkusa.org/qa/the-solution/. Accessed March 19, 2025.
65. Shlomo Winner, "Neturei Karta in Iran," YouTube, https://www.youtube.com/watch?v=CKRhFzVJKMc.
66. Joseph Telushkin, *Jewish Literacy* (New York: William Morrow, 1991), 335-336.
67. Robert Wistrich, *A Lethal Obsession* (New York: Random House, 2010), 768, 863, 919.
68. Howard S. Sachar, *A History of Israel: From the Rise of Zionism to Our Time* (New York: Alfred A. Knopf, 1996), 600.

CHAPTER 12—TAKING A STAND AGAINST END-TIMES ANTISEMITISM

1. Ian Kershaw, *Popular Opinion and Political Dissent in the Third Reich: Bavaria 1933–45* (Oxford, UK: Oxford University Press, 1983), 277.
2. "Freedom and Liberty vs. Islam and Sharia," https://nosharia.wordpress.com/list-of-muslim-majority-countries-with-sectstategovernment/. Accessed March 11, 2025.
3. "Muslim Population by Country 2025," *World Population Review*, https://worldpopulationreview.com/country-rankings/muslim-population-by-country. Accessed March 11, 2025.
4. "Elie Wiesel Acceptance Speech," *The Nobel Prize*, https://www.nobelprize.org/prizes/peace/1986/wiesel/acceptance-speech/. Accessed March 11, 2025.
5. "Munich Pact signed," *History*, https://www.history.com/this-day-in-history/munich-pact-signed. Accessed March 11, 2025.
6. "Estimated War Dead WWII," *War Chronicle*, https://warchronicle.com/world-war-2-death-toll-of-all-nations/. Accessed March 11, 2025.
7. Jim Hoft, "Muslims Demand that 'Offensive Crosses' Be Removed From Catholic University," *Gateway Pundit*, December 4, 2015, https://www.thegatewaypundit.com/2015/12/muslims-demand-that-offensive-crosses-be-removed-from-catholic-university/. Accessed March 11, 2025.

8. Jessilyn Lancaster, "Church of England Removes Christ's Cross so Muslims Won't Be Offended," *Charisma News*, July 5, 2016, https://charismanews.com/news/world/church-of-england-removes-christ-s-cross-so-muslims-won-t-be-offended/. Accessed March 11, 2025.
9. "Sharia, the fundamental religious concept of Islam—namely, its law." The religious law of Islam is seen as the expression of God's command for Muslims and, in application, constitutes a system of duties that are incumbent upon all Muslims by virtue of their religious belief. Known as the sharīʿah (literally, "path leading to the watering place"), the law represents a divinely ordained path of conduct that guides Muslims toward a practical expression of religious conviction in this world and the goal of divine favour in the world to come." *Britannica*, "sharia," https://www.britannica.com/topic/sharia. Accessed March 19, 2025.
10. "The World's Muslims: Religion, Politics and Society," *Pew Research Center*, https://www.pewresearch.org/religion/2013/04/30/the-worlds-muslims-religion-politics-society-overview/. Accessed January 6, 2025.
11. Dr. Richard D. Land, "Radical Islamic Jihadism: A Mortal Threat to Western Civilization," *The Christian Post*, January 13, 2025, https://www.christianpost.com/news/radical-islamic-jihadism-a-mortal-threat-to-western-civilization-132455/. Accessed January 11, 2025.
12. *Dhimmitude:* the Islamic system of governing populations conquered by jihad wars, encompassing all of the demographic, ethnic, and religious aspects of the political system. The word *dhimmitude* comes from *dhimmi*, an Arabic word meaning "protected." *Dhimmi* was the name applied by the Arab-Muslim conquerors to indigenous non-Muslim populations who surrendered by a threat (*dhimma*) to Muslim domination. Islamic conquests expanded over vast territories globally for more than a millennium (638–1683). The Muslim empire incorporated numerous varied peoples. Although these populations differed, they were ruled by the same type of laws, based on the *shari'a* (Bat Ye'or, *dhimmitude.org*).
13. "Act Now Against These Companies Profiting from the Genocide of the Palestinian People," *BDS*, December 25, 2023, https://bdsmovement.net/Act-Now-Against-These-Companies-Profiting-From-Genocide. Accessed March 11, 2025.
14. Lists intended for boycotting Israel can be turned around and used to support Israel—you'll find such lists at Boycott-Israel.org (https://boycott-israel.org/boycott.html) and BDS (https://www.bdsmovement.net/Guide-to-BDS-Boycott).

CHAPTER 13—WHY WE SHOULD FIGHT END-TIMES ANTISEMITISM

1. "The ADL Global 100: Index of Antisemitism," *ADL*, https://www.adl.org/adl-global-100-index-antisemitism. Accessed March 19, 2025.
2. The rescue network acts as an "underground railroad for Jews," gathering people across the USA and parts of the world. It is a vetted, secure, and volunteer network made up of Christians who are willing to make sacrifices to help rescue and shelter Jewish people at risk for their lives. One can become part of the network by starting the process at https://www.shalominmessiah.com/connect/ and checking the box labeled "I am interested in joining the network that Olivier spoke about."